Music Teacher's BOOK OF LISTS

Cynthia Meyers Ross

Karen Meyers Stangl

PARKER PUBLISHING COMPANY
West Nyack, New York 10995

Library of Congress Cataloging-in-Publication Data

Ross, Cynthia Meyers.
    The music teacher's book of lists / Cynthia Meyers Ross, Karen
Meyers Stangl.
      p.   cm.
    ISBN 0-13-093832-7 (spiral)—ISBN 0-13-673500-2 (paperback)
    1. School music—Instruction and study—Handbooks, manuals, etc.
I. Stangl, Karen Meyers.   II. Title.
MT10.R775 1994   94-2407
780'.2'02—dc20   CIP
                                             MN

10 9 8 7 6 5 4

*Some of the illustrations within are reproductions from the fine Dover Press Pictorial
Archives series. The reproductions are used with the permission of Dover Publications, Inc.*

Acknowledgments

We would like to thank Margaret Beattie and Linda Von Kelsch of the Central
Rappahannock Regional Library; and Marilyn Cooley of WETA radio in Washington,
D.C. for their assistance with our research.

    We would especially like to acknowledge the help and encouragement of Audrey
Adair-Hauser.

ISBN 0-13-093832-7 (spiral)

ISBN 0-13-673500-2 (pbk)

ATTENTION: CORPORATIONS AND SCHOOLS

Parker Publishing Company books are available at quantity discounts with bulk purchase for
educational, business, or sales promotional use. For information, please write to: Prentice Hall Special
Sales, 240 Frisch Court, Paramus, NJ 07652. Please supply: title of book, ISBN number, quantity,
how the book will be used, date needed.

PARKER PUBLISHING COMPANY
West Nyack, NY 10994

A Simon & Schuster Company

On the World Wide Web at http://www.phdirect.com

Prentice-Hall International (UK) Limited, *London*
Prentice-Hall of Australia Pty. Limited, *Sydney*
Prentice-Hall Canada Inc., *Toronto*
Prentice-Hall Hispanoamericana, S.A., *Mexico*
Prentice-Hall of India Private Limited, *New Delhi*
Prentice-Hall of Japan, Inc., *Tokyo*
Simon & Schuster Asia Pte. Ltd., *Singapore*
Editora Prentice-Hall do Brasil, Ltda., *Rio de Janeiro*

About This Book

Music is an integral part of a well-rounded education. It plays an important role in the curriculum from elementary through secondary school. This book is a unique information source developed for music teachers of all levels of experience and all levels of instruction. It provides nearly 300 lists useful in developing instructional materials and planning lessons. It can be used by the elementary general music teacher, as well as by teachers of music appreciation, history, or theory. Chorus, band, and orchestra directors will find the lists helpful to prepare their students for performances. Even private studio teachers can use this book effectively to stimulate interest among their students. The student teacher and beginning teacher will find many applications for these lists, which will provide a fun and motivational vehicle for learning. The veteran teacher, as well, will find these lists a valuable resource that provides a multitude of information that can inject new life into the "same old" curriculum.

The demands being placed on music teachers these days are ever increasing. Scheduling often does not allow adequate preparation time for each class. The lack of ready-to-use materials is a problem. For elementary music teachers, compiling daily ideas and activities appropriate to varying abilities and grade levels can be an overwhelming task. Upper-level teachers are often expected to "travel" and teach a wide diversity of classes. They may start their day with a band class and a music appreciation class at the middle school, and then be off to the high school to teach music theory! In addition, the newest trends in education encourage music teachers to integrate their curricula with other topics being studied in the regular classroom (i.e., Native Americans, seasons of the year, etc.). This single volume contains a wealth of information packaged in a convenient, time-saving resource designed to alleviate these daily demands.

The book includes a broad range of lists, divided into nine main sections:

   I. **Rudiments of Music**—Contains thirty-three lists of the basics of music, such as "Notes and Their Pitch Names," "Major Scales and Their Key Signatures," and "Famous Compositions Illustrating Various Rhythms."

  II. **Music Theory**—Presents such helpful lists as "Some Rules of Four-Part Harmony," "Cadences," and "Forms and Compositional Techniques."

 III. **Composers and Their Works**—Provides the most comprehensive list of composers, from Isaac Albeniz to Ellen T. Zwilich, broken down by major works, countries of origin, birthdates, historical periods, and so on.

  IV. **Instruments and Instrumental Ensembles**—Includes varied lists for each instrument, such as "Predecessors of the Piano," "Orchestral Compositions Featuring the Various Woodwind Instruments," and "Brass Instrument Virtuosi."

   V. **Opera and Vocal Music**—Features such lists as "Types of Voices," "Famous American Choral Groups," "Famous Opera Stars Past and Present," and "Some Operas with Historical Themes."

  VI. **Music History**—Offers some general characteristics of each period, as well as lists covering the development of the orchestra and musical instruments over the centuries.

 VII. **Popular Music**—"Jazz" up your curriculum with lists such as "Some Rock and Roll Notables," "Country Music Artists," and "Top Tunes of the 1960's."

VIII. **Dance**—Offers useful lists such as "Famous Ballet Companies," "Baroque Dances," and "Representative Dances of Various Nations."

  IX. **Integrating Music with the Content Areas**—Keep abreast of the latest trends in education. To correlate your music lessons to the classroom curriculum quickly, useful lists such as "Negro Spirituals," "World War II Songs," and "Holiday Songs" are included. Lists of current children's literature, videos, and CD ROMs are provided as well.

The lists within these categories are designed for use with students of various grades and skill levels. They are printed in full-page format to allow for easy photocopying. You may utilize the lists individually to accommodate your curriculum and the needs of your students. In addition, there is a comprehensive cross-referencing system to refer you to additional material if you wish to expand your lessons to include related topics.

Music is one of the oldest disciplines. It deals with many fields, including history, the comparative study of various cultures, and the more technical aspects, such as acoustics, pedagogy, and theory. But music is not just a subject—it is an art! The art of music transcends the realm of knowledge. It deals with thoughts and emotions, making it truly complex.

In order to distill the myriad aspects of music into list form, it becomes necessary to resort to oversimplification of subject matter. The knowledgeable musician will be able to expand upon the topics and explain any paradoxes, using the lists as a starting point.

This book cannot serve as a replacement for the many valuable resources musical scholars have provided. Because of their format, music texts, dictionaries, and encyclopedias can go into much greater depth. It is our hope that the lists in this book will be a valuable supplement to the subjects you are covering. Many are meant to challenge your students to broaden their knowledge through more in-depth research.

The Music Teacher's Book of Lists is a compilation of research that is both informative and fun to read, even for the knowledgeable musician. We invite you to learn some fascinating facts and use your creativity to broaden, enrich, and enliven the musical education of your students.

Cynthia Meyers Ross & Karen Meyers Stangl

About the Authors

The authors are sisters who used the unique combination of their varied skills and experiences to develop this resource book for teachers.

Cynthia Meyers Ross holds a bachelor of music degree from the State University of New York at Potsdam, Crane School of Music. Her post-graduate work has been done at the University of Tennessee, Knoxville, as well as Catholic University in Washington, D.C. She has taught music in the public schools (nursery through grade 12) for ten years in New York and Virginia. In 1989, she left the public schools to devote herself full-time to building a Suzuki studio in the Fredericksburg, Virginia, area. She is a member of the Suzuki Association of the Americas, as well as the Suzuki Association of the Greater Washington Area, for which she serves on the board of directors and as chairman of the string division. She is the Suzuki mother of a violinist, Catherine, age 9.

Karen Meyers Stangl received her B.A. from the State University of New York at Oneonta. As a classroom teacher for the last twenty years she has taught grades 1 through 6. She has been active on many committees, involved in writing and editing a variety of curriculum materials, and has taught staff-development seminars. In the past, she has worked with the gifted program and has recently been the lead teacher for a newly developed program for at-risk students. She is currently working as a first grade teacher in Stafford County, Virginia, where she integrates the fine arts into her whole-language program.

Contents

Section I

RUDIMENTS OF MUSIC

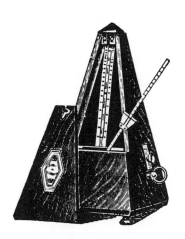

LIST 1.1   BASIC NOTE VALUES

Notes have no absolute numerical (beat) value until they are used within the context of a time signature. Below is a list of notes with their names.

double whole note

dotted whole note

whole note

dotted half note

half note

dotted quarter note

quarter note

dotted eighth note   or   (in groups)

eighth note   (in groups)

dotted sixteenth note   or

sixteenth note   (in groups)

dotted thirty-second note   or

thirty-second note   (in groups)

dotted sixty-fourth note   or

sixty-fourth note   (in groups)

See Also List 1.21, Time Signatures

LIST 1.2   DUPLE RELATIONSHIPS

Below is a list of notes with their names. Each note is worth *double* the value of the note directly below it.

LIST 1.3   DOTTED NOTES

All notes can be "dotted" by placing a dot after them. The dot increases the value of the note by half, making the dotted note worth one-and-a-half times the value of the original note.

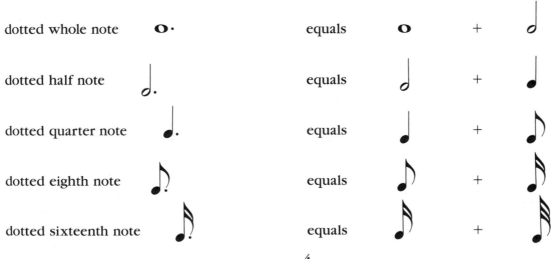

4

LIST 1.4   TRIPLE RELATIONSHIPS

The following relationships are listed to facilitate understanding the use of compound time signatures such as $\frac{6}{8}$, $\frac{9}{8}$, $\frac{12}{8}$, and so on.

A dotted half note equals twice the value of a dotted quarter note.

The dotted quarter note is the basic pulse.

A quarter note/eighth note combination equals two-thirds and one-third of a dotted quarter note.

Each eighth note equals one-third of a dotted quarter note.

LIST 1.5   RESTS

Rests carry the same names and relative values as notes (see Lists 1.1–1.4). They serve as symbols for silence in music.

whole rest

half rest

quarter rest

eighth rest

sixteenth rest

The whole rest can receive the same value as a whole note, or it can be used to signify silence for one whole measure, whatever the value of that measure might be.

Rests can also be "dotted," thus increasing their value to one-and-a-half that of the original rest.

Multiple measures of rests can be indicated as shown below. The number over the rest indicates how many *measures* should be silent.

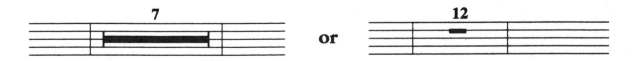

LIST 1.6 MODERN CLEFS

The function of the clef is to give the lines and spaces of the staff their pitch designations. Different clefs indicate different ranges of notes on each staff. Thus some instruments are better suited to having music written in one clef than another.

CLEF NAME		NICKNAME	INSTRUMENTS USING CLEF
Treble clef		G clef 2nd line = G	violin, flute, clarinet, trumpet, oboe, piano–right hand, female voices, tenor voice (high male), etc.
Alto clef		C clef/"viola" clef 3rd line = C	viola
Bass clef		F clef 4th line = F	cello, trombone, bassoon, piano-left hand, male voices, tympani, etc.
Tenor clef		4th line = C	tenor trombone, higher notes for cello, etc.

LIST 1.7 OTHER CLEFS

Octave Clefs: These clefs are read as their counterparts above, but an octave higher or lower, depending on the location of the 8. The double treble clef is read an octave lower than normal.

Percussion Clef: This clef is used with instruments of indefinite pitch.

See Also List 4.39, Percussion Instruments

6

© 1994 by Parker Publishing Company

LIST 1.8   OBSOLETE CLEFS

Clefs appeared in music around the eleventh century. The three most common clefs identified the locations of either G, C, or F. These were placed in various locations on the staff and looked in some way like the letters they represented.

SOPRANINO OR FRENCH VIOLIN CLEF

SOPRANO CLEF

MEZZO-SOPRANO CLEF

BARITONE CLEF

SUB-BASS CLEF

LIST 1.9   NOTES AND THEIR PITCH NAMES

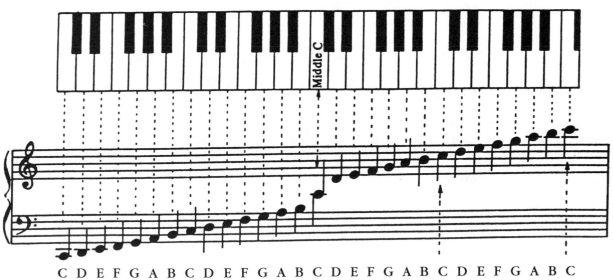

C D E F G A B C D E F G A B C D E F G A B C D E F G A B C

LIST 1.10   NOTE NAMES IN VARIOUS LANGUAGES

ENGLISH	GERMAN	FRENCH	ITALIAN
C	C	ut	do
D	D	re	re
E	E	mi	mi
F	F	fa	fa
G	G	sol	sol
A	A	la	la
B	H	si	si
C-sharp	cis	ut diese	do diesis
D-sharp	dis	re diese	re diesis
E-sharp	eis	mi diese	mi diesis
F-sharp	fis	fa diese	fa diesis
G-sharp	gis	sol diese	sol diesis
A-sharp	ais	la diese	la diesis
B-sharp	B	si diese	si diesis
C-flat	ces	ut bemol	do bemolle
D-flat	des	re bemol	re bemolle
E-flat	es	mi bemol	mi bemolle
F-flat	fes	fa bemol	fa bemolle
G-flat	ges	sol bemol	sol bemolle
A-flat	as	la bemol	la bemolle
B-flat	B	si bemol	si bemolle
double-sharp	-isis	double-diese	doppio diesis
double-flat	-eses	double-bemol	doppio bemolle

LIST 1.11   RHYTHMIC WORDS IN VARIOUS LANGUAGES

AMERICAN ENGLISH	BRITISH ENGLISH	ITALIAN	FRENCH	GERMAN
double whole note	breve	breve	carrée	Doppeltaktnote
whole note	semibreve	semibreve	ronde	Ganzetaktnote
half note	minim	minima or bianca	blanche	Halbenote
quarter note	crotchet	semiminima or nera	noire	Viertel
eighth note	quaver	croma	croche	Achtel
sixteenth note	semiquaver	semicroma	double croche	Sechzehntel
thirty-second note	demisemiquaver	biscroma	triple croche	Zweiunddreissigstel
sixty-fourth note	hemidemisemiquaver	semibiscroma	quadruple croche	Vierundsechzigstel

8

LIST 1.12   OTHER MUSICAL TERMS IN VARIOUS LANGUAGES

Composers have come to use Italian words for instructions to the musician. In more recent times, composers of various nations have used their native tongue to write instructions to the performer. Below is a list of often-seen words and phrases and the corresponding English instruction. These are not always literal translations from one language to another.

ITALIAN	GERMAN	FRENCH	ENGLISH
maggiore	dur	majeur	major
minore	moll	mineur	minor
lento	langsam	lent	slow
accelerando/stringendo	dringend	pressez	getting faster
coda	Anhang	coda	ending
crescendo	anwachsend	croitre	getting louder
molto	sehr	tres	very
leggiero	leicht	leger	lightly
moderato	massig	modere	moderately
como posible	moglich	possible	as possible
pesante	schwer	pesant	heavy
poco	wenig	peu	little
piu	mehr	plus	more
subito	plotzlich	subit	suddenly
non	nicht	pas	not
tempo	Zeitmass	temps	time/beat/speed
pacifico	ruhig	pacifique	peaceful
vivo	lebhaft	vite	quick
animato	munter	vif	lively

LIST 1.13   HAND SIGNALS FOR NOTES

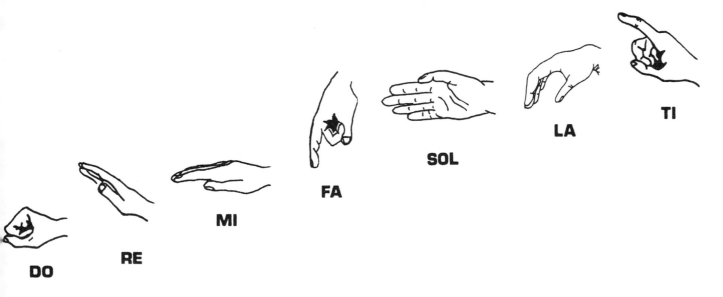

9

LIST 1.14 SOLFÈGE

Solfège is a system of using syllables to sing the various pitches in music. There are two systems of solfège: "movable do" and "fixed do." In movable do, the tonic, or key note, is assigned the syllable "do." In fixed do, the note C is always "do." In C major, the two systems are identical; in other keys the difference is apparent.

C Major Scale:

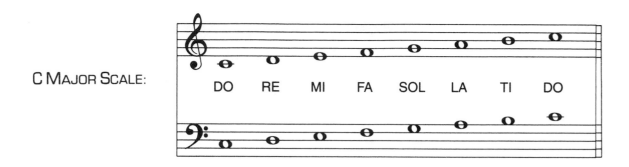

C Chromatic Scale:

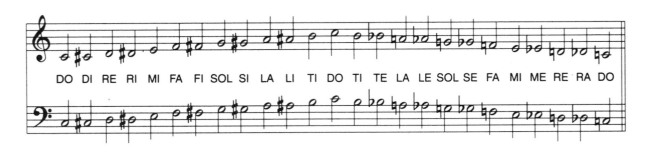

E Melodic Minor:

LIST 1.15 ACCIDENTALS

Accidentals are notes appearing in music which are not specified or implied in the key signature. Below is a list of the accidental signs with their functions.

Double-flat	♭♭	lowers a note by two half-steps
Flat	♭	lowers a note by one half-step
Natural	♮	not flat, not sharp (cancels a previous sign)
Sharp	♯	raises a note by one half-step
Double-sharp	𝄪	raises a note by two half-steps

LIST 1.16 RULES OF ACCIDENTALS

1. Accidentals appear *before* the note in printed music, but, when spoken, are said after the note.

   (We say, "F-sharp," but in music the sharp is printed first:  .)

2. The "center" of the accidental should rest on the line or space of the note it affects.

3. Accidentals last for one measure. Every note of that name and octave that follows the accidental will be affected.

4. When the new measure begins, the key signature again takes precedence.

5. Sometimes the composer will put the new sign (from the key signature) into the music on the next note of that name to appear. In this case, the sign will be seen in parentheses ().

6. If an accidental ties over into the next bar, keep the accidental until the tie is over.

LIST 1.17 MAJOR SCALES AND THEIR KEY SIGNATURES

C Major   No sharps or flats

G Major   1 sharp: F#

D Major   2 sharps: F# and C#

A Major   3 sharps: F#, C#, and G#

E Major   4 sharps: F#, C#, G#, and D#

B Major   5 sharps: F#, C#, G#, D#, and A#

F# Major   6 sharps: F#, C#, G#, D#, A#, and E#

C# Major   7 sharps: F#, C#, G#, D#, A#, E#, and B#

F Major   1 flat: B♭

B♭ Major   2 flats: B♭ and E♭

E♭ Major   3 flats: B♭, E♭, and A♭

A♭ Major   4 flats: B♭, E♭, A♭, and D♭

D♭ Major   5 flats: B♭, E♭, A♭, D♭, and G♭

G♭ Major   6 flats: B♭, E♭, A♭, D♭, G♭, and C♭

C♭ Major   7 flats: B♭, E♭, A♭, D♭, G♭, C♭, and F♭

LIST 1.18 MINOR SCALES AND
THEIR KEY SIGNATURES

a minor   No sharps or flats

e minor   1 sharp: F♯

b minor   2 sharps: F♯ and C♯

f♯ minor   3 sharps: F♯, C♯, and G♯

c♯ minor   4 sharps: F♯, C♯, G♯, and D♯

g♯ minor   5 sharps: F♯, C♯, G♯, D♯, and A♯

d♯ minor   6 sharps: F♯, C♯, G♯, D♯, A♯, and E♯

a♯ minor   7 sharps: F♯, C♯, G♯, D♯, A♯, E♯, and B♯

d minor   1 flat: B♭

g minor   2 flats: B♭ and E♭

c minor   3 flats: B♭, E♭, and A♭

f minor   4 flats: B♭, E♭, A♭, and D♭

b♭ minor   5 flats: B♭, E♭, A♭, D♭, and G♭

e♭ minor   6 flats: B♭, E♭, A♭, D♭, G♭, and C♭

a♭ minor   7 flats: B♭, E♭, A♭, D♭, G♭, C♭, and F♭

a minor   e minor   b minor   f♯ minor   c♯ minor   g♯ minor   d♯ minor   a♯ minor

d minor   g minor   c minor   f minor   b♭ minor   e♭ minor   a♭ minor

13

See Also List 1.20, Variations in the Minor Mode

LIST 1.19   PARALLEL AND RELATIVE MINORS

Parallel minors start on the same note as their parallel major; they have different key signatures. The starting note of a relative minor scale is the same as the sixth note of its relative major. The key signatures will be identical.

PARALLEL MINORS

C Major—c minor

G Major—g minor	F Major—f minor
D Major—d minor	B♭ Major—b♭ minor
A Major—a minor	E♭ Major—e♭ minor
E Major—e minor	A♭ Major—a♭ minor
B Major—b minor	D♭ Major—d♭ minor
F♯ Major—f♯ minor	G♭ Major—g♭ minor
C♯ Major—c♯ minor	C♭ Major—c♭ minor

RELATIVE MINORS

C Major—a minor

G Major—e minor	F Major—d minor
D Major—b minor	B♭ Major—g minor
A Major—f♯ minor	E♭ Major—c minor
E Major—c♯ minor	A♭ Major—f minor
B Major—g♯ minor	D♭ Major—b♭ minor
F♯ Major—d♯ minor	G♭ Major—e♭ minor
C♯ Major—a♯ minor	C♭ Major—a♭ minor

See Also List 1.17, Major Scales and Their Key Signatures; and List 1.18, Minor Scales and Their Key Signatures

LIST 1.20   VARIATIONS IN THE MINOR MODE

Although the key signatures in list 1.18 are used for music written in the minor keys, there are three variations of minor scales in use today:

1. Natural Minor (Pure Minor): Uses the key signatures as shown in List 1.18, thus:

2. Harmonic Minor: Uses the key signature, but raises the seventh step of the scale one half-step to achieve the leading tone-tonic relationship found in major scales. This creates the interval of an augmented second between the sixth and seventh notes, giving the harmonic minor scale its distinctive sound.

3. Melodic Minor: The sixth and seventh notes are raised one half-step in the ascending scale, then lowered (to follow the key signature) in the descending scale:

LIST 1.21 TIME SIGNATURES

Time (or meter) signatures appear at the beginning of a piece of music. They give the performer the precise value of all rhythmic symbols, as well as the accent pattern and beat division.

Simple meters divide the beats into 2's or 4's: ("1 &, 2 e & a")
Compound meters divide the beat into thirds: ("1 & a, 2- a")
Asymmetrical meters have both simple and compound elements.

TIME SIGNATURE	DIVISION OF BEAT	ACCENT PATTERN		SYMBOLS
$\frac{2}{4}$	simple	duple		
$\frac{3}{4}$	simple	triple		
$\frac{4}{4}$	simple	quadruple	𝄴	Common Time
$\frac{2}{2}$	simple	duple	𝄵	Cut Time; alla breve
$\frac{3}{2}$	simple	triple		
$\frac{3}{8}$	simple	triple		
$\frac{6}{8}$	compound	duple		
$\frac{9}{8}$	compound	triple		
$\frac{12}{8}$	compound	quadruple		
$\frac{5}{4}$	asymmetrical	2 + 3 or 3 + 2		
$\frac{7}{4}$	asymmetrical	4 + 3, 3 + 4, or 2 + 3 + 2		

LIST 1.22   CONDUCTING PATTERNS

1:

2:

3: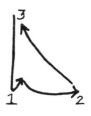

4: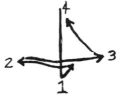

5 (2 + 3):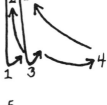

5 (3 + 2):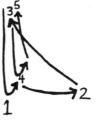

6 (3 + 3):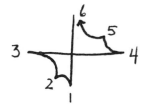

6 (2 + 2 + 2):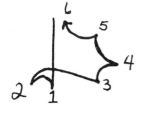

7 (3 + 4):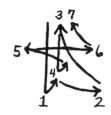

7 (4 + 3):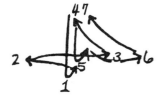

7 (2 + 3 + 2):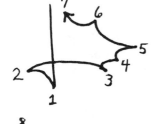

8:

LIST 1.23 FAMILIAR TUNES ILLUSTRATING VARIOUS METERS

Different editions of songs are often printed in different time signatures. The following list gives the general accent pattern and beat divisions of familiar songs.

SIMPLE DUPLE

"Buffalo Gals"
"This Old Man"
"Ruben and Rachel"
"Love Somebody"
"Dixie"
"This Land Is Your Land"
"She'll Be Comin' 'Round the Mountain"

COMPOUND DUPLE

"When Johnny Comes Marching Home"
"Greensleeves"
"Row, Row, Row Your Boat"
"The Farmer in the Dell"
"Three Blind Mice"
"Pop! Goes the Weasel"

SIMPLE TRIPLE

"Clementine"
"America (My Country 'Tis of Thee)"
"Kumbaya"
"The Star Spangled Banner"
"Home on the Range"
"Lavender's Blue"
"Daisy Bell (Bicycle Built for Two)"

COMPOUND TRIPLE

"Beautiful Dreamer"
"Down in the Valley"

SIMPLE QUADRUPLE

"Alouette"
"America the Beautiful"
"I've Been Workin' on the Railroad"
"Au Claire de la Lune"
"Bingo"
"London Bridge Is Falling Down"

See Also List 1.21, Time Signatures

LIST 1.24 FAMOUS COMPOSITIONS ILLUSTRATING VARIOUS TIME SIGNATURES

4/4
Eine Kleine Nachtmusik, K.#525, 1st mvt., Allegro — Mozart
"Sabre Dance" from *Gayane* — Khachaturian
March Slave — Tchaikovsky
Symphony no. 9 (*From the New World*), 2nd mvt., Largo — Dvořák
Overture to *Die Meistersinger* — Wagner
Symphony no. 1, 4th mvt., un poco allegretto e grazioso — Brahms
"Procession of the Sardar" from *Caucasian Sketches* — Ippolitoff-Ivanoff

2/4
Pomp and Circumstance March, op. 39, no. 1 — Elgar
"Toreador Song" from *Carmen* — Bizet
"To a Wild Rose" — MacDowell
"Hopak" from *The Fair at Sorochinsk* — Mussorgsky
Symphony no. 94 in G (*Surprise*), 2nd mvt., Andante — Haydn
Marche Militaire — Schubert
Symphony no. 7, 2nd mvt., Allegretto — Beethoven

3/4
Symphony no. 3 (*Eroica*), 1st mvt., Allegro con brio — Beethoven
"Skaters' Waltz" — Waldteufel
Symphony no. 8 (*Unfinished*), 1st mvt., Allegro moderato — Schubert
"Waltz" from *Sleeping Beauty* — Tchaikovsky
"Procession of the Nobles" from *Mlada* — Rimsky-Korsakov

2/2
"Stars and Stripes Forever March" — Sousa
"La Cinquantaine" — Gabriel-Marie

6/8
"Washington Post March" — Sousa
"Morning" from *Peer Gynt Suite* — Grieg
The Moldau — Smetana
"Barcarolle" from *The Tales of Hoffman* — Offenbach
"The Young Prince and Princess" from *Scheherezade* — Rimsky-Korsakov

OTHERS:

Overture to *Candide*	(7/4)	Bernstein
Symphony no. 6 (*Pathetique*), 2nd mvt., Allegro con grazia	(5/4)	Tchaikovsky
"Mars" from *The Planets*	(5/4)	Holst
"Neptune" from *The Planets*	(5/4)	Holst
Symphony no. 2, 1st mvt., Allegretto-Poco allegro-Tranquillo, ma poco a poco ravvivando il tempo al allegro	(6/4)	Sibelius
"Arabian Dance" from *The Nutcracker*	(3/8)	Tchaikovsky
Symphony no. 8 (*Unfinished*), 2nd mvt., Andante con moto	(3/8)	Schubert
"Pastoral Symphony" from *Messiah*	(12/8)	Händel
Symphony no. 5 Andante cantabile, con alcuna licenza	(12/8)	Tchaikovsky

CHANGING TIME SIGNATURES

The Rite of Spring — Stravinsky
Appalachian Spring — Copland
Adagio for Strings — Barber
"Promenade" from *Pictures at an Exhibition* — Mussorgsky

LIST 1.25 COMMON RHYTHMS

All rhythms are essentially variations on basic rhythmic patterns. For each set below, the top line shows several basic rhythmic patterns with their appropriate counting. Below each basic pattern are variations which utilize the same counting.

Basic Eighth Note Patterns:

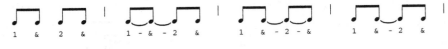

Variations:

Basic Sixteenth Note Patterns:

Variations:

Basic Triplet Patterns:

Variations:

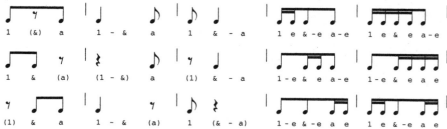

20

LIST 1.26 POPULAR SONGS AND RHYMES ILLUSTRATING VARIOUS RHYTHMS

"Battle Hymn of the Republic"

"Ten Little Indian Boys"

"One Potato, Two Potato"

"Twinkle, Twinkle, Little Star"

"Reuben and Rachel"

"Auld Lang Syne"

"Anniversary Waltz"

"Pop Goes the Weasel"

See Also List 1.27, "Famous Compositions Illustrating Various Rhythms."

LIST 1.27 FAMOUS COMPOSITIONS ILLUSTRATING VARIOUS RHYTHMS

	Romeo and Juliet Suite, op. 64, no. 2, 1st mvt., "The Montagues and Capulets"	Prokofiev
	Holberg Suite, 1st mvt., Prelude	Grieg
	Serenade in D, K250, "Haffner" 4th mvt.	Mozart
	Symphony #9, "Choral," 4th mvt., Main Theme	Beethoven
	Symphony #4 in F minor, op 36, 3rd mvt.	Tchaikovsky
	Hungarian Dance no. 1 in g minor	Brahms
	"Jesu, Joy of Man's Desiring," from Cantata no. 147, Vocal Theme	J.S. Bach
	Royal Fireworks	Händel
	St. Paul Suite 1st mvt., Jig	Holst

See Also List 1.26, Popular Songs & Rhymes Illustrating Various Rhythms.

LIST 1.28 ORNAMENTS AND GRACE NOTES

There are many variations in performing ornaments and grace notes that depend on the historical period of the music and other factors. Below is a general list of ornaments, by name, their appearance in music, and one common way of performing them.

NAME	WRITTEN	PLAYED
ACCIACCATURA		
APPOGGIATURA		
INVERTED MORDENT		
INVERTED TURN		
MORDENT		
TRILL		
TURN		

LIST 1.29 DYNAMIC MARKINGS

SYMBOL	ITALIAN TERM	DEFINITION
pp	pianissimo	very soft
p	piano	soft
mp	mezzo piano	moderately soft
mf	mezzo forte	moderately loud
f	forte	loud
ff	fortissimo	very loud
cresc.	crescendo	getting louder
<	crescendo	getting louder
dim.	diminuendo	getting softer
decresc.	decrescendo	getting softer
>	decrescendo	getting softer

LIST 1.30   ITALIAN TEMPO INDICATIONS

Adagietto   diminutive of adagio; somewhat faster than adagio

Adagio   at ease (slow)

Adagissimo   extremely slow

Allegretto   diminutive of allegro; somewhat slower than allegro

Allegro   cheerful (fast)

Andante   walking

Andantino   diminutive of andante; somewhat faster than andante

Grave   grave; solemn

Largamente   broadly

Larghetto   diminutive of largo; somewhat faster than largo

Largo   broad

Lento   slow

Moderato   moderate

Prestissimo   as fast as possible

Presto   very fast

Vivace   quick, lively

CHANGE OF TEMPO TERMS

accelerando   becoming faster

allargando   slowing down

allentando   slowing down

largando   slowing down

meno mosso   less motion (slower)

piu mosso   more motion (faster)

rallentando (rall.)   gradual slackening in speed

ritardando (ritard., rit.)   gradual slackening in speed

ritenuto   immediate reduction of speed

rubato   deliberate unsteadiness of tempo

stringendo (string.)   "drawing tight" (faster)

sustenuto   slackening the tempo

See Also List 1.31, Rudimentary Phrasing, Style, and Articulation Terms

LIST 1.31 RUDIMENTARY PHRASING, STYLE, AND ARTICULATION TERMS

a piacere	performer uses his discretion as to tempo and rhythm
accent	emphasis on a note or chord
agitato	excited
amabile	graceful
amoroso	tender and affectionate
animato	animated; lively
appassionato	with intense emotion
articulation	clarity of musical performance
attack	promptness and decision in beginning a tone
bel canto	vocal style emphasizing beauty of sound
brillante	bright
calando	gradually softer and slower
calmo	calm, tranquil
cantabile	in a singing style
comodo	easy, agreeable
con anima	with life and animation
con fuoco	with energy or passion (fire)
con brio	with vigor and spirit
con moto	with motion
con spirito	spirited
decay	the resolution of a note or chord
deciso	boldly, decisively
delicato	delicate
deliberatamente	deliberately
desto	brisk, sprightly
detache	detached
dolce	sweetly
doloroso	sorrowfully
energico	energetic
espressivo	expressively
flessibile	flexible
furioso	furious
giocoso	humorous
grandioso	with grandeur
grazioso	with grace
incalzando	getting faster and louder
innocente	innocently
legato	connected, smoothly

26

leggiero	lightly
lugubre	sad, mournful
maestoso	majestically
marcato	marked, stressed
marziale	martial, in the style of a march
mesto	sad, mournful
morendo	dying away
passionato	passionate
perdendosi	dying away
pesante	heavy
phrase	a complete musical thought; a musical sentence
piacevole	pleasing, agreeable
pomposo	pompous, grand
religioso	religiously, solemn
risoluto	bold
rubato	freely with respect to tempo
rustico	rural, rustic
scherzando	playful, lively
semplice	simple
sempre	always, continuously
sentimentale	sentimentally
sentito	expressive
serioso	serious
simile	similarly, continue in the same manner
slur	two or more notes connected by a single articulation
solenne	solemn
sordamente	muted, softly
sostenuto	sustained, legato
sospirando	sighing, doleful
sotto voce	in an undertone
spiccato	bounced bowing
spiritoso	spirited
staccato	short, detached
sustain	the continuous sound between attack and decay
tenuto (ten.)	sustained, held out
tranquillo	tranquilly
veloce	fast

LIST 1.32 RUDIMENTARY VOCABULARY AND SYMBOLS

accent	>	emphasis on a note or chord
alto clef	𝄡	indicates middle C on third line of staff
bar line		separates a staff into measures
bass clef	𝄢	indicates F below middle C on the fourth line of the staff
caesura	//	pause
coda	⊕	ending (sign indicates go to coda)
crescendo	<	get louder
da capo	D.C.	"from the head" (go back to the beginning)
decrescendo	>	get softer
del segno	D.S.	"from the sign" (go back to sign)
diminuendo	>	get softer
double bar	‖	indicates the end of a piece or section
fermata	𝄐	"hold" hold note longer than rhythm indicated
fine	*Fine*	ending
first ending		ending to be used the first time
flat	♭	lowers a note one half-step
forte-piano	*fp*	loud immediately followed by soft
forzando, forzato	*fz*	sudden, strong accent
key signature		tells what notes to play sharp or flat in a piece or section
Generalpause (grand pause)	G.P.	silence
Maelzel Metronome	M.M. ♩ = 80	metronome marking indicating number of beats per minute

28

List 1.32 (continued)

measure		a group of beats, recurring consistently, divided by bar lines
measure repeat	./.	repeat the previous measure
natural	♮	cancels a sharp or flat
octave	8va	play the music one octave (8 notes) higher (sometimes lower)
phrase	,	breathe
repeat sign	:‖	repeat back to the beginning or to the last facing repeat sign
second ending	2.	ending to be used upon taking a repeat
sforzando, sforzato	*sf*	sudden, strong accent
sforzando, sforzato	*sfz*	sudden, strong accent
sharp	♯	raises a note one half-step
sign (segno)	𝄋	go back to this sign at a D.S.
slur		two different pitches which are connected (in one breath, bow stroke, etc.)
staff		5 lines and 4 spaces, upon which music is written
tie		two of the same (pitch) notes to be played together as one longer note
time signature	$\frac{3}{4}$	numbers at the beginning of a piece of music which relate information about the rhythms, accent patterns, beat divisions, etc.
treble clef	𝄞	indicates G above middle C on the second line of the staff
trill	*tr*	ornamentation consisting of alternation of two consecutive notes

LIST 1.33 TYPES OF NOTATION

Ecphonetic	A.D. 600–1000
Chironomy	8th Century
Neumatic	8th–14th Centuries
Daseian Notation	9th–10th Centuries
Modal Notation	c. 1175–1250
Mensural	c. 1250–1600
White Mensural Notation	c. 1450–1600
Tablature	15th–17th Centuries
Figured Bass	1600–1750
Thoroughbass	1600–1750
Fasola	17th–18th Centuries
Tonic Sol-Fa	developed c. 1840
Modern Notation	after 1600 (to present)

Section II

MUSIC THEORY

LIST 2.1   THE MODES

MODE	HALF-STEPS BETWEEN	EXAMPLE
Ionian	3 & 4; 7 & 8	
Dorian	2 & 3; 6 & 7	
Phrygian	1 & 2; 5 & 6	
Lydian	4 & 5; 7 & 8	
Mixolydian	3 & 4; 6 & 7	
Aeolian	2 & 3; 5 & 6	
Locrian	1 & 2; 4 & 5	

LIST 2.2 TYPES OF SCALES

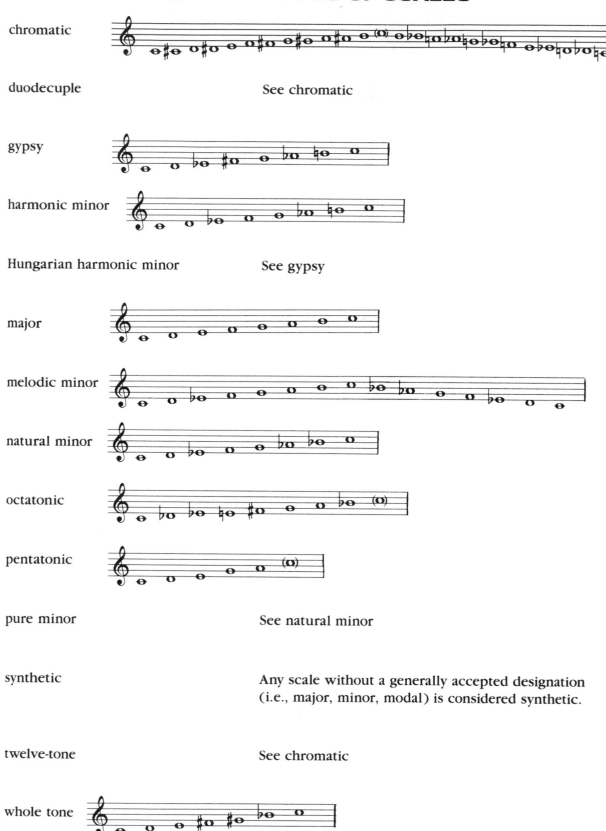

chromatic

duodecuple   See chromatic

gypsy

harmonic minor

Hungarian harmonic minor   See gypsy

major

melodic minor

natural minor

octatonic

pentatonic

pure minor   See natural minor

synthetic   Any scale without a generally accepted designation (i.e., major, minor, modal) is considered synthetic.

twelve-tone   See chromatic

whole tone

LIST 2.3 SCALE DEGREE NAMES

1. tonic   the keynote
2. supertonic   one whole step above the tonic
3. mediant   halfway between the tonic and the dominant
4. subdominant   a perfect fifth below the tonic
5. dominant   a perfect fifth above the tonic
6. submediant   halfway between the tonic and the subdominant
7. (subtonic)   one whole step below the tonic
7. leading tone   one half-step below the tonic

C MAJOR:

1. tonic   2. supertonic   3. mediant   4. subdominant   5. dominant   6. submediant   ♭7. subtonic   7. leading tone

LIST 2.4 FAMOUS COMPOSITIONS ILLUSTRATING VARIOUS TONALITIES AND SCALE PATTERNS

whole tone	"Nuages" from *Nocturnes*	Claude Debussy
pentatonic	Prelude no. 2, "Voiles"	Claude Debussy
major	"Hallelujah Chorus" from *Messiah*	Georg Friedrich Händel
melodic minor	"Carol of the Bells"	Traditional
harmonic minor	"Marche Slave"	Peter Tchaikovsky
natural minor	"Oh Come, Oh Come, Emanuel"	15th Century
pandiatonic	*Trois Gymnopédies* *Appalachian Spring*	Erik Satie Aaron Copland
polytonal	*Le Boeuf sur la toit* *Three Places in New England*	Darius Milhaud Charles Ives
octatonic	"Theme" from *Octet*	Igor Stravinsky
dorian mode	Violin Concerto op. 47, 1st mvt., Allegro moderato	Jean Sibelius
phrygian mode	String Quartet in F, 1st mvt., Allegro moderato (2nd theme, melody)	Maurice Ravel
lydian mode	Lydia	Gabriel Fauré
mixolydian mode	"Prologue" from *Serenade for Tenor, Horn and Strings*	Benjamin Britten
locrian mode	Violin Concerto in D minor (1940), 2nd mvt., Andante sostenuto	Aram Khachaturian
gypsy scale	Nocturne in C Minor, op. 48, no. 1	Frédéric Chopin

LIST 2.5   INTERVALS

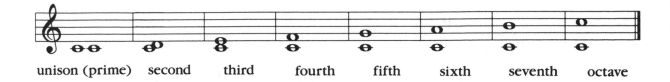

unison (prime)   second   third   fourth   fifth   sixth   seventh   octave

See Also List 2.7, Compound Intervals

LIST 2.6   QUALITIES OF INTERVALS

An interval is called either perfect or major if the top note exists in the key of the bottom note. Unisons, fourths, fifths, and octaves are perfect, while seconds, thirds, sixths, and sevenths are major.

Relation of top to bottom note:	unisons, fourths, fifths, octaves	seconds, thirds, sixths, sevenths	Examples
Top note in the key of the bottom note	perfect (P)	major (M)	P4 M3
Top note one half-step lower	diminished (d)	minor (m)	d5 m3
Top note two half-steps lower	doubly diminished (dd)	diminished (d)	dd5 d3
Top note one half-step higher	augmented (A)	augmented (A)	A4 A3

36

© 1994 by Parker Publishing Company

LIST 2.7 COMPOUND INTERVALS

Compound intervals are those which are larger than an octave. They follow the same rules as their smaller counterparts, for example:

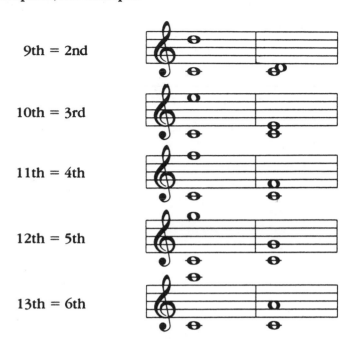

9th = 2nd

10th = 3rd

11th = 4th

12th = 5th

13th = 6th

LIST 2.8 INVERSIONS OF INTERVALS

Inversion of an interval occurs when one of the notes is moved by an octave so that the top note/bottom note relationship is reversed.

Interval

seconds become sevenths
sevenths become seconds

thirds become sixths
sixths become thirds

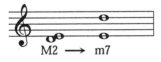

fourths become fifths
fifths become fourths

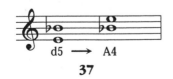

Quality

Major intervals become
minor intervals

Minor intervals become
major intervals

Perfect intervals remain
perfect intervals

Augmented intervals become
diminished intervals

Diminished intervals become
augmented intervals

37

LIST 2.9 SONGS TO AID THE TEACHING OF INTERVALS

INTERVAL	ASCENDING	DESCENDING
minor 2nd	"Stormy Weather" (Arlen)	"Button Up Your Overcoat" from *Follow Through* (Desylva, Brown, Henderson)
Major 2nd	"Do-Re-Mi" from *The Sound of Music* (Rodgers)	"Mary Had a Little Lamb" (Traditional)
minor 3rd	"So Long, Farewell" from *The Sound of Music* (Rodgers)	"The Star Spangled Banner" (Key)
Major 3rd	"Kumbaya" (Folk Song)	"Swing Low, Sweet Chariot" (Spiritual)
Perfect 4th	"Bridal Chorus" from *Lohengrin* (Wagner)	"Clementine" (Folk Song)
Augmented 4th/ Diminished 5th	"Maria" from *West Side Story* (Bernstein)	4th Theme from *The Incredible Flutist* (Piston)
Perfect 5th	"Twinkle, Twinkle, Little Star" (Traditional)	"Feelings" (Albert)
minor 6th	"Go Down, Moses" (Spiritual)	Theme from *Love Story* (Lai)
Major 6th	"My Bonnie Lies Over the Ocean" (Traditional)	"Nobody Knows the Trouble I've Seen" (Spiritual)
Minor 7th	"Somewhere" from *West Side Story* (Bernstein)	"How Am I to Know?" (King)
Major 7th/ Diminished octave	"I Love You" (Porter)	"Back in Your Own Backyard" (Jolson, Rose, Dreyer)
Octave	"Over the Rainbow" from *The Wizard of Oz* (Arlen)	"It's D'lovely" from *Red Hot and Blue* (Porter)

LIST 2.10 TRIADS

A triad is made up of three notes, each having the interval of a third between them.

TRIAD TYPE	BOTTOM INTERVAL	TOP INTERVAL	EXAMPLES
Major	Major third	minor third	
minor	minor third	Major third	
Augmented	Major third	Major third	
diminished	minor third	minor third	

LIST 2.11 INVERSIONS OF TRIADS

INVERSION	DESCRIPTION	EXAMPLE	FIGURED BASS
root position	root of the chord is the lowest note		(none)
first inversion	third of the chord is the lowest note		6
second inversion	fifth of the chord is the lowest note		6 4

LIST 2.12 INVERSIONS OF SEVENTH CHORDS

INVERSION	EXAMPLE	FIGURED BASS
root position		7
first inversion		6 5
second inversion		4 3
third inversion (seventh in bass)		4 2

LIST 2.13 RULES OF FOUR-PART HARMONY

CHORD CONSTRUCTION

1. Use a complete chord whenever possible; omit fifth if necessary.
2. Double the bass in root position.
3. Double the soprano in first inversion.
4. Double the bass in second inversion.
5. Avoid doubling the leading tone or any altered tone.
6. Avoid spacing upper voices more than an octave apart.

VOICE LEADING

1. Repeat tones whenever possible.
2. Conjunct motion is preferable to disjunct motion.
3. Use consonant rather than dissonant leaps.
4. Avoid parallel unisons, octaves, and perfect fifths.
5. Resolve active tones to stable tones.
6. Avoid overlapping or crossing voices.
7. Strive for a balance of similar, contrary, oblique, and parallel motions between parts.

LIST 2.14 COMMON HARMONIC PROGRESSIONS

CHORD	USUALLY FOLLOWED BY	SOMETIMES FOLLOWED BY	LESS OFTEN FOLLOWED BY
I	V	IV	ii or iii
ii	V	IV or vi	I or iii
iii	vi	IV	I, ii or V
IV	V	I or ii	iii or vi
V	I	IV or vi	ii or iii
vi	I or V	iii or IV	I
vii	iii	I	

LIST 2.15   NON-HARMONIC TONES

A non-harmonic tone is a note which is not consonant with the other notes in the chord to which it belongs, and therefore must be "resolved."

NON-HARMONIC TONE	ABBREVIATION/ EXAMPLE	PRECEDED BY	RESOLVED BY
anticipation	ANT	step or leap	change of harmony
appoggiatura	APP	leap	step
cambiata	CAMB	leap in the same direction as the resolution	step
escape tone (échappée)	ET	step in the opposite direction as the resolution	leap
neighboring group	NG	step	step

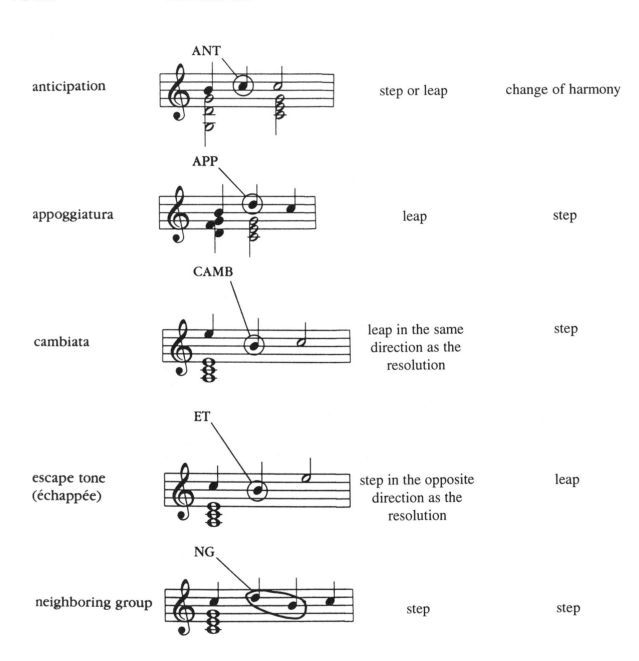

© 1994 by Parker Publishing Company

NON-HARMONIC TONE	ABBREVIATION/ EXAMPLE	PRECEDED BY	RESOLVED BY
neighboring tone (auxiliary tone)	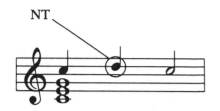	step	step in the opposite direction
passing tone		step	step in the same direction
pedal tone	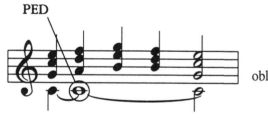	oblique motion	change of harmony
retardation	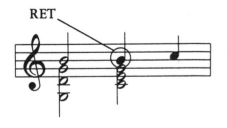	oblique motion	step (ascending)
suspension	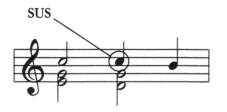	oblique motion	step (descending)

LIST 2.16 CADENCES

Two chords that end a musical phrase are known as a cadence.

CADENCE   EXAMPLE/FIGURED BASS   DEFINITION

Authentic

V   I

A cadence with a progression from dominant to tonic.

Cadential 6/4

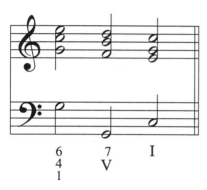

6   7   I
4   V
1

A cadence containing three chords in which the tonic six-four is resolved by a step to the dominant, then to its resolution.

Deceptive

V^7 v i

A cadence in which the dominant progresses to a substitute for the tonic.

Half

I   V

A cadence which ends on the dominant.

CADENCE   EXAMPLE/FIGURED BASS   DEFINITION

Imperfect Authentic

V   I

An authentic cadence which is not perfect.

Perfect Authentic

V   I

An authentic cadence with both chords in root position *and* the root of the tonic chord is in the soprano.

Phrygian

v i⁶   V

A half cadence in which the root of the dominant chord is in both soprano and bass, *and* is approached by a step from opposite directions.

Plagal

IV   I

A cadence which progresses from subdominant to tonic.

Progressive

Any cadence which concludes a phrase with a chord other than the tonic.

Terminal

Any cadence in which the final chord is heard as the tonic.

LIST 2.17 CHROMATIC AND OTHER HARMONIES

CHORD NAME	EXAMPLES	DEFINITIONS
Appoggiatura Chord		A suspended chord which resolves after the harmonic change
Augmented Chord		A chord built in major thirds. The fifth of an augmented chord generally resolves up to the third or root of the following harmony.
Augmented Sixth Chords	 Italian German French	A chord in which the interval of the augmented sixth in the first harmony resolves out to the interval of an octave in the second harmony. The three types are Italian, German and French.
Borrowed Harmonies		Harmonies borrowed from the parallel minor key.
Cluster		Chords of three or more consecutive seconds.
Diminished Seventh		A harmony constructed of three minor thirds.
Eleventh Chord		An extended tertian harmony which encompasses the interval of an eleventh. The eleventh is generally raised.

List 2.17 (continued)

CHORD NAME	EXAMPLES	DEFINITIONS
Mystic Chord		A harmony built with perfect, augmented and diminished fourths, devised and employed by Alexander Scriabin.
Neapolitan Sixth		A major triad built on the lowered supertonic; most frequently used in first inversion.
Non-tertian Harmonies	quartal quintal	Harmonies built with intervals other than the third (secundal, quartal, quintal).
Polychord		Combinations of conventional chords sounding simultaneously.
Secondary Dominant		A chord of dominant function used to create temporary tonics.
Secondary Leading Tone		Acts as a leading tone to the temporary tonic.
Whole Tone Chord		A harmonic structure composed of notes from the whole tone scale.

LIST 2.18 FORMS AND COMPOSITIONAL TECHNIQUES

FORM	COMPOSITION	COMPOSER
SONG FORMS		
simple binary	"America"	Traditional
ternary	"Sidmung," op. 25, no. 1	Robert Schumann
through-composed	"Restless Love," op. 5, no. 1	Franz Schubert
da capo aria	"Where E'er You Walk"	Georg Friedrich Händel
SINGLE MOVEMENT FORMS		
rondo	Piano Sonata in C, K. 545, 3rd mvt., Rondo	Wolfgang Amadeus Mozart
sonata	Symphony no. 40 in G Minor, K. 550, 1st mvt., Molto allegro	Wolfgang Amadeus Mozart
minuet and trio	Quintet in E, op. 13, no. 5, 3rd mvt., Minuetto	Luigi Boccherini
theme and variations	Variations on a Theme of Haydn	Johannes Brahms
COMPOSITIONAL TECHNIQUES		
invention	Two- and Three-Part Inventions	Johann Sebastian Bach
fugue	Concerto Grosso no. 1 in D Minor for Strings and Piano Obbligato, 4th mvt., Fugue: Allegro	Ernest Bloch
passacaglia	"Dido's Lament" from *Dido and Aeneas*	Henry Purcell
chaconne	Chaconne in D minor	Johann Sebastian Bach
dodecaphony (twelve-tone)	Violin Concerto	Alban Berg
pointillism	Octet in E-flat, op. 20, 3rd mvt., Scherzo: Allegro leggierissimo	Felix Mendelssohn
hemiola	Slavonic Dance no. 8	Antonín Dvořák
pedal point	Finale from *The Firebird*	Igor Stravinsky
canon	Violin Sonata in A, 4th mvt., Allegretto poco mosso	César Franck
minimalism	In C	Terry Reilly

Section III

COMPOSERS AND THEIR WORKS

LIST 3.1   PRE-BAROQUE COMPOSERS

Léonin	12th century	France
Pérotin	1160–1220	France
Guillaume de Mauchaut	c. 1300–c. 1377	France
John Dunstable	c. 1385–c. 1453	England
Guillaume Dufay	c. 1400–c.1474	Netherlands
Josquin Des Prez	c. 1440–1521	Franco-Flemish
Andrea Gabrieli	1510–1586	Italy
Giovanni Pierluigi da Palestrina	1525–1594	Italy
Orlando di Lasso	1532–1594	Netherlands
William Byrd	1543–1623	England
Tomás Luis de Victoria	c. 1548–1611	Spain
Thomas Morley	1557–1602	England
Giovanni Gabrieli	c. 1557–1612	Italy
Carlo Gesualdo	c. 1560–1613	Italy
John Dowland	1563–1626	England
Claudio Monteverdi	1567–1643	Italy
Michael Praetorius	1571–1621	Germany
Girolamo Frescobaldi	1583–1643	Italy
Orlando Gibbons	1583–1625	England
Heinrich Schütz	1585–1672	Germany

LIST 3.2   REPRESENTATIVE BAROQUE PERIOD COMPOSERS AND THEIR COUNTRIES

The Baroque Period in Europe began around 1600 and lasted approximately 150 years. The music of the following composers exhibits certain stylistic characteristics associated with this era. (See Section VI)

Tommaso Albinoni	1671–1751	Italy
Thomas Arne	1710–1778	England
Johann Sebastian Bach	1685–1750	Germany
William Boyce	1711–1779	England
Dietrich Buxtehude	c. 1637–1707	Denmark
Jeremiah Clarke	1673–1707	England
Archangelo Corelli	1653–1713	Italy
François Couperin	1668–1693	France
Johann Joseph Fux	1660–1741	Austria
Francesco Geminiani	1687–1762	Italy
Georg Friedrich Händel	1685–1759	Germany/England
Jean Baptiste Lully	1632–1687	France
Pietro Nardini	1722–1793	Italy
Johann Pachelbel	1653–1706	Germany
Henry Purcell	1659–1695	England
Jean Phillipe Rameau	1683–1764	France
Alessandro Scarlatti	1660–1725	Italy
Domenico Scarlatti	1685–1757	Italy/Spain
John Stanley	1712–1786	England
Giuseppe Tartini	1692–1770	Italy
Georg Philipp Telemann	1681–1767	Germany
Antonio Vivaldi	1678–1741	Italy

See Also List 6.4, Some General Characteristics of Baroque Music

LIST 3.3 REPRESENTATIVE CLASSICAL PERIOD COMPOSERS AND THEIR COUNTRIES

The Classical Period in European music began circa 1750 and lasted until about 1825. The following composers' works exhibit certain stylistic characteristics associated with this era. (See Section VI)

Carl Philipp Emanuel Bach	1714-1788	Germany
Johann Christian Bach	1735-1782	Germany
Ludwig van Beethoven	1770-1827	Germany/Austria
Luigi Boccherini	1743-1805	Italy
Muzio Clementi	1752-1832	Italy/England
Carl Czerny	1791-1857	Austria
Anton Diabelli	1781-1858	Austria
Carl von Dittersdorf	1739-1799	Austria
Christoph Gluck	1714-1787	Germany
Franz Joseph Haydn	1732-1809	Austria
Friedrich Kuhlau	1786-1832	Denmark
Wolfgang Amadeus Mozart	1756-1791	Austria
Ignaz Pleyel	1757-1831	Austria
Antonio Salieri	1750-1825	Italy
Giovanni Sammartini	1700-1775	Italy
Franz Schubert	1797-1828	Austria
Carl Stamitz	1745-1801	Germany

See Also List 6.6, General Characteristics of Classical Period Music

LIST 3.4 REPRESENTATIVE ROMANTIC PERIOD COMPOSERS AND THEIR COUNTRIES

The Romantic Era in European music began around 1825 and lasted until the turn of the twentieth century. The composers in this list wrote music which exhibits the characteristics of "Romantic Music." (See Section VI)

Hector Berlioz	1803-1869	France
Johannes Brahms	1833-1897	Germany/Austria
Frédéric Chopin	1810-1849	Poland/France
Franz Liszt	1811-1886	Hungary
Felix Mendelssohn	1809-1847	Germany
Niccolò Paganini	1782-1840	Italy
Giacomo Puccini	1712-1781	Italy
Camille Saint-Saëns	1835-1921	France
Robert Schumann	1810-1856	Germany
Johann Strauss, Jr.	1825-1899	Austria
Richard Strauss	1864-1949	Germany
Peter Tchaikovsky	1840-1893	Russia
Giuseppe Verdi	1813-1901	Italy
Richard Wagner	1813-1883	Germany

See Also List 3.5, Nationalist Composers; and List 6.7, General Characteristics of Romantic Era Music

LIST 3.5 NATIONALIST COMPOSERS

Nationalism, a movement which began in the second half of the nineteenth century, can be observed in history as well as in the arts. It can be described as an urge composers felt to represent their native heritage through their music.

EASTERN EUROPE

Béla Bartók	1881–1945
Frédéric Chopin	1810–1849
Antonín Dvořák	1841–1904
Franz Erkel	1810–1893
Zoltán Kodály	1882–1967
Stanislaw Moniuszko	1819–1872
Moritz Moszkowski	1854–1925
Carl Orff	1895–1982
Ignace Jan Paderewski	1860–1941
Ludwig Philipp Scharwenka	1847–1917
Karl Šebor	1843–1903
Jan Nepomuk Škroup	1811–1892
Bedrich Smetana	1824–1884
Henri Wieniawski	1835–1880

ENGLAND

Granville Bantock	1868–1946
Arnold Bax	1883–1953
Edward Elgar	1857–1934
Gustav Holst	1874–1934
Ralph Vaughan Williams	1872–1958

FRANCE

Hector Berlioz	1803–1869
Emmanuel Chabrier	1841–1894
Claude Debussy	1862–1918
Gabriel Fauré	1845–1924
César Franck	1822–1890
Maurice Ravel	1875–1937
Camille Saint-Saëns	1835–1921

GERMANY

Anton Bruckner	1824–1896
Johannes Brahms	1833–1897
Gustav Mahler	1860–1911
Robert Schumann	1810–1856
Richard Strauss	1864–1949
Richard Wagner	1813–1883

ITALY

Giuseppe Verdi	1813–1901

RUSSIA

Mily Balakirev	1837–1910
Alexander Borodin	1833–1887
Cesar Cui	1835–1918
Alexander Dargomijski	1813–1869
Mikhail Glinka	1804–1857
Modest Mussorgsky	1839–1881
Nicolai Rimsky-Korsakov	1844–1908
Anton Rubinstein	1829–1894
Nicholai Rubinstein	1835–1881
Peter Tchaikovsky	1840–1893

SCANDANAVIA

Niels W. Gade	1817–1890
Edvard Grieg	1843–1907
Armas Järnefelt	1869–1958
Selim Palmgren	1878–1951
Ludwig Schytte	1848–1909
Jean Sibelius	1865–1957
Emil Sjögren	1853–1918

SPAIN

Isaac Albeniz	1860–1909
Manuel de Falla	1876–1946
Enrique Granados	1867–1916

UNITED STATES

Aaron Copland	1900–1990
George Gershwin	1898–1937
Roy Harris	1898–1979

See Also List 6.11, Les Six; and List 6.12, The Mighty Handful

LIST 3.6 20TH CENTURY COMPOSERS

John Adams	U.S.A.	1947–
Malcolm Arnold	England	1921–
Georges Auric	France	1899–1978
Milton Babbitt	U.S.A.	1916–1983
Samuel Barber	U.S.A.	1910–1981
Arthur Benjamin	Australia	1893–1960
Béla Bartók	Hungary	1881–1945
Arnold Bax	England	1883–1953
Leon Beiderbecke	U.S.A.	1903–1931
Alban Berg	Austria	1885–1935
Luciano Berio	Italy	1925–
Irving Berlin	U.S.A.	1888–1989
Leonard Bernstein	U.S.A.	1918–1990
Arthur Bliss	England	1891–1975
Pierre Boulez	France	1925–
Benjamin Britten	England	1913–1976
John Cage	U.S.A.	1912–1992
Elliot Carter	U.S.A.	1908–
Carlos Chavez	Mexico	1899–1978
Aaron Copland	U.S.A.	1900–1990
John Corigliano	U.S.A.	1938–
Henry Cowell	U.S.A.	1897–1965
Paul Creston	U.S.A.	1906–1985
George Crumb	U.S.A.	1929–
Luigi Dallapiccola	Italy	1904–1975
Walter Damrosch	U.S.A.	1862–1950
Peter Maxwell Davies	England	1934–
Claude Debussy	France	1862–1918
Norman Dello-Joio	U.S.A.	1913–
David Del Tredici	U.S.A.	1937–
David Diamond	U.S.A.	1915–
Ernst von Dohnanyi	Hungary	1877–1960
Sir Edward Elgar	England	1857–1934
Manuel de Falla	Spain	1867–1946
Gerald Finzi	England	1901–1956
Carlisle Floyd	U.S.A.	1926–
Lukas Foss	U.S.A.	1922–
George Gershwin	U.S.A.	1898–1937
Alberto Ginastera	Argentina	1916–1983
Philip Glass	U.S.A.	1937–
Reinhold Glière	Russia	1875–1956
Morton Gould	U.S.A.	1913-1996
Ferde Grofé	U.S.A.	1892–1972
William Christopher Handy	U.S.A.	1873–1958
Howard Hanson	U.S.A.	1896–1981
Roy Harris	U.S.A.	1898–1979
Lou Harrison	U.S.A.	1917–

List 3.6 (continued)

Hans Werner Henze	Germany	1926–
Paul Hindemith	Germany	1895–1963
Gustav Holst	England	1874–1934
Arthur Honegger	Switzerland	1892–1955
Alan Hovhaness	U.S.A.	1911–
Karel Husa	Czechoslovakia/U.S.A.	1921–
Charles Ives	U.S.A.	1874–1954
Dimitri Kabalevsky	Russia	1904–1987
Aram Khachaturian	Russia	1903–1978
Zoltán Kodály	Hungary	1882–1967
Erich Korngold	Austria	1897–1957
György Ligeti	Hungary	1923–
Charles Loeffler	U.S.A.	1861–1935
Frederick Loewe	U.S.A.	1901–1988
Otto Luening	U.S.A.	1900–
Witold Lutoslawski	Poland	1913–
Gian-Carlo Menotti	U.S.A.	1911–
Oliver Messiaen	France	1908–1992
Darius Milhaud	France	1892–1974
Douglas Moore	U.S.A.	1893–1969
Karl Orff	Germany	1895–1982
Arvo Pärt	Estonia	1935–
Krystof Penderecki	Poland	1933–
Walter Piston	U.S.A.	1894–1976
Francis Poulenc	France	1899–1963
Sergei Prokofiev	Russia	1891–1953
Sergei Rachmaninoff	Russia	1873–1943
Priaulx Rainier	South Africa	1903–1986
Maurice Ravel	France	1875–1937
Steve Reich	U.S.A.	1936–
Ottorino Respighi	Italy	1879–1936
Emil von Reznicek	Austria	1860–1945
George Rochberg	U.S.A.	1918–
Ned Rorem	U.S.A.	1923–
Carl Ruggles	U.S.A.	1876–1971
Franz Schmidt	Austria	1874–1939
Arnold Schoenberg	Austria	1874–1951
William Schuman	U.S.A.	1910–1992
Roger Sessions	U.S.A.	1896–1985
Dimitri Shostakovich	Russia	1906–1975
Jean Sibelius	Finland	1865–1957
Stephen Sondheim	U.S.A.	1930–
Karlheinz Stockhausen	Germany	1928–
Richard Strauss	Germany	1864–1949
Igor Stravinsky	Russia	1882–1971
Virgil Thomson	U.S.A.	1896–1989
Michael Tippett	England	1905–
Joaquin Turina	Spain	1882–1949

List 3.6 (continued)

Edgard Varèse	U.S.A.	1883–1965
Ralph Vaughan Williams	England	1872–1958
Heitor Villa-Lobos	Brazil	1887–1959
William Walton	England	1902–1983
Peter Warlock	England	1894–1930
Anton Webern	Austria	1883–1945
Kurt Weill	Germany	1900–1950
Malcolm Williamson	Australia	1931–
Charles Widor	France	1844–1937
Jannis Xenakis	Greece	1922–
Riccardo Zandonai	Italy	1883–1944

See Also List 3.19, Women Composers; List 3.20, African-American Composers; and List 6.5, General Characteristics of Twentieth Century Music

LIST 3.7   AMERICAN COMPOSERS

Leroy Anderson	1908-1975	Ferde Grofé	1892-1972
John Adams	1947-	Howard Hanson	1896-1981
Milton Babbitt	1916-1983	Roy Harris	1898-1979
Leon Beiderbecke	1903-1931	Victor Herbert	1859-1924
Irving Berlin	1888-1989	Alan Hovhaness	1911-
Leonard Bernstein	1918-1990	Charles Ives	1874-1954
William Billings	1746-1800	Scott Joplin	1869-1917
James Bland	1854-1911	Otto Luening	1900-
Harry Burleigh	1866-1949	Edward MacDowell	1861-1908
John Cage	1912-1992	Gian Carlo Menotti	1911-
John Carpenter	1876-1951	Douglas Moore	1893-1969
Elliot Carter	1908-	Harry Partch	1901-1976
Edgar Clark	1913-	Walter Piston	1894-1976
Aaron Copland	1900-1990	Cole Porter	1892-1965
John Corigliano	1938	Quincy Porter	1897-1966
Henry Cowell	1897-1965	Richard Rodgers	1902-1979
Paul Creston	1906-1985	Sigmund Romberg	1887-1951
George Crumb	1929-	Ned Rorem	1923-
Walter Damrosch	1862-1950	Carl Ruggles	1876-1971
Norman Dello-Joio	1913-	William Schuman	1910-1992
David Diamond	1915-	Roger Sessions	1896-1985
Emma Lou Diemer	1927-	Stephen Sondheim	1930-
Carlisle Floyd	1926-	John Philip Sousa	1854-1932
Lukas Foss	1922-	Deems Taylor	1885-1966
Stephen Foster	1826-1864	Virgil Thompson	1896-1989
George Gershwin	1898-1937	Edgar Varèse	1883-1965
Philip Glass	1937-	Vincent Youmans	1898-1946
Morton Gould	1913-1996	Ellen Zwilich	1939-
Charles Griffes	1884-1920		

See Also List 3.19, Women Composers; and List 3.20, African-American Composers

LIST 3.8 AUSTRIAN COMPOSERS

Alban Berg	1885-1935	Gustav Mahler	1860-1911
Marie Léopoldine Blahetka	1811-1887	Marianne von Martinez	1744-1812
Anton Bruckner	1824-1896	Wolfgang Amadeus Mozart	1756-1791
Carl Czerny	1791-1857	Ignaz Pleyel	1757-1831
Anton Diabelli	1781-1858	Emil von Reznicek	1860-1945
Marianne Di Martinez	1744-1812	Franz Schmidt	1874-1939
Carl Dittersdorf	1739-1799	Arnold Schoenberg	1874-1951
Gottfried von Einem	1918-	Franz Schreker	1878-1934
Johann Fux	1660-1741	Franz Schubert	1797-1828
Carl Goldmark	1830-1915	Johann Strauss, Jr.	1825-1899
Franz Joseph Haydn	1732-1809	Franz von Suppe	1819-1895
Michael Haydn	1737-1806	Georg Wagenseil	1715-1777
Erich Korngold	1897-1957	Anton von Webern	1883-1945
Ernst Krenek	1900-	Hugo Wolf	1860-1903
Josef Lanner	1801-1843		

See Also List 3.19, Women Composers

LIST 3.9 BRITISH COMPOSERS

Thomas Arne	1710-1778	Edward German	1862-1936
Malcolm Arnold	1921-	Orlando Gibbons	1585-1625
Thomas Attwood	1765-1838	Ivor Gurney	1890-1973
Charles Avison	1709-1770	Hamilton Harty	1879-1941
Arnold Bax	1883-1953	Alun Hoddinott	1929-
Richard Bennett	1936-	Gustav Holst	1874-1934
William Bennett	1816-1875	John Ireland	1879-1962
Lennox Berkeley	1903-1989	Matthew Locke	1621-1677
Arthur Bliss	1891-1975	Thea Musgrave	1928-
John Blow	1649-1708	Hubert Parry	1848-1918
William Boyce	1711-1779	Roger Quilter	1877-1953
Frank Bridge	1879-1941	Thomas Ravenscroft	1582-1635
Benjamin Britten	1913-1976	Alan Rawsthorne	1905-1971
John Bull	1810-1880	Cyril Scott	1879-1970
William Byrd	1543-1623	John Stainer	1840-1901
Jeremiah Clarke	1673-1707	Charles Stanford	1852-1924
Eric Coates	1886-1957	John Stanley	1712-1786
Samuel Coleridge-Taylor	1875-1912	Arthur Sullivan	1842-1900
William Croft	1678-1727	Thomas Tallis	1505-1585
William Crotch	1775-1847	John Taverner	1944-
Peter Maxwell Davies	1934-	Michael Tippett	1905-
Frederick Delius	1862-1934	Thomas Tomkins	1572-1656
John Dowland	1563-1626	Christopher Tye	1505-1572
John Dunstable	1390-1453	Ralph Vaughan Williams	1872-1958
John Eccles	1668-1735	William Walton	1902-1983
Edward Elgar	1857-1934	Peter Warlock	1894-1930
Giles Farnaby	1563-1640	Thomas Weelkes	1576-1623
John Field	1782-1837	Samuel Wesley	1766-1837
Gerald Finzi	1901-1956	Samuel Sebastian Wesley	1810-1876
Balfour Gardiner	1877-1950	John Wilbye	1574-1638
John Gardner	1917-		

See Also List 3.19, Women Composers

© 1994 by Parker Publishing Company

LIST 3.10 EASTERN EUROPEAN COMPOSERS

Cornelius Abrányi	1822-1903	Witold Lutoslawski	1913-
Béla Bartók	1881-1945	Bohuslav Martinu	1890-1959
Frédéric Chopin	1810-1849	Ignacy Paderewski	1860-1941
Ernst von Dohnanyi	1877-1960	Andrzej Panufnik	1914-
Jan Dussek	1760-1812	Krystof Penderecki	1933-
Antonín Dvořák	1841-1904	Marta Ptasynska	1943-
Stephen Heller	1814-1888	Bedrich Smetana	1824-1884
Johann Hummel	1778-1837	Johann Stamitz	1717-1757
Leoš Janáček	1854-1928	Josef Suk	1874-1935
Zoltán Kodály	1882-1967	Maria Agata Szymanowska	1789-1831
Franz Lehar	1870-1948	Karol Szymanowski	1882-1937
György Ligeti	1923-	Alexandre Tansman	1897-1986
Franz Liszt	1811-1886		

See Also List 3.19, Women Composers

LIST 3.11 FLEMISH COMPOSERS

Jean Absil	1893-1974	Pierre di Manchicourt	d. 1564
Jacobus Clemens	c. 1510-1556	Jean Mouton	c. 1459-1522
Thomas Crequillon	d. 1557	Jacob Obrecht	1453-1505
Josquin Des Prez	1440-1521	Johannes Ockeghem	1425-1495
César Franck	1822-1890	Willem Pijper	1894-1947
Nicolas Gombert	c. 1490-1556	Jan Sweelinck	1562-1621
Isaac Henricus	c. 1450-1517	Philippe Verdelot	d. c. 1545
Pierre de La Rue	c. 1460-1518	Adrian Willaert	1480-1562
Orlando di Lasso	1532-1594		

See Also List 3.19, Women Composers

LIST 3.12   FRENCH COMPOSERS

Adolphe Adam	1803-1856	André Grétry	1741-1813
Charles Alkan	1813-1888	Jacques Halévy	1799-1862
Daniel Auber	1782-1871	Ferdinand Hérold	1791-1833
Georges Auric	1899-1978	Vincent d'Indy	1851-1931
Hector Berlioz	1803-1869	Edouard Lalo	1823-1892
Georges Bizet	1838-1875	Jean-Marie Leclair	1697-1764
François Boïeldieu	1775-1834	Léonin	12th century
Lili Boulanger	1893-1918	Jean-Baptiste Lully	1632-1687
Nadia Boulanger	1887-1979	Guillaume de Machaut	1304-1377
Pierre Boulez	1925-	Jules Massenet	1842-1912
Emmanuel Chabrier	1841-1894	Oliver Messiaen	1908-1992
Cécile Chaminade	1857-1944	Darius Milhaud	1892-1974
Marc-Antione Charpentier	1634-1704	Jacques Offenbach	1819-1880
Gustave Charpentier	1860-1956	Pérotin	1160-1220
Ernest Chausson	1855-1899	Francis Poulenc	1899-1963
François Couperin	1668-1733	Jean-Phillipe Rameau	1683-1764
Claude Debussy	1862-1918	Maurice Ravel	1875-1937
Léo Delibes	1836-1891	Albert Roussel	1869-1937
Paul Dukas	1865-1935	Camille Saint-Saëns	1835-1921
Henri Duparc	1848-1933	Erik Satie	1866-1925
Gabriel Fauré	1845-1924	Henri Sauget	1901-
Jean Françaix	1912-	Germaine Tailleferre	1892-1983
César Franck	1822-1890	Charles Widor	1844-1937
Charles Gounod	1818-1893		

See Also List 3.19, Women Composers

LIST 3.13   GERMAN COMPOSERS

Carl Philipp Emanuel Bach	1714-1788	Fanny Mendelssohn	1805-1847
Johann Christian Bach	1735-1782	Felix Mendelssohn	1809-1847
Johann Sebastian Bach	1685-1750	Giacomo Meyerbeer	1791-1864
Wilhelm Friedmann Bach	1710-1784	Moritz Moszkowske	1854-1925
Ludwig van Beethoven	1770-1827	Otto Nicolai	1810-1849
Julius Benedict	1804-1885	Carl Orff	1895-1982
Johannes Brahms	1833-1897	Johann Pachelbel	1653-1706
Max Bruch	1838-1920	Hans Pfitzner	1869-1949
Hans von Bulow	1830-1894	Johann Quantz	1697-1773
Christian Cannabich	1731-1798	Max Reger	1873-1916
Peter Cornelius	1824-1874	Julius Reubke	1834-1858
Johann Cramer	1771-1858	Franz Schreker	1878-1934
Werner Egk	1901-1983	Clara Wieck Schumann	1819-1896
Friedrich von Flotow	1812-1883	Robert Schumann	1810-1856
Robert Franz	1815-1892	Heinrich Schütz	1585-1672
Christoph Gluck	1714-1787	Ludwig Spohr	1784-1859
Carl Graun	1704-1759	Carl Philipp Stamitz	1745-1801
Carl Halle	1819-1895	Karlheinz Stockhausen	1928-
Georg Friedrich Händel	1685-1759	Richard Strauss	1864-1949
Hans Werner Henze	1926-	Georg Philipp Telemann	1681-1767
Paul Hindemith	1895-1963	Richard Wagner	1813-1883
Engelbert Humperdinck	1854-1921	Carl Maria von Weber	1786-1826
Carl Loewe	1796-1869	Kurt Weill	1900-1950
Albert Lortzing	1801-1851		

See Also List 3.19, Women Composers

LIST 3.14   ITALIAN COMPOSERS

Tommaso Albinoni	1671–1751	Gian Francesco Malipiero	1882–1973
Vincenzo Bellini	1801–1835	Luca Marenzio	1553–1599
Luciano Berio	1925–	Pietro Masacagni	1863–1945
Luigi Boccherini	1743–1805	Saverio Mercandante	1795–1870
Arrigo Boito	1842–1918	Claudio Monteverdi	1567–1643
Ferruccio Busoni	1866–1924	Pietro Nardini	1722–1793
Giulio Caccini	1545–1618	Luigi Nono	1924–
Giacomo Carissimi	1605–1674	Niccolò Paganini	1782–1840
Alfredo Casella	1883–1947	Giovanni Paisiello	1740–1816
Emilio di Cavalieri	1550–1602	Giovanni Palestrina	1525–1594
Pietro Cavalli	1602–1676	Giovanni Pergolesi	1710–1736
Marc Cesti	1623–1669	Jacopo Peri	1561–1633
Luigi Cherubini	1760–1842	Goffredo Petrassi	1904–
Francesco Cilea	1866–1950	Niccolo Piccinni	1728–1800
Domenico Cimarosa	1749–1801	Ildebrando Pizzetti	1880–1968
Muzio Clementi	1752–1832	Amilcare Ponchielli	1834–1886
Archangelo Corelli	1653–1713	Giacomo Puccini	1858–1924
Luigi Dallapiccola	1904–1975	Ottorino Respighi	1879–1936
Gaetano Donizetti	1797–1848	Gioacchino Rossini	1792–1868
Alfonso Ferrabosco	1543–1588	Antonio Salieri	1750–1825
Girolamo Frescobaldi	1583–1643	Giovanni Battista Sammartini	1698–1775
Andrea Gabrieli	1510–1586	Alessandro Scarlatti	1660–1725
Giovanni Gabrieli	1557–1612	Domenico Scarlatti	1685–1757
Francesco Geminiani	1687–1762	Gasparo Spontini	1774–1851
Carlo Gesualdo	1560–1613	Giuseppe Tartini	1692–1770
Umberto Giordano	1867–1948	Francesco Tosti	1846–1916
Francesco Landini	1325–1397	Fortunio Giuseppe Verdi	1813–1901
Ruggiero Leoncavallo	1858–1919	Antonio Vivaldi	1678–1741
Pietro Locatelli	1695–1764	Ermanno Wolf-Ferrari	1876–1948
Bruno Maderna	1920–1972	Riccardo Zandonai	1883–1944

See Also List 3.19, Women Composers

LIST 3.15 RUSSIAN COMPOSERS

Anton Arensky	1861–1906	Modest Mussorgsky	1839–1881
Mily Balakirev	1837–1910	Sergei Prokofiev	1891–1953
Alexander Borodin	1833–1887	Sergei Rachmaninoff	1873–1943
Cesar Cui	1835–1918	Nicolai Rimsky-Korsakov	1844–1908
Alexander Dargomizhjsky	1813–1869	Anton Rubinstein	1829–1894
Alexander Glazunov	1865–1936	Dmitri Shostakovich	1906–1975
Reinhold Glière	1875–1956	Alexander Scriabin	1872–1915
Mikhail Glinka	1804–1857	Igor Stravinsky	1882–1971
Aram Khachaturian	1903–1978	Peter Tchaikovsky	1840–1893
Anatol Liadov	1855–1914		

See Also List 3.19, Women Composers

LIST 3.16 SCANDINAVIAN COMPOSERS

Hans Abrahamsen	1952–	Helvi Leiviskä	1902–
Agathe Backer-Grøndahl	1847–1907	Carl Nielsen	1865–1931
Franz Berwold	1796–1868	Johan Helmich Roman	1694–1758
Ulf Björlin	1933–	Jean Sibelius	1865–1957
Karl-Birger Blomdahl	1916–1968	Erzsébet Szönyi	1924–
Dietrich Buxtehude	1637–1707	Karl-Erik Welin	1934–1992
Edvard Grieg	1843–1907	Dag Wirgen	1905–1986
Lars-Erik Larsson	1908–1986		

See Also List 3.19, Women Composers

LIST 3.17 SPANISH COMPOSERS

Marcial del Adalid y Gurréa	1826–1881	Enrique Granados	1867–1916
Isaac Albeniz	1860–1909	Cristobal Halffter	1930–
Juan Cristostomo Arriaga	1806–1826	Pablo de Sarasate	1844–1908
Garbriel Balart	1824–1893	Fernando Sor	1778–1839
Anselmo Clavé	1824–1874	Joaquin Turina	1882–1949
Oscar Espla	1886–1976	Tomás Luis de Victoria	1549–1611
Manuel de Falla	1867–1946		

LIST 3.18   COMPOSERS OF OTHER COUNTRIES

Komei Abe	Japan	1911–
Motohiko Adachi	Japan	1940–
Fikret Dzhamil Amirov	Azerbaijan	1922–1984
Dennis Ap Ivor	Ireland	1916–
Violet Archer	Canada	1913–
Bulent Arel	Turkey	1919–1990
João Jose Baldi	Portugal	1770–1816
Milton Barnes	Canada	1931–
Sadao Bekku	Japan	1922–
Arthur Benjamin	Australia	1893–1960
Cachao	Cuba	1918–
Turlough Carolan	Ireland	1670–1738
Ronald Center	Scotland	1913–1973
Carlos Chavez	Mexico	1899–1978
Skinner Chávez-Melo	Mexico	d. 1992
Chou Wen-Chung	China/U.S.A.	1923–
Roque Cordero	Panama	1917–
Jean Coulthard	Canada	1908–
Ram Da-Oz	Israel	1929–
Chevalier De Saint Georges	West Indies	1745–1799
Manu Dibango	Cameroon	1934–
Halim El-Dabh	Egypt/U.S.A.	1921–
John Field	Ireland	1782–1837
Alberto Ginastera	Argentina	1916–1983
Percy Grainger	Australia	1882–1961
Hamilton Harty	Ireland	1879–1941
Arthur Honegger	Switzerland	1892–1955
Helen Hopekirk	Scotland	1856–1945
Emile Jaques-Dalcroze	Switzerland	1865–1950
Douglas Lilburn	New Zealand	1915–
Frank Martin	Switzerland	1890–1974
Colin McPhee	Canada	1901–1964
Barbara Pentland	Canada	1912–
Priaulx Rainier	South Africa	1903–1986
Ahmed Adnan Saygun	Turkey	1907–1991
Toru Takemitsu	Japan	1930–
Heitor Villa-Lobos	Brazil	1887–1959
Gillian Whitehead	New Zealand	1941–
Grace Williams	Wales	1906–1977
Jannis Xenakis	Greece	1922–
Youmei Xiao	China	d. 1940

See Also List 3.19, Women Composers

LIST 3.19 WOMEN COMPOSERS

Beth Aderson	U.S.A.	1950–
Maria Teresa Agnesi	Italy	1720–1795
Laurie Anderson	U.S.A.	1947–
Ruth Anderson	U.S.A.	1928–
Anna Amalia, Princess of Prussia	Prussia	1723–1787
Violet Archer	Canada	1913–
Agathe Backer-Grøndahl	Norway	1847–1907
Thekla Badarzewska	Poland	1834–1861
Katharine Bainbridge	U.S.A.	1863–1967
Esther Ballou	U.S.A.	1915–1973
Ethel Barnes	England	1880–1948
Elsa Barraine	France	1910–
Marion Bauer	U.S.A.	1887–1955
Mrs. H.H.A. Beach	U.S.A.	1867–1944
Martha Beck	U.S.A.	1900–
Johanna Beyer	Germany/U.S.A.	1888–1944
Mélanie Bonis	France	1858–1937
Lili Boulanger	France	1893–1918
Nadia Boulanger	France	1887–1979
Gena Branscombe	Canada/U.S.A.	1881–1977
Marguerite Canal	France	1890–1978
Mary Carmichael	England	1851–1935
Cecile Chaminade	France	1857–1944
Rebecca Clarke	England	1886–1979
Elizabeth Coolidge	U.S.A.	1864–1953
Ruth Crawford	U.S.A.	1901–1953
Lucile Crews	U.S.A.	1888–1972
Pearl Curran	U.S.A.	1875–1941
Mabel Daniels	U.S.A.	1878–1971
Hilda Dianda	Argentina	1925–
Emma Lou Diemer	U.S.A.	1927–
Marianne Di Martinez	Austria	1744–1812
Vivian Fine	U.S.A.	1913–
Lorraine Finley	U.S.A.	1899–1972
Fay Foster	U.S.A.	1886–1960
Jennifer Fowler	Australia	1939–
Mary Ann Gabriel	England	1825–1877
Peggy Glanville-Hicks	Australia	1912–
Karen Griebling	U.S.A.	1957–
Doris Hays	U.S.A.	1941–
Helen Hopekirk	Scotland	1856–1945
Mary Howe	U.S.A.	1882–1964
Betsy Jolas	France/U.S.A.	1926–
Eunice Katunda	Brazil	1915–
Clara Anna Korn	Germany	1866–1940
Elisabeth Jacquet de La Guerre	France	1659–1729
Margaret Ruthven Lang	U.S.A.	1867–1972
Helvi Leiviskä	Finland	1902–1982
Elisabeth Lutyens	England	1906–1983
Nina Makarova	Russia	1908–1976

List 3.19 (continued)

Mathilde McKinney	U.S.A.	1904–
Fanny Mendelssohn	Germany	1805–1847
Thea Musgrave	Scotland	1928–
Dika Newlin	U.S.A.	1923–
Tatiana Nikolayeva	Russia	1924–
Pauline Oliveros	U.S.A.	1932–
Priaulx Rainier	South Africa	1903–1986
Shulamit Ran	Israel	1949–
Marga Richter	U.S.A.	1926–
Megan Roberts	U.S.A.	1952–
Clara Wieck Schumann	Germany	1819–1896
Sheila Silver	U.S.A.	1946–
Alice Mary Smith	England	1839–1884
Dame Ethal Smyth	England	1858–1944
Laurie Spiegel	U.S.A.	1945–
Emma Steiner	U.S.A.	1850–1928
Elizabeth Sterling	England	1819–1895
Lily Strickland	U.S.A.	1887–1958
Dana Suesse	U.S.A.	1911–1987
Margaret Sutherland	Australia	1897–1984
Ewa Synowiec	Poland	1942–
Erzsebet Szönyi	Hungary	1924–
Maria Agata Szymanowska	Poland	1789–1831
Germaine Tailleferre	France	1892–1983
Louise Talma	France/U.S.A.	1906–
Phyllis Tate	England	1911–1987
Auguste Thomas	U.S.A.	1964–
Joan Tower	U.S.A.	1938–
Calliope Tsoupaki	Greece	1963–
Alicia Urreta	Mexico	1935–1986
Galina Ustvolskaya	Russia	1919–
Mary Jeanne Van Appledorn	U.S.A.	1927–
Nancy Van de Vate	U.S.A.	1930–
Henrietie Van den Boorn-Coclet	Belgium	1866–1945
Elizabeth Vercoe	U.S.A.	1941–
Slava Vorlova	Czech Republic	1894–1973
Harriet Ware	U.S.A.	1877–1962
Elinor Warren	U.S.A.	1900–1991
Valery Weigl	Austria/U.S.A.	1894–1982
Judith Weir	Scotland	1954–
Yulia Weissbers	Russia	1880–1942
Maude White	England	1855–1937
Ruth White	U.S.A.	1925–
Florence Wickham	U.S.A.	1880–1962
Mary Lou Williams	U.S.A.	1910–1981
Grace Williams	Wales	1906–1977
Mary Wood	U.S.A.	1857–1944
Ruth Zechlin	Germany	1926–
Agnes Zimmerman	Germany	1845–1925
Ellen Zwilich	U.S.A.	1939–

LIST 3.20   AFRICAN-AMERICAN COMPOSERS

Thomas J. Anderson	1928–	Azalia Hackley	1867–1922
Walter Anderson	1915–	W.C. Handy	1873–1958
David Baker	1931–	Hall Johnson	1887–1970
Thomas Bethune	1849–1908	J. Rosamund Johnson	1873–1954
Eubie Blake	1883–1983	Quincy Jones	1934–
James Bland	1854–1911	Scott Joplin	1868–1917
Oscar Brown, Jr.	1926–	Ulysses Kay	1917–
Harry Burleigh	1866–1949	Carman Moore	1936–
Charles Cooke	1891–1958	Coleridge-Taylor Perkinson	1932–
William Dawson	1898–1990	Julia Perry	1924–1979
Noel De Costa	1929–	Hale Smith	1925–
R. Nathaniel Dett	1882–1943	William Grant Still	1895–1978
Carl Diton	1886–1969	Howard Swanson	1907–1978
Shirley DuBois	1906–1977	Clarence White	1880–1960
Duke Ellington	1899–1974	Olly Wilson	1937–
Louis Moreau Gottschalk	1829–1869	John Work	1901–1968

See Also List 9.28, The Afro-American Five

LIST 3.21   FAMOUS COMPOSERS OF BALLETS

Adolphe Adam	Arthur Honegger
George Antheil	Aram Khachaturian
Anton Arensky	Gian Francesco Malipiero
Béla Bartók	Bohuslav Martinu
Leonard Bernstein	Felix Mendelssohn
Arthur Bliss	Darius Milhaud
Benjamin Britten	Francis Poulenc
Carlos Chavez	Sergei Prokofiev
Aaron Copland	Maurice Ravel
Henry Cowell	Ottorino Resphigi
Claude Debussy	Nicolai Rimsky-Korsakov
Manuel de Falla	Arnold Schoenberg
Leo Delibes	Igor Stravinsky
Charles Griffes	Germaine Tailleferre
Hans Werner Henze	Alexander Tcherepnin
Ferdinand Hérold	Peter Tchaikovsky
Paul Hindemith	Ralph Vaughan Williams
Gustav Holst	

See Also List 8.7, Great Ballets

LIST 3.22 COMPOSERS OF MASSES

A mass is a musical setting for the Roman liturgy called the Ordinary, consisting of the Kyrie, Gloria, Credo, Sanctus, and Agnus Dei. Earlier masses were written for church use. Later masses and requiem masses were written more for the concert hall than the actual church setting.

Johann Sebastian Bach	Germany	1685-1750
Ludwig van Beethoven	Germany	1770-1827
Hector Berlioz	France	1803-1869
Anton Bruckner	Austria	1824-1896
William Byrd	England	1543-1623
Giacomo Carissimi	Italy	1605-1674
Luigi Cherubini	Italy	1760-1842
Josquin Des Prez	Franco-Flemish	1440-1521
Guillame Dufay	Netherlands	c.1400-1474
Antonín Dvořák	Bohemia (Czech)	1841-1904
Antoine de Fevin	France	1474-1512
Francisco Guerrero	Spain	1528-1599
Franz Joseph Haydn	Austria	1732-1809
Michael Haydn	Austria	1737-1806
Ferdinand Hummel	Germany	1855-1928
Orlando di Lasso	Netherlands	1532-1594
Franz Liszt	Hungary	1811-1886
Cristóbal de Morales	Spain	c.1500-1553
Jean Mouton	France	c.1459-1522
Wolfgang Amadeus Mozart	Germany	1756-1791
Jacob Obrecht	Netherlands	1450-1505
Johannes Ockeghem	Netherlands	c.1410-1496
Giovanni Pierluigi da Palestrina	Italy	c.1525-1594
Giovanni Battista Pergolesi	Italy	1710-1736
Alessandro Scarlatti	Italy	1660-1725
Franz Schubert	Austria	1797-1828
Robert Schumann	Germany	1810-1856
Claudin Sermisy	France	c.1490-1562
Ludwig Spohr	Germany	1784-1859
John Taverner	England	1944-
Christopher Tye	England	c.1500-c.1572
Giuseppe Verdi	Italy	1813-1901
Lodovico da Viadana	Italy	1560-1627
Tomás Luis de Victoria	Spain	1548-1611

LIST 3.23   FAMOUS COMPOSERS OF SYMPHONIC POEMS

COMPOSER	REPRESENTATIVE WORK
Hector Berlioz	*Symphonie Fantastique*
Alexander Borodin	*In the Steppes of Central Asia*
Claude Debussy	*La Mer (The Sea)*
Paul Dukas	*L'apprenti sorcier (The Sorcerer's Apprentice)*
Antonín Dvořák	*Vodnik (The Water Goblin)*
George Gershwin	*An American in Paris*
Ferde Grofé	*Grand Canyon* Suite
Arthur Honegger	*Pacific 231*
Vincent d'Indy	*Max et Thelca (Max and Thelca)*
Modest Mussorgsky	*A Night on Bald Mountain*
Sergei Prokofiev	*Sni (Dreams)*
Sergei Rachmaninoff	*The Isle of the Dead*
Maurice Ravel	*La valse*
Ottorino Respighi	*Fontane di Roma (The Fountains of Rome)*
Nicolai Rimsky-Korsakov	*Scheherazade*
Albert Roussel	*Résurrection (Resurrection)*
Camille Saint-Saëns	*Dance macabre*
Arnold Schoenberg	*Pélleas und Mélisande (Pelleas and Melisande)*
Jean Sibelius	*Swan of Tuonela*
Betrich Smetana	*Ma vlast (My Country)*
Richard Strauss	*Till Eulenspiegel*
Igor Stravinsky	*Feu d'artife (Fireworks)*
Peter Tchaikovsky	*Romeo and Juliet*

LIST 3.24   FAMOUS COMPOSERS OF MOTETS AND MADRIGALS

As a rule, a motet is an unaccompanied sacred choral work based on a Latin verse. The peak of its existence was 1220–1750. A madrigal is a secular song for one or more voices. The madrigal was popular between the fourteenth and seventeenth centuries.

Jacob Arcadelt	Netherlands	c.1505–1568
Johann Michael Bach	Germany	1648–1694
Johann Sebastian Bach	Germany	1685–1750
Adriano Banchieri	Italy	1568–1634
Jacobo da Bologna	Italy	14th C.
Dietrich Buxtehude	Denmark	1637–1707
William Byrd	England	1543–1623
Antonio Caldara	Italy	1670–1736
Giovanni da Cascia	Italy	14th C.
Marc-Antoine Charpentier	France	1634–1704
Jacobus Clemens	Netherlands	c.1510–1556
François Couperin	France	1668–1733
Josquin Des Prez	Franco Flemish	1440–1521
John Dowland	England	1563–1626
Guillame Dufay	Netherlands	c.1400–1474
John Dunstable	England	c.1385–1453
Constanzo Festa	Italy	c.1480–1545
Johann Joseph Fux	Austria	1660–1741
Andrea Gabrieli	Italy	c.1510–1586
Giovanni Gabrieli	Italy	c.1554–1612
Jhan Gero	Netherlands	16th C.
Don Carlo Gesualdo	Italy	c.1560–1613
Orlando Gibbons	England	1583–1625
Nicolas Gombert	Netherlands	c.1490–1556
Claude Goudimel	France	c.1510–1572
Andreas Hammerschmidt	Germany	1612–1675
Han Leo Hassler	Germany	1564–1612
Johann Adolf Hasse	Germany	1699–1783
Niccolo Jommelli	Italy	1714–1774
Francesco Landini	Italy	1325–1397
Orlando di Lasso	Netherlands	1532–1594
Jean-Baptiste Lully	France	1632–1687
Guillaume de Machaut	France	c.1300–1377
Luca Marenzio	Italy	1553–1599
Philippe de Monte	Belgium	1521–1603
Claudio Monteverdi	Italy	1567–1643
Cristóbal de Morales	Spain	c.1500–1553
Thomas Morley	England	c.1557–1602
Jacob Obrecht	Netherlands	1450–1505
Johannes Ockeghem	Netherlands	c.1410–1496
Johann Pachelbel	Germany	1653–1706
Giovanni Pierluigi da Palestrina	Italy	c.1525–1594

List 3.24 (continued)

Thomas Ravenscroft	England	c.1590–1633
Cipriano de Rore	Netherlands	1516–1565
Alessandro Scarlatti	Italy	1660–1725
Heinrich Schütz	Germany	1585–1672
Ludwig Senfl	Germany	c.1486–1543
Thomas Tallis	England	c.1505–1585
Domingo Terradellas	Spain/Italy	1713–1751
Orazio Vecchi	Italy	1550–1605
Lodovico da Viadana	Italy	1560–1627
Tomás Luis de Victoria	Spain	1548–1611
Francesco Viola	Italy	16th C.
Thomas Weelkes	England	c.1575–1623
John Wilbye	England	1574–1638
Adrian Willaert	Netherlands	c.1490–1562

LIST 3.25 FAMOUS COMPOSERS OF FUGUES

Johann Sebastian Bach
Béla Bartók
Ludwig van Beethoven
Alban Berg
Hector Berlioz
Johannes Brahms
Dietrich Buxtehude
Archangelo Corelli

César Franck
Georg Friedrich Händel
Roy Harris
Franz Josef Haydn
Paul Hindemith
Felix Mendelssohn
Wolfgang Amadeus Mozart
Johann Pachelbel

Max Reger
Camille Saint-Saëns
Robert Schumann
Dmitri Shostakovich
Jan P. Sweelinck
Giuseppe Verdi
Anton Webern

LIST 3.26   FAMOUS COMPOSERS OF SONATAS

Isaac Albeniz
George Antheil
Carl Philipp Emanuel Bach
Johann Sebastian Bach
Béla Bartók
Mrs. H.H.A. Beach
Ludwig van Beethoven
Ernest Bloch
Luigi Boccherini
Johannes Brahms
Luigi Cherubini
Muzio Clementi
Archangelo Corelli
Claude Debussy
Karl von Dittersdorf
Ernst von Dohnanyi
Paul Dukas
Johann Dussek
Gabriel Fauré
César Franck
Alexander Glazunov
Edvard Grieg
Charles Griffes
Georg Friedrich Händel

Roy Harris
Joseph Haydn
Paul Hindemith
Arthur Honegger
Johann Hummel
John Ireland
Zoltán Kodály
Erich Korngold
Jean-Marie Leclair
Franz Liszt
Pietro Locatelli
Edward MacDowell
Felix Mendelssohn
Darius Milhaud
Leopold Mozart
Wolfgang Amadeus Mozart
Pietro Nardini
Ignacy Paderewski
C. Hubert Parry
Gaetano Pugnani
Sergei Rachmaninoff
Maurice Ravel
Max Reger
Anton Rubinstein

Camille Saint-Saëns
Giovanni Sammartini
Domenico Scarlatti
Franz Schubert
Robert Schumann
Alexander Scriabin
Roger Sessions
Johann Stamitz
Karl Stamitz
Igor Stravinsky
Germaine Tailleferre
Giuseppe Tartini
Alexander Tcherepnin
Georg Philipp Telemann
Giovanni Battista Viotti
Giovanni Vitali
Tommaso Vitali
Antonio Vivaldi
Carl Maria von Weber
Samuel Wesley
Charles Widor
Alexander Zemlinsky

LIST 3.27 FAMOUS COMPOSERS OF CONCERTOS

Anton Arensky
Carl Phillip Emanuel Bach
Johann Sebastian Bach
Béla Bartók
Ludwig van Beethoven
Alban Berg
Ernest Bloch
Johannes Brahms
Max Bruch
Ernest Chausson
Frédéric Chopin
Samuel Coleridge-Taylor
Aaron Copland
Archangelo Corelli
Frederick Delius
Ernst von Dohnanyi
Jan Dussek
Antonín Dvořák
Gabriel Fauré
César Franck
Alexander Glazunov
Edvard Grieg
Johan Halvorsen
Georg Friedrich Händel

Franz Joseph Haydn
Paul Hindemith
Jenö Hubay
Johann Hummel
Joseph Joachim
Edouard Lalo
Franz Liszt
Edward MacDowell
Gian Francesco Malipiero
Felix Mendelssohn
Darius Milhaud
Wolfgang Amadeus Mozart
Ignacy Paderewski
Niccolò Paganini
Sergei Prokofiev
Sergei Rachmaninoff
Jean-Philippe Rameau
Maurice Ravel
Max Reger
Carl Reinecke
Ottorino Respighi
Franz Ries
Nicolai Rimsky-Korsakov
Anton Rubinstein

Camille Saint-Saëns
Arnold Schoenberg
Robert Schumann
Alexander Scriabin
Roger Sessions
Jean Sibelius
Christian Sinding
Louis Spohr
Richard Strauss
Igor Stravinsky
Johan Svendsen
Germaine Tailleferre
Giuseppe Tartini
Peter Tchaikovsky
Alexander Tcherepnin
Giuseppe Torelli
Francesco Veracini
Henri Vieuxtemps
Antonio Vivaldi
William Walton
Carl Maria von Weber
Charles Widor
Józef Wieniawski
Eugeǹe Ysaÿe

LIST 3.28 FAMOUS COMPOSERS OF SYMPHONIES

COMPOSER	NUMBER OF SYMPHONIES	COMPOSER	NUMBER OF SYMPHONIES
Ludwig van Beethoven	9	Wolfgang Amadeus Mozart	41
Hector Berlioz	4	Carl Nielsen	6
Johannes Brahms	4	Sergei Prokofiev	7
Anton Bruckner	9	Franz Schubert	10
Antonín Dvořák	9	Robert Schumann	4
Edward Elgar	2	Dmitri Shostakovich	15
Franz Joseph Haydn	104	Jean Sibelius	7
Hans Werner Henze	6	Peter Tchaikovsky	6
Gustav Mahler	10	Michael Tippett	4
Felix Mendelssohn	5	Ralph Vaughan Williams	9

LIST 3.29 FAMOUS COMPOSERS OF VOCAL MUSIC

Isaac Albeniz
Anton Arensky
Thomas Arne
Louis Aubert
George Auric
Carl Philipp Emanuel Bach
Johann Sebastian Bach
Mily Balakirev
Samuel Barber
Joseph Barnby
Béla Bartók
Arnold Bax
Mrs. H.H.A. Beach
Ludwig van Beethoven
Hector Berlioz
Leonard Bernstein
Georges Bizet
Arthur Bliss
Ernest Bloch
John Blow
Alexander Borodin
Johannes Brahms
Frank Bridge
Max Bruch
George Butterworth
Giulio Caccini
Giacomo Carissimi
John Carpenter
Emilio del Cavalieri
Cécile Chaminade
Gustave Charpentier
Ernest Chausson
Luigi Cherubini
Frédéric Chopin
Domenico Cimarosa
Samuel Coleridge-Taylor
Frederick Converse
Aaron Copland
William Crotch
Cesar Cui
Claude Debussy
Frederick Delius
Ernst von Dohnanyi
Gaetano Donizetti
Henri Duparc
Antonín Dvořák
Edward Elgar
Manuel de Falla

Gabriel Fauré
Gerald Finzi
Arthur Foote
Cecil Forsyth
Stephen Foster
César Franck
Johann Fux
Balfour Gardiner
Orlando Gibbons
Alexander Glazunov
Reinhold Glière
Mikhail Glinka
Christoph Gluck
Charles Gounod
Percy Grainger
Enrique Granados
Edvard Grieg
Charles T. Griffes
Ivor Gurney
Georg Friedrich Händel
Johann Hasse
Franz Joseph Haydn
Paul Hindemith
Gustav Holst
Arthur Honegger
Engelbert Humperdinck
Jacques Ibert
Vincent d'Indy
John Ireland
Leoš Janáček
Nicola Jommelli
Zoltán Kodály
Edouard Lalo
Liza Lehmann
Ruggiero Leoncavallo
Franz Liszt
Edward MacDowell
Gustav Mahler
Jules Massenet
Johann Mattheson
Felix Mendelssohn
Darius Milhaud
Thomas Morley
Modest Mussorgsky
Wolfgang Amadeus Mozart
Nicolas Nabokov
Carl Nielsen
Horatio Parker

Hubert H. Parry
Gabriel Pierné
Francis Poulenc
Roger Quilter
Sergei Rachmaninoff
Maurice Ravel
Max Reger
Ottorino Respighi
Nicolai Rimsky-Korsakov
Luigi Rossi
Gioacchino Rossini
Alec Rowley
Anton Rubinstein
Camille Saint-Saëns
Antonio Salieri
Alessandro Scarlatti
Arnold Schoenberg
Franz Schubert
Robert Schumann
Heinrich Schütz
Jean Sibelius
Bedrich Smetana
Albert Spalding
Louis Spohr
John Stainer
Charles Stanford
John Stanley
Alessandro Stradella
Richard Strauss
Igor Stravinsky
Arthur Sullivan
Karol Szymanowski
Alexandre Tansman
Peter Tchaikovsky
Georg Philipp Telemann
Joaquin Turina
Ralph Vaughan Williams
Giuseppe Verdi
Richard Wagner
William Walton
Peter Warlock
Carl Maria von Weber
Anton von Webern
Kurt Weill
Charles Widor
Hugo Wolf
Ermanno Wolf-Ferrari

LIST 3.30   FAMOUS COMPOSERS OF OPERA

John Adams
Samuel Barber
Béla Bartók
Vincenzo Belini
Alban Berg
Hector Berlioz
Georges Bizet
Arrigo Baito
Alexander Borodin
Benjamin Britten
Gustave Charpentier
Luigi Cherubini
Francesco Cilea
Claude Debussy
Léo Delibes
Gaetano Donizetti
Friedrich von Flotow
George Gershwin
Alberto Ginastera

Umberto Giordano
Philip Glass
Christoph Gluck
Charles Gounod
Georg Friedrich Händel
Engelbert Humperdinck
Leos Janacek
Scott Joplin
Ruggiero Leoncavallo
Pietro Mascagni
Jules Massenet
Gian Carlo Menotti
Giacomo Meyerbeer
Claudio Monteverdi
Douglas Moore
Modest Mussorgsky
Wolfgang Amadeus Mozart
Jacques Offenbach
Giovanni Pergolesi

Francis Poulenc
Sergei Prokofiev
Giacomo Puccini
Henry Purcell
Maurice Ravel
Nicolai Rimsky-Korsakov
Gioacchino Rossini
Camille Saint-Saëns
Bedrich Smetana
Johann Strauss, Jr.
Richard Strauss
Peter Tchaikovsky
Ambroise Thomas
Virgil Thomson
Giuseppe Verdi
Richard Wagner
Carl Maria von Weber

See Also List 5.9, Famous Operas and Their Composers

LIST 3.31   PULITZER PRIZE-WINNING COMPOSERS

For compositions by an American in larger forms of chamber music, orchestra, or choral music, or for an operatic work containing a ballet.

Year	Composer	Year	Composer	Year	Composer
1943	William Schuman	1961	Walter Piston	1979	Joseph Schwanter
1944	Howard Hansen	1962	Robert Ward	1980	David Del Tredici
1945	Aaron Copland	1963	Samuel Barber	1981	no prize given
1946	Leo Sowerby	1964	no prize given	1982	Roger Sessions
1947	Charles Ives	1965	no prize given	1983	Ellen T. Zwillich
1948	Walter Piston	1966	Leslie Bassett	1984	Bernard Rands
1949	Virgil Thomson	1967	Leon Kirchner	1985	Stephen Albert
1950	Gian-Carlo Menotti	1968	George Crumb	1986	George Perle
1951	Douglas Moore	1969	Karel Husa	1987	John Harbison
1952	Gail Kubik	1970	Charles W. Wuorinen	1988	William Bolcom
1953	no prize given	1971	Mario Davidovsky	1989	Roger Reynolds
1954	Quincy Porter	1972	Jacob Druckman	1990	Mel Powell
1955	Gian-Carlo Menotti	1973	Elliot Carter	1991	Shulamit Ran
1956	Earnest Toch	1974	Donald Martino	1992	Wayne Peterson
1957	Norman Dello Joio	1975	Dominick Argento	1993	Christopher Rouse
1958	Samuel Barber	1976	Ned Rorem	1994	Gunther Schuller
1959	John La Montaine	1977	Richard Wernick	1995	Morton Gould
1960	Elliot Carter	1978	Michael Colgrass	1996	George Walker

© 1994 by Parker Publishing Company

LIST 3.32 COMPOSERS BORN IN JANUARY

Juan Cristostomo Arriaga	27	1806-1826	Henri Duparc	21	1848-1933
Daniel Auber	29	1782-1871	Edouard Lalo	27	1823-1892
Mily Balakirev	2	1837-1910	Wolfgang Amadeus Mozart	27	1756-1791
Max Bruch	6	1838-1920	Francis Poulenc	7	1899-1963
Emmanuel Chabrier	18	1841-1894	Franz Schubert	31	1797-1828
Ernest Chausson	20	1855-1899	Alexander Scriabin	6	1872-1915
Frederick Delius	29	1862-1934	Michael Tippett	2	1905-

LIST 3.33 COMPOSERS BORN IN FEBRUARY

Georges Auric	15	1899-1978	Léo Delibes	21	1836-1891
Alban Berg	9	1885-1935	André Gretry	11	1741-1813
Arrigo Boito	24	1842-1918	Georg Friedrich Händel	23	1685-1759
Pietro Cavalli	14	1602-1676	Felix Mendelssohn	3	1809-1847
Archangelo Corelli	17	1653-1713	Gioacchino Rossini	29	1792-1868

LIST 3.34 COMPOSERS BORN IN MARCH

Thomas Arne	12	1710-1778	Maurice Ravel	7	1875-1937
Carl Philipp Emanuel Bach	8	1714-1788	Max Reger	19	1873-1916
Johann Sebastian Bach	21	1685-1750	Nicolai Rimsky-Korsakov	6	1844-1908
Samuel Barber	9	1910-1981	Franz Schreker	23	1878-1934
Béla Bartók	25	1881-1945	Bedrich Smetana	2	1824-1884
Frédéric Chopin	1	1810-1849	Georg Philipp Telemann	14	1681-1767
Franz Joseph Haydn	31	1732-1809	Heitor Villa-Lobos	5	1887-1959
Arthur Honnegger	10	1892-1955	Antonio Vivaldi	4	1678-1741
Vincent d'Indy	27	1851-1931	William Wallace	11	1812-1865
Ruggiero Leoncavallo	8	1858-1919	William Walton	29	1902-1983
Gian Francesco Malipiero	18	1882-1973	Kurt Weill	2	1900-1950
Modest Mussorgsky	21	1839-1881	Hugo Wolf	13	1860-1903

LIST 3.35 COMPOSERS BORN IN APRIL

Friedrich von Flotow	26	1812-1883	Ludwig Spohr	5	1784-1859
Josef Lanner	12	1801-1843	Franz von Suppe	18	1819-1895
Franz Lehár	30	1870-1948	Giuseppe Tartini	8	1692-1770
Sergei Prokofiev	23	1891-1953	Francesco Tosti	9	1846-1916
Sergei Rachmaninoff	1	1873-1943			

LIST 3.36   COMPOSERS BORN IN MAY

Isaac Albeniz	29	1860–1909	Hans Pfitzner	5	1869–1949
Michael Balfe	15	1808–1870	Erik Satie	17	1866–1925
Johannes Brahms	7	1833–1897	Alessandro Scarlatti	2	1660–1725
Gabriel Fauré	12	1845–1924	Arthur Sullivan	13	1842–1900
Carl Goldmark	18	1830–1915	Jan Sweelinck	★	1562–1621
Jules Massenet	12	1842–1912	Peter Tchaikovsky	7	1840–1893
Claudio Monteverdi	★	1567–1643	Richard Wagner	22	1813–1883
Giovanni Paisiello	8	1740–1816			

LIST 3.37   COMPOSERS BORN IN JUNE

Edward Elgar	2	1857–1934	Carl Nielsen	9	1865–1931
Mikhail Glinka	1	1804–1857	Jacques Offenbach	20	1819–1880
Charles Gounod	18	1818–1893	Robert Schumann	8	1810–1856
Edvard Grieg	15	1843–1907	Richard Strauss	11	1864–1949
Aram Khachaturian	6	1903–1978	Igor Stravinsky	17	1882–1971

LIST 3.38   COMPOSERS BORN IN JULY

Franz Berwold	23	1796–1868	Enrique Granados	27	1867–1916
Ernst Bloch	24	1880–1959	Hans Werner Henze	1	1926–
Francesco Cilea	26	1866–1950	Leoš Janáček	3	1854–1928
Ernst von Dohnanyi	27	1877–1960	Gustav Mahler	7	1860–1911
John Field	26	1782–1837	Gian Carlo Menotti	7	1911–
Stephen Foster	4	1826–1864	Carl Orff	10	1895–1982
Alexander Glazunov	29	1865–1936	Ottorino Respighi	9	1879–1936
Christoph Gluck	2	1714–1787			

LIST 3.39   COMPOSERS BORN IN AUGUST

Leonard Bernstein	25	1918–1990	John Ireland	13	1879–1962
Arthur Bliss	2	1891–1975	Ernst Krenek	23	1900–
Claude Debussy	22	1862–1918	Karlheinz Stockhausen	22	1928–
Umberto Giordano	27	1867–1948			

© 1994 by Parker Publishing Company

LIST 3.40 COMPOSERS BORN IN SEPTEMBER

Johann Christian Bach	5	1735–1782	Engelbert Humperdinck	1	1854–1921
Anton Bruckner	4	1824–1896	Saverio Mercandante	17	1795–1870
Luigi Cherubini	14	1760–1842	Giacomo Meyerbeer	5	1791–1864
Antonín Dvořák	8	1841–1904	Darius Milhaud	4	1892–1974
Girolamo Frescobaldi	9	1583–1643	Amilcare Ponchielli	1	1834–1886
George Gershwin	26	1898–1937	Jean-Phillipe Rameau	25	1683–1764
Michael Haydn	14	1737–1806	Arnold Schoenberg	13	1874–1951
Gustav Holst	21	1874–1934	Dmitri Shostakovich	25	1906–1975

LIST 3.41 COMPOSERS BORN IN OCTOBER

Malcolm Arnold	21	1921–	Camille Saint-Saëns	9	1835–1921
Luciano Berio	10	1925–	Domenico Scarlatti	26	1685–1757
Georges Bizet	25	1838–1875	Heinrich Schütz	8	1585–1672
Charles Ives	20	1874–1954	Johann Strauss, Jr.	25	1825–1899
Franz Liszt	22	1811–1886	Karol Szymanowski	6	1882–1937
Albert Lortzing	23	1801–1851	Ralph Vaughan Williams	12	1872–1958
Niccolò Paganini	17	1782–1840	Giuseppe Verdi	10	1813–1901

LIST 3.42 COMPOSERS BORN IN NOVEMBER

Charles Alkan	30	1813–1888	Gaetano Donizetti	29	1797–1848
Arnold Bax	8	1883–1953	Manuel de Falla	23	1876–1946
Vincenzo Bellini	3	1801–1835	Paul Hindemith	16	1895–1963
Alexander Borodin	12	1833–1887	Carl Loewe	30	1796–1869
Benjamin Britten	22	1913–1976	Jean-Baptiste Lully	29	1632–1687
Aaron Copland	14	1900–1990	Gasparo Spontini	14	1774–1851
François Couperin	10	1668–1733	Virgil Thomson	25	1896–1989
Carl Dittersdorf	2	1739–1799	Carl Maria von Weber	18	1786–1826

LIST 3.43 COMPOSERS BORN IN DECEMBER

Ludwig van Beethoven	16	1770–1827	Pietro Masacagni	7	1863–1945
Hector Berlioz	11	1803–1869	Giacomo Puccini	22	1858–1924
François Boïeldieu	16	1775–1834	Franz Schmidt	22	1874–1939
Domenico Cimarosa	17	1749–1801	Jean Sibelius	8	1865–1957
César Frank	10	1822–1890	Edgar Varèse	22	1883–1965
Zoltán Kodály	16	1882–1967	Anton von Webern	3	1883–1945
Bohuslav Martinu	8	1890–1959			

LIST 3.44   THE MAJOR WORKS OF JOHANN SEBASTIAN BACH

Vocal Music:

Magnificat in D Major	1723
St. John Passion	1723
St. Matthew Passion	1729
St. Mark Passion	1731
Christmas Oratorio	1734
Easter Oratorio	1735
Mass in B Minor	1738

over 200 sacred and secular cantatas
7 motets
numerous chorales, sacred songs, and arias
4 missa breves
5 settings of Sanctus

Organ Works:

6 trio sonatas for organ
20 preludes and fugues
4 fantasias and fugues
4 toccata and fugues
6 concerti
independent preludes, fantasias, and fugues
Das Orgel-Buchlein

Keyboard Works:

15 inventions
15 sinfonias
6 English suites
6 French suites
Clavier-Ubung
6 partitas
Das wohltemperirte Clavier I
   and II   1722/1744
Italian Concerto
Goldberg Variations
miscellaneous suites, preludes, fugues,
   fantasias, toccatas
Clavierbuchlein I and II

Lute Works:

2 suites
2 partitas
prelude, fugue, and allegro

Chamber Music:

6 sonatas and partitas for solo violin	1720
6 sonatas for violin and harpsichord	1717-1723
2 sonatas for violin and basso continuo	c. 1717
6 suites for solo cello	c. 1720
3 sonatas for harpsichord, viol da gamba	c. 1720
4 sonatas for flute and basso continuo	c. 1720

Orchestral Music:

2 concerti for violin	c. 1720
1 concerto for two violins	c. 1720
1 concerto for flute	c. 1720
6 Brandenburg concerti	c. 1717-1720
14 harpsichord concerti	1735-1740
4 orchestral suites	c. 1717-1723

LIST 3.45   THE MAJOR WORKS OF LUDWIG VAN BEETHOVEN

VOCAL MUSIC:

Opera: *Fidelio*	1814
Mass in C Major	1807
Missa Solemnis	1823

ORCHESTRAL MUSIC:

9 symphonies	1800–1825
Coriolanus Overture	1807
Egmont Overture	1810
Leonora Overture no. 1	1807
Leonora Overture no. 2	1805
Leonora Overture no. 3	1806

CONCERTI:

5 piano concerti	1797–1809
1 violin concerto	1806

SMALLER WORKS:

16 string quartets	1798–1826
16 piano trios	1791–1815
10 violin sonatas	1797–1812
32 piano sonatas	1783–1822
29 sets of piano variations	1783–1823

LIST 3.46   THE MAJOR WORKS OF HECTOR BERLIOZ

OPERAS:

Benvenuto Cellini	1838
Les Troyens	1859
Beatrice et Benedict	1862

CHORAL MUSIC:

Requiem	1837
La Damnation de Faust	1846
Te Deum	1849
L'Enfance du Christ	1854

ORCHESTRAL MUSIC:

Symphanie Fantastique	1830
Harold en Italy	1834
Romeo et Juliet	1839

OVERTURES:

Les Francs-Juges	1827
Le Carnival Romain	1844
Le Corsaire	1855

SHORTER WORKS:

Sara la Baigneuse	1834
La Mort d'Ophelie	1848
Nuits d'Été	1856

LIST 3.47   THE MAJOR WORKS OF JOHANNES BRAHMS

CHORAL MUSIC:

Deutsches Requiem	1868	*Akademische Fest-Ouvertüre*	1881
Alto Rhapsody	1869	*Tragische Ouvertüre*	1880
many motets and part songs		Variations on a Theme by Haydn	1873
4 symphonies	1876–1885	Hungarian Dances	1873
2 piano concerti	1858 & 1881	Liebeslieder Waltzes	1874
1 violin concerto	1878	Choral Preludes for Organ	1896
double concerto for violin and cello	1887		

LIST 3.48   THE MAJOR WORKS OF CLAUDE DEBUSSY

OPERA:

Pelléas et Mélisande	1892–1902

CHORAL MUSIC:

L'Enfant prodigue	1884
La Damoiselle élue	1888

ORCHESTRAL MUSIC:

Prélude à l'après-midi d'un faune Nocturnes	1892–1894
La Mer	1903–1905
Images pour orchestre	1906–1909

CHAMBER MUSIC:

String Quartet in G Minor	1893
Sonata for cello and piano	1915
Sonata for flute, viola, and harp	1916
Sonata for violin and piano	1917

PIANO MUSIC:

Suite bergamasque	1890–1905
Estampes	1903
Images I	1905
Images II	1907
Children's Corner	1908
Twelve Préludes, Book i	1910
Twelve Préludes, Book ii	1913
Twelve Études, Book i	1915
Twelve Études, Book ii	1915

LIST 3.49   THE MAJOR WORKS OF ANTONÍN DVOŘÁK

9 symphonies	1865–1893	*Dumky* Trio	1894
concert overtures	1871	*American* Quartet	1894
Slovanic Dances and Rhapsodies	1878–1879	cello concerto	1896
Quintet in E-flat Major	1893		

LIST 3.50   THE MAJOR WORKS OF EDWARD ELGAR

CHORAL MUSIC:

The Black Knight (cantata)	1893
The Light of Life (oratorio)	1896
Caractacus (cantata)	1898
The Dream of Gerontius (oratorio)	1900
The Apostles (oratorio)	1903
The Kingdom (oratorio)	1906
The Music Makers (choral ode)	1912

ORCHESTRAL MUSIC:

Variations on an original theme, the "Enigma"	1899
"Pomp and Circumstance" Marches 1–5	1901–1930
Cockaigne (In London Town) Overture	1901

ORCHESTRAL MUSIC (continued):

Introduction and Allegro (strings)	1905
Symphony no. 1 in A-flat	1908
Symphony no. 2 in E-flat	1911
Falstaff (symphonic poem)	1913

CONCERTI:

Concerto for violin and orchestra	1910
Concerto for cello and orchestra	1919

CHAMBER MUSIC:

String Quartet in E Minor	1918
Quintet for piano and strings, in A Minor	1918
Sonata for violin and piano, in E Minor	1918

© 1994 by Parker Publishing Company

LIST 3.51　THE MAJOR WORKS OF GEORG FRIEDRICH HÄNDEL

OPERAS:

Almira	1705
Rinaldo	1711
Giulio Cesare	1724
Rodelinda	1725
Berenice	1737
Serse	1738
Deidamia	1741

ORATORIOS:

Israel in Egypt	1739
Messiah	1741
Samson	1743
Belshazzar	1745
Judas Maccabaeus	1747
Solomon	1749
Theodora	1750
Jephtha	1752

CHORAL MUSIC:

11 Chandos anthems	1717–1720
4 Coronation anthems for King George II	1727
Acis and Galatea	1720
Alexander's Feast	1736
Semele	
Hercules	

ORCHESTRAL MUSIC:

Water Music
Fireworks Music
12 concerti grossi (op. 6)

LIST 3.52 THE MAJOR WORKS OF FRANZ JOSEF HAYDN

OPERAS:

L'incontro improvviso	1775
Il mondo della luna	1777
L'isola disabitata	1779
Armida	1784
Orfeo ed Euridice	1791

CHORAL MUSIC:

St. Cecilia Mass	1772
Nelson Mass	1798
The Creation	1798
Creation Mass	1801
The Seasons	1801

104 SYMPHONIES:

No. 45 in F-sharp Minor (*Farewell*)	1772
No. 82 in C Major (*Bear*)	1786
No. 92 in G Major (*Oxford*)	1788
No. 94 in G Major (*Surprise*)	1791
No. 100 in G Major (*Military*)	1794
No. 101 in D Major (*Clock*)	1794
No. 103 in E-flat Major (*Drum Roll*)	1795
No. 104 in D Major (*London*)	1795

LIST 3.53   THE MAJOR WORKS OF WOLFGANG AMADEUS MOZART

OPERAS:

Idomeneo	1781
Entfuhrung aus dem Serail	1782
Le nozze di Figaro	1786
Così fan tutte	1787
Don Giovanni	1787
Die Zauberflöte	1791
La Clemenza di Tito	1791

CHURCH MUSIC:

Mass in C, K. 257 (Credo)	1776
Mass in C, K. 317 (Coronation)	1779
Mass in C, K. 337 (Solemn Vespers)	1780
Mass in D minor, K. 626 (Requiem)	1791

41 SYMPHONIES:

Symphony no. 35, K. 385 (*Haffner*)	1782
Symphony no. 36, K. 425 (*Linz*)	1783
Symphony no. 38, K. 504 (*Prague*)	1786
Symphony no. 39 in E-flat, K. 543	1788
Symphony no. 40 in G Minor, K. 550	1788
Symphony no. 41, K. 551 (*Jupiter*)	1788

CONCERTI:

27 for piano
5 for violin
4 for horn
2 for flute
1 for bassoon
1 for clarinet
symphonia concertante for violin and viola

CHAMBER WORKS:

24 string quartets
42 violin sonatas
23 piano sonatas
6 string quintets
divertimenti
serenades (such as *Eine Kleine Nachtmusik*)
cassations

See Also List 5.21, The Operas of Wolfgang Amadeus Mozart

85

LIST 3.54   THE MAJOR WORKS OF HENRY PURCELL

OPERAS:

Dido and Aeneas	1689
The History of Dioclesian	1690
King Arthur	1691
The Fairy Queen	1692
The Indian Queen	1695
The Tempest	1695

CHORAL MUSIC:

"Welcome to all the pleasures" (Ode for St. Cecilia's day)	1683
"Come ye sons of Art" (Ode for Queen Mary's birthday)	1694
"Swifter Isis, swifter flow" (Welcome Song for Charles II)	1681
"Sound the Trumpet" (Welcome Song for James II)	1687

INSTRUMENTAL MUSIC:

3 fantasias in three parts	1680?
9 fantasias in four parts	1680
12 sonatas in three parts	1683
Musick's Hand-Maid	1689
10 sonatas in four parts	1697

LIST 3.55 THE MAJOR WORKS OF FRANZ SCHUBERT

OPERAS:

Alfonso und Estrella	1822
Fierrabras	1823

CHORAL MUSIC:

Mass in A-flat	1822
Mass in E-flat	1828

10 SYMPHONIES:

No. 4 in C Minor (*Tragic*)	1816
No. 5 in B-flat Major	1816
No. 6 in C Major	1818
No. 8 in B Minor (*Unfinished*)	1822
No. 9 in C Major (*Great C major*)	1828

CHAMBER MUSIC:

Piano Quintet in A Major (*Trout*)	1819
String Quartet in D Minor (*Death and the Maiden*)	1824
Octet in F Major	1824
String Quintet in C Major	1828
14 piano sonatas	
Fantasy in C Major (*Wanderer*)	1822

SONGS:

Die Schöne Müllerin	1823
Die Winterreise	1828
over 600 *Lieder*	

LIST 3.56   THE MAJOR WORKS OF ROBERT SCHUMANN

OPERA:

Genoveva	1850

CHORAL MUSIC:

Das Paradies und die Peri	1841
The Rose Pilgrimage	1851
Scenes from Goethe's Faust	1853

SYMPHONIES:

No. 1 in B flat (*Spring*)	1841
No. 2 in C Major	1846
No. 3 in E-flat (*Rhenish*)	1850
No. 4 in D Minor	1851

CONCERTI:

Piano Concerto in A Minor	1841–1845
Cello Concerto in A Major	1850

CHAMBER MUSIC:

Piano Quartet	1842
Piano Quintet	1842
Piano Trio no. 1 in D Minor	1847
Piano Trio no. 2 in F Major	1847
Piano Trio no. 3 in G Minor	1851

PIANO MUSIC:

Papillons	1832
Carnaval	1835
Davidsbündlertänze	1837
Kinderszenen	1838
Faschingsschwank aus Wien	1839

SONGS:

Frauenliebe und -leben	1840
Dichterliebe	1840
over 250 *Lieder*	

LIST 3.57   THE FAMOUS MARCHES OF JOHN PHILIP SOUSA

"El Capitan" ("We Love the U.S.A.")	1896	"Manhattan Beach"	c.1888
"The Gladiator"	1886	"Semper Fidelis"	1888
"Hands Across the Sea"	1899	"Stars and Stripes Forever"	1896
"Hail to the Spirit of Liberty"	1900	"The Thunderer"	1889
"The High School Cadets"	1890	"U.S. Field Artillery"	1917
"King Cotton"	1895	"The Washington Post"	1889
"The Liberty Bell"	1893		

LIST 3.58   THE MAJOR WORKS OF IGOR STRAVINSKY

BALLETS AND OTHER STAGE WORKS:

The Firebird (L'oiseau de feu)	1910
Petrushka (Pétrouchka)	1911
The Rite of Spring (La sacre du printemps)	1913
Pulcinella	1920
The Wedding (Les noces)	1923
Apollo (Appollon musgète)	1928
The Fairy's Kiss (Le baiser de la fée)	1928
Persephone (Perséphone)	1934
The Card Party (Jeu de cartes)	1937
Orpheus	1947
Agon	1957

STAGE WORKS:

The Nightingale (Le rossignol)	1914
The Soldier's Tale (l'Histoire du soldat)	1918
Mavra	1921
Oedipus Rex	1927
The Rake's Progress	1951
The Flood	1962

WORKS FOR CHORUS AND ORCHESTRA:

Symphony of Psalms	1930
Mass	1948
Canticum Sacrum	1955
Threni	1958
Requiem Canticles	1966

ORCHESTRAL WORKS:

Symphonies for Wind Instruments	1920
Concerto for Piano and Wind Orchestra	1924
Concerto for Violin and Orchestra	1932
Dumbarton Oaks Concerto	1938
Symphony in C	1940
Danses Concertantes	1941–1942
Concerto in D for String Orchestra	1946

orchestra Suites from the various ballets mentioned above

LIST 3.59   THE MAJOR WORKS OF PETER TCHAIKOVSKY

Operas:

Eugene Onegin	1878
The Queen of Spades	1890

Ballets:

Swan Lake	1876
The Sleeping Beauty	1889
The Nutcracker	1892

Symphonies:

No. 1 in G Minor (*Winter Dreams*)	1866, revised 1874
No. 2 in C Minor (*Little Russian*)	1872, revised 1879
No. 3 in D Major	1875
No. 4 in F Minor	1878
Manfred Symphony	1885
No. 5 in E Minor	1888
No. 6 in B Minor (*Pathétique*)	1893

Orchestral Works:

Overture, *Romeo and Juliet*	1869, revised 1870 and 1880
Symphonic Fantasy, *The Tempest*	1873
Symphonic Fantasy, *Francesca da Rimini*	1876
1812 Overture	1880
Overture-Fantasy, *Hamlet*	1888

Concerti:

Piano Concerto no. 1 in B-flat Minor	1874–1875
Variations on a Rococo Theme (cello and orchestra)	1876
Violin Concerto in D Major	1878
Piano Concerto no. 2 in G Major	1879–1880, revised 1893
Piano Concerto no. 3 in E-flat Major	1893

LIST 3.60   THE MAJOR WORKS OF RALPH VAUGHAN WILLIAMS

OPERAS:

Hugh the Drover	1914,
	revised 1956
Riders to the Sea	1925–1932
Sir John in Love	1928
The Pilgrim's Progress	1951

BALLETS:

Job	1930

SYMPHONIES:

Sea Symphony	1909
London Symphony	1913,
	revised 1918, 1920, 1933
Pastoral Symphony	1921
Symphony no. 4 in F Minor	1934
Symphony no. 5 in D	1943
Symphony no. 6 in E Minor	1947
Sinfonia Antartica	1952
Symphony no. 8 in D Minor	1955
Symphony no. 9 in E Minor	1957

ORCHESTRAL WORKS:

Norfolk Rhapsody	1906
Incidental music, *The Wasps*	1909
Fantasia on a theme by Thomas Tallis	1910
Five variants of "Dives and Lazarus"	1939
Partita for Double String Orchestra	1948

WORKS FOR VOICE OR CHORUS AND ORCHESTRA:

Toward the Unknown Region	1906
On Wenlock Edge	1909
Sancta Civitas	1925
Benedicite	1929
Five Tudor Portraits	1935
Serenade to Music	1938
Hodie	1954

LIST 3.61   THE MAJOR WORKS OF GIUSEPPE VERDI

OPERAS:

Nabucco	1842
Ernani	1844
Macbeth	1847,
	revised 1867
Rigoletto	1851
Il Trovatore	1853
La Traviata	1857,
	revised 1881
Simon Boccanegra	1859
Un Ballo in Maschera	1862
La Forza del Destino	1862
Don Carlos	1867,
	revised 1884
Aida	1871
Otello	1887
Falstaff	1893

OTHER WORKS:

Requiem	1873
String Quartet	1873

Section IV

INSTRUMENTS AND INSTRUMENTAL ENSEMBLES

LIST 4.1 PREDECESSORS OF THE PIANO

clavichord
dulcimer
harpsichord
spinet
virginal

LIST 4.2 TYPES OF PIANOS

baby grand
concert grand
console
electric
player
spinet
upright

LIST 4.3 PARTS OF THE MODERN PIANO

1. bridges
2. case
3. damper pedal
4. hammer
5. hammer rail
6. hitch pin
7. key/keyboard
8. keybed
9. metal frame
10. muffler felt
11. muffler pedal
12. pin block
13. pressure bar
14. soft pedal
15. soundboard
16. strings
17. tuning pin
(See page 260 for full page reproducible.)

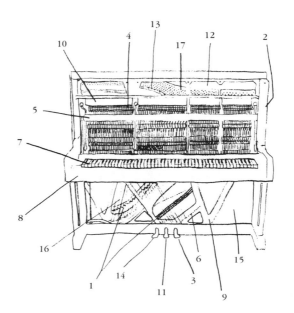

LIST 4.4 DEVELOPERS AND MAKERS OF PIANOS

Alpheus Babcock

Americus Backers

Dwight Hamilton Baldwin

Wilhelm Carl Bechstein   (Blüthner & Bechstein)

Julius Blüthner   (Blüthner & Bechstein)

Ignaz Bösendorfer

John Broadwood

Jonas Chickering

Bartolomeo Cristofori   (earliest piano)

Christian Friederici   (first upright)

Emmons Hamlin   (Mason & Hamlin)

Emil Heckel

Ferdinand Heckel

Ernest Knabe

William Knabe

William Knabe

Henry Mason   (Mason & Hamlin)

Johann Daniel Silberman

Johann Heinrich Silberman

Johann Andreas Stein

Charles Steinway   (Steinway & Sons)

Henry Steinway   (Steinway & Sons)

Theodore Steinway   (Steinway & Sons)

Robert Stodart

Johann Andreas Streicher

Torakusu Yamaha

Johannes Zumpe   (first square piano)

LIST 4.5 PIANO VIRTUOSI PAST AND PRESENT

Charles Alkan	France
Geza Anda	Hungary
Claudio Arrau	Chile
Vladimir Ashkenazy	Russia
Emanuel Ax	Poland/U.S.A.
William Backhaus	German/Swiss
Daniel Barenboim	Argentina
Ludwig van Beethoven	Germany
Leonard Bernstein	U.S.A.
Michel Beroff	France
Jorge Bolet	Cuba/U.S.A.
Alfred Brendel	Austria
John Browning	U.S.A.
Han von Bulow	Germany
Ferrucio Busoni	Italian/German
Robert Casadesus	France
Frédéric Chopin	French/Polish
Muzio Clementi	It./Eng.
Van Cliburn	U.S.A.
Jean-Philippe Collard	France
Alfred Cortot	France
Dennis Russell Davis	U.S.A.
Alicia deLarrocha	Spain
Misha Dichter	Poland/U.S.A.
Barry Douglas	Ireland
Philippe Entremont	France
Christoph Eschenbach	Germany
Anna Essipoff	Russia
John Field	Ireland
Rudolf Firkusny	Czechoslovakia
Leon Fleischer	U.S.A.
Malcolm Frager	U.S.A.
Walter Gieseking	Germany
Emil Gilels	Russia
Louis Gottschalk	U.S.A.
Glenn Gould	Canada
Gary Graffman	U.S.A.
Percy Grainger	Australia/U.S.A.
Dame Myra Hess	Great Britain
Joseph Hofmann	Polish/American
Vladimir Horowitz	Russia/U.S.A.
Johann Hummel	Austria
Paul Jacobs	U.S.A.
Byron Janis	U.S.A.
Zoltán Kocsis	Hungary
Ruth Laredo	U.S.A.
Bennett Lerner	U.S.A.

List 4.5 (continued)

Rosina Lhévinne	Russia
Dinu Lipatti	Rumania
Franz Liszt	Hungary
Radu Lupu	Rumania
Fanny Mendelssohn	Germany
Felix Mendelssohn	Germany
Ivan Moravec	Czechoslovakia
Wolfgang Amadeus Mozart	Austria
Guiomar Novães	Brazil
Garrick Ohlsson	U.S.A.
Ignacy Paderewski	Poland
Murray Perahia	U.S.A.
Ivo Pogorelich	Yugoslavia
André Previn	Germany/U.S.A.
Sergei Prokofiev	Russia
Sergei Rachmaninoff	Russian/American
Sviatoslav Richter	Ukraine
Pascal Roge	France
Anton Rubinstein	Russia
Artur Rubinstein	Polish-American
Camille Saint-Saëns	France
Artur Schnabel	Austria
Clara Schumann	Germany
Hilde Somer	Austria/American
Sigismond Thalberg	Switzerland
Alexander Thoradze	Russia
Tamás Vasary	Hungary
Andre Watts	U.S.A.
Alexis Wisenberg	Bulgaria
Fannie Bloomfield Zeisler	Austria/U.S.A.

LIST 4.6 FAMOUS COMPOSERS OF PIANO MUSIC

Isaac Albeniz
George Antheil
Anton Arensky
Mily Balakiev
Granville Bantock
Béla Bartók
Arnold Bax
Mrs. H.H.A. Beach
Ludwig van Beethoven
Alexander Borodin
Johannes Brahms
Frank Bridge
Cecil Burleigh
Emmanuel Chabrier
Cécile Chaminade
Frédéric Chopin
Samuel Coleridge-Taylor
Aaron Copland
Henry Cowell
Cesar Cui
Claude Debussy
R. Nathaniel Dett
Ernst von Dohnanyi
Johann Dussek
Antonín Dvořák
Manuel de Falla
Gabriel Fauré
John Field
César Franck
Balfour Gardiner
Alexander Glazunov

Reinhold Glière
Mikhail Glinka
Louis Gottschalk
Percy Grainger
Enrique Granados
Edvard Grieg
Charles Griffes
Johan Halvorsen
Stephan Heller
Arthur Honegger
Johann Hummel
Jacques Ibert
Vincent d'Indy
John Ireland
Zoltán Kodály
Erich Korngold
Ernst Krenek
Fridrich Kuhlau
Anatole Liadov
Franz Liszt
Otto Luening
Edward MacDowell
Gian Francesco Malipiero
Fanny Mendelssohn
Felix Mendelssohn
Darius Milhaud
Modest Mussorgsky
Wolfgang Amadeus Mozart
Carl Nielson
Ignacy Paderewski
Francis Poulenc

Sergei Prokofiev
Roger Quilter
Sergei Rachmaninoff
Maurice Ravel
Max Reger
Nicolai Rimsky-Korsakov
Anton Rubinstein
Camille Saint-Saëns
Erik Satie
Artur Schnabel
Arnold Schoenberg
Franz Schubert
Clara Wieck Schumann
Robert Schumann
Cyril Scott
Alexander Scriabin
Dmitri Shostikovich
Jean Sibelius
Christian Sinding
Igor Stravinsky
Josef Suk
Alexandre Tansman
Peter Tchaikovsky
Alexander Tcherepnin
Joaquin Turina
Heitor Villa-Lobos
Carl Maria von Weber
August Winding
Ermanno Wolf-Ferrari
Alexander Zelimsky

LIST 4.7 ORCHESTRAL COMPOSITIONS FEATURING THE PIANO

There are many fine solo piano works and piano concerti; the following is a list of pieces which feature piano in an orchestral setting:

Bartók:	Dance Suite; Sonata for Two Pianos and Percussion	Shostakovitch:	Piano Concerto no. 2
		Stravinsky:	*Petrushka*
Bloch:	Concerto Grosso no. 1	Tippett:	Concerto for Orchestra
Brahms:	Piano Concerto no. 2	Copland:	"Hoedown" from *Rodeo*
Saint-Saëns:	*Carnival of the Animals*		

LIST 4.8 PREDECESSORS AND RELATIVES OF THE ORGAN

barrel organ
hand organ
harmonica
hydraulus
monkey organ
panpipes
regal
street organ
syrinxes

LIST 4.9 TYPES OF ORGANS

Pipe: Tracker or mechanical electropneumatic, direct electric

Reed: American, cabinet, melodeon, harmonium

Electronic: Different from electropneumatic or direct electric in that the sound is electronically produced

LIST 4.10 PARTS OF THE MODERN ORGAN

1. choir organ manual
2. console
3. coupler-tilt tablet
4. crescendo pedal
5. great organ manual
6. pedal key/keyboard
7. stop knobs
8. swell organ manual
9. swell pedals
10. thumb piston
11. toe piston

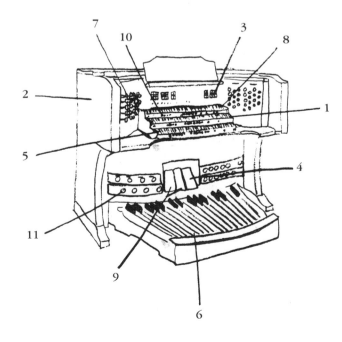

LIST 4.11   ORGAN FAMILIES OF TONE

diapason/principal
flute
string
reed

LIST 4.12   ORGAN STOPS

Aeolian
Aeoline
Bass Coupler
Bass Flute
Bassoon
Bourdon
Celeste
Celestina
Cello
Choral
Clarabella
Clarinet
Clarion
Clarionet
Contrebasse
Cor Anglais
Cornet
Cornet Echo
Corno
Coupler
Coup. Harmonique
Cremona
Diapason
Diapason Bass
Diapason Forte
Dolce
Double Diapason
Dulcet
Dulciana
Echo
Echo Horn

Expression
Fife
Flute
Flute d'Amour
Flute Forte
Forte
Forte I
Forte II
French Horn
Full Organ
Gamba
Gemshorn
Grand Expressione
Grand jeu
Grand Organ
Great to Pedals
Harp Aeoline
Harp Aeolienne
Harp eollienne
Hautbois
Hautboy
Horn
Knee Swell
Manual Sub-Bass
Melodia
Oboe
Octave Coupler
Open Diapason
Orchestral Forte
Pedal Bourdon
Pedal Dulciana

Piano
Piccolo
Principal
Principal Forte
Saliconal
Saxophone
Stop Diapason
Sub-Bass
Sub-Octave Coupler
Swell
Swell Organ
Swell to Great
Swell to Pedals
Treble Coupler
Treble Forte
Tremolo
Trumpet
Viola
Viola Dolce
Viol da Gamba
Violette
Violin
Violina
Voix Celeste
Voix Florante
Vox Angelicus
Vox Celeste
Vox Humana
Vox Jubilante
Waldflöte

LIST 4.13 ORGAN BUILDERS

Rudolf von Beckerath	Germany
Richard Bridge	England
John Brombaugh	U.S.A.
Aristide Cavaillé-Coll	France
Dominique Hyacinth Cavaillé-Coll	France
François-Henri Clicquot	France
Jean-Baptiste Clicquot	France
Louis-Alexandre Clicquot	France
Charles Brenton Fisk	U.S.A.
Joseph Gabler	Germany
Zacharias Hildebrandt	Germany
Holtkamp Organ Co.	U.S.A.
Christian Müller	Germany
Arp Schnitger	Germany, Holland
Johann Georg (Jurgen) Schnitger	
Franz Caspar Schnitger	
Johann Andreas Schulze	
Johann Friedrich Schulze	Switzerland, Germany; active in England
Heinrich Edmund Schulze	
Herward Schulze	
Eduard Schulze	
Andreas Silbermann	Saxony
Gottried Silbermann	Germany
David Tannenberg	U.S.A.
Henry Willis I	England
Henry Willis II	England
Henry Willis III	England
Henry Willis IV	England
Wurlitzer Co. (theater organs)	U.S.A.

LIST 4.14   FAMOUS ORGANISTS

Jehan Alain	Dietrich Buxtehude	Jean Langlais
Marie-Claire Alain	David Craighead	John Longhurst
Johann Sebastian Bach	Catharine Crozier	Wolfgang Amadeus Mozart
Jennifer Bate	Marcel Dupré	Robert Sanders
E. Power Biggs	Virgil Fox	Russell Saunders
Guy Bovet	Christopher Herrick	Albert Schweitzer
David Britton	Peter Hurford	Gillian Weir

LIST 4.15   FAMOUS COMPOSERS OF ORGAN MUSIC

Jehan (Ariste) Alain	1911–1940	Georg Friedrich Händel	1685–1759
Johann Sebastian Bach	1685–1750	Jean Langlais	1907–1991
Johannes Brahms	1833–1897	Felix Mendelssohn	1809–1847
Dietrich Buxtehude	1637–1707	Oliver Messiaen	1908–1993
François Couperin	1668–1733	Wolfgang Amadeus Mozart	1756–1791
Marcel Dupré	1886–1971	Louis Vierne	1870–1937
Edward Elgar	1857–1934	Charles Widor	1844–1937
César Franck	1822–1890		

LIST 4.16   REPRESENTATIVE WORKS FOR THE ORGAN

Toccata and Fugue in D Minor	Johann Sebastian Bach
Organ Concerto no. 1 in C Major	Franz Joseph Haydn
"Toccata" from Organ Symphony no. 5	Charles Widor
L'Ascension (Four Meditations)	Oliver Messiaen
Litanies op. 79	Jehan Alain
Chorale Preludes op. 122	Johannes Brahms
Hommagge a Frescobaldi	Jean Langlais
Organ Concerto op. 7	Georg Friedrich Händel
Sonata in G, op. 28	Edward Elgar
Sonata no. 6 in D Minor	Felix Mendelssohn

LIST 4.17   ORGAN TERMINOLOGY

action
blower
choir organ
console
couplers
diapason
direct electric
divisions
echo organ
electropneumatic
flue pipe
flutes
great organ

key channel
keyboard
manual
organ case
pallet
pedal board
pedal organ
pipes
positive organ
principal
ranks
reed pipe

slider
solo organ
stop knobs
stops
strings
swell box
swell organ
tracker
under expression
volume-control pedals
wind chests
wind supply

LIST 4.18   THE VIOLIN FAMILY

violin
viola

violoncello (cello)
double bass (string bass, bass viol, bass fiddle)

LIST 4.19   PREDECESSORS AND RELATIVES OF THE VIOLIN

cellone
cithara
fiddles
kit
lira da braccio
octabass
pochette
rebec

taschengeige
vielle
viola da gamba
viola d'amore
viola da spalla
violio piccolo
viols

LIST 4.20   THE PARTS OF THE MODERN VIOLIN AND BOW

VIOLIN:

1. bouts
2. bridge
3. chin rest
4. end button
5. f hole
6. fingerboard
7. neck
8. nut
9. pegbox
10. pegs
11. purfling
12. ribs
13. scroll
14. shoulder
15. strings
16. tailpiece
17. top
18. tuners

BOW:

1. eye
2. ferrule
3. frog
4. hair
5. ivory
6. screw
7. slide
8. stick
9. tip
10. wrapping

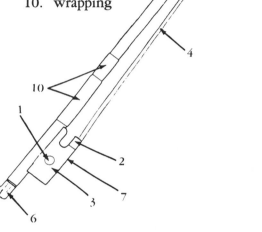

The parts of the violin and bow are numbered to correspond with the two accompanying illustrations. You may reproduce the illustrations and hand them out to your students for a quiz, a self-check exercise, or as a homework assignment. See pages 258 and 259 for full page reproducibles.

LIST 4.21   DEVELOPERS AND MAKERS OF STRINGED INSTRUMENTS AND BOWS

Amati Family
    Andrea
    Antonio
    Girolamo
    Girolamo
    Niccolò
Giovanni Battista Guadagnini
Guarneri Family
    Andrea
    Pietro Giovanni
    Giuseppe
    Pietro
    Giuseppe Antonio

Carleen Hutchins
Klotz Family
    Matthias Klotz
    Sebastian Klotz
Nicolas Lupot
Giovanni Paolo Maggini
Gasparo da Salo
Ludwig Spohr
Jakob Stainer
Antonio Stradiveri
François Tourte
Jean-Baptiste Vuillaume

LIST 4.22 STRINGED INSTRUMENT VIRTUOSI
PAST AND PRESENT

VIOLINISTS

Leopold Auer
Johann Sebastian Bach
Joshua Bell
Sarah Chang
Kyung Wha Chung
Archangelo Corelli
Pablo deSarasate
Mischa Elman
Toshiya Eto
Eugène Fodor
Pierre Gaviniès
Francesco Geminiani
Jascha Heifetz
Joseph Joachim
Ani Kavafian
Nigel Kennedy
Young-Uck Kim
Fritz Kreisler
Gidon Kremer
Rodolphe Kreutzer
Jean-Marie Leclair
Cho-Liang Lin
Yehudi Menuhin
Midori
Nathan Milstein
Shlomo Mintz
Leopold Mozart
Wolfgang Amadeus Mozart
Anne-Sophie Mutter
David Oistrakh
Niccolò Paganini
Itzhak Perlman
Ruggiero Ricci
Nadja Salerno-Sonnenberg
Louis Spohr
Isaac Stern
Joseph Szigeti
Giuseppe Tartini
Francesco Veracini
Henry Vieuxtemps
Giovanni Battista Viotti
Tomaso Vitali
Antonio Vivaldi
Henryk Wieniawski
Eugène Ysaÿe
Efrem Zimbalist
Pinchas Zuckerman

VIOLISTS

Paul Hindemith
Kim Kashkashian
Ida Kavafian
Yehudi Menuhin
William Primrose
Lionel Tertis
Michael Tree
William Walton

CELLISTS

Pablo Casals
J.F. Dotzauer
Jacqueline duPré
Pierre Fournier
Georg Goltermann
Lynn Harrell
Julius Klengel
Yo Yo Ma
Mischa Maisky
Gregor Piatigorsky
David Popper
Bernhard Romberg
Leonard Rose
Mstislav Rostropovich
Janos Starker
Paul Tortelier
Julian Lloyd Webber

DOUBLE BASSISTS

Jerry Fuller
Yoan Goilav
Bjorn Ianke
Gary Karr
Yasunori Kawahara
Barbara Sanderling
Ludwig Streicher

LIST 4.23 FAMOUS COMPOSERS OF STRINGED INSTRUMENT MUSIC

Johann Sebastian Bach
Béla Bartók
Alban Berg
Ludwig van Beethoven
Hector Berlioz
Johannes Brahms
Aaron Copland
Antonín Dvořák

Edward Elgar
Franz Joseph Haydn
Paul Hindemith
Zoltán Kodály
Gustav Mahler
Felix Mendelssohn
Wolfgang Amadeus Mozart

Camille Saint-Saëns
Robert Schumann
Jean Sibelius
Igor Stravinsky
Peter Tchaikovsky
Georg Telemann
William Walton

LIST 4.24 COMPOSITIONS FEATURING THE VIOLIN

There are many fine solo violin works, sonatas, and concerts; the following is a list of just a few of the pieces which feature the violin in an orchestral context:

Music for Strings, Percussion, and Celeste; Divertimento for String Orcherstra	Béla Bartók
Four Dance Episodes from *Rodeo*	Aaron Copland
"The Lark Ascending"	Ralph Vaughan Williams
Romanian Rhapsodies	Georges Enesco
Symphony no. 4	Gustav Mahler
Scheherazade	Nicolai Rimsky-Korsakov
Overture to *La Scala di Seta;* Overture to *Il Signor Bruschino*	Gioacchino Rossino
Concerto for Double String Orchestra	Michael Tippett
Grand Canyon Suite	Ferde Grofé
Concerti	Bach, Bartók, Beethoven, Berg, Brahms, Mendelssohn, Mozart, Schoenberg, Shostakovich, Sibelius, Tchaikovsky

LIST 4.25 COMPOSITIONS FEATURING THE VIOLA

Harold in Italy	Hector Berlioz
Enigma Variations	Edward Elgar
Hary Janos Suite	Zoltán Kodály
Sinfonia Concertante	Wolfgang Amadeus Mozart
Brandenburg Concerto No. 6	Johann Sebastian Bach
Holberg Suite, 5th mvt., Rigaudon	Edvard Grieg
Concerti	Bartók, Copland, Hindemith, Walton

LIST 4.26   COMPOSITIONS FEATURING THE CELLO

Concerto for Violin and Cello; Piano Concerto no. 2	Johannes Brahms
Enigma Variations	Edward Elgar
"Swan" from *Carnival of the Animals*	Camille Saint-Saëns
Violin Concerto	Jean Sibelius
Firebird Suite	Igor Stravinsky
"Aria und Ob Die Wolke Sie Verhulle" from *Der Freischutz*	Carl Maria con Weber
Serenade for Strings, op. 48, 4th mvt.	Peter Tchaikovsky
Concerti	Dvořák, Elgar, Haydn, Schumann, Saint-Saëns

LIST 4.27   COMPOSITIONS FEATURING THE DOUBLE BASS

Symphonies no. 5 and no. 6	Ludwig van Beethoven
Four Dance Episodes from *Rodeo*	Aaron Copland
The Creation	Franz Josef Haydn
Symphony no. 1, 3rd mvt.	Gustav Mahler
L'Enfant et les Sortileges	Maurice Ravel
Scheherazade	Nicolai Rimsky-Korsakov
"Elephant" from *Carnival of the Animals*	Camille Saint-Saëns

LIST 4.28   OTHER STRINGED INSTRUMENTS

Aeolian harp
arpeggione
balalaika
banjo
dulcimer
guitar
harp
hurdy-gurdy
lute
lyre
mandolin
sitar
ukelele
zither

LIST 4.29 WOODWIND INSTRUMENTS

basset horn
bassoon
clarinet
contrabass clarinet
contrabassoon
English horn
flute
oboe
piccolo
recorder
Sarrusophone
saxophone

LIST 4.30 EARLY WOODWINDS

bass flute
bassonore
bombard
chalumeau
cornett
cortaut
crumhorn
curtal
fagotto
heckelphone
pommer
recorder
shawm
sordoni
tenor flute
treble flute

LIST 4.31 DEVELOPERS AND MAKERS OF WOODWIND INSTRUMENTS

Eugène Albert	clarinet
Carol Almenräder	bassoon
Theobald Boehm	flute
Jacob Denner	recorder, flute, oboe, clarinet
Johann Christoph Denner	various woodwinds (recorders, oboes, bassoons, clarinets)
William Haynes	flute
Johann Adam Heckel	clarinet, bassoon
Wilhelm Heckel	oboe (Hecklephone)
Hotteterre family	flute
Jean Hotteterre	oboe
Michel Philidor	oboe
Adolph Sax	saxophone

LIST 4.32   WOODWIND VIRTUOSI

FLUTE:

Julius Baker
Samuel Baron
Georges Barrère
Frans Bruggen
James Galway
Philippe Gaubert
William Kincaid
Hans-Martin Linde
Gareth Morris
Marcel Moyse
William Murchie
Aurèle Nicolet
Emil Prill
Jean-Pierre Rampal
Kurt Redel
René leRoy
Gustav Scheck
Hans Peter Schmitz
Karl-Heinz Zöller
Eugenia Zukerman

OBOE:

John Anderson
Theodore Baskin
Neil Black
Jacques Chambon
Janet Craxton
Peter Crist
Nicholas Daniel
Paul Domnbecht
Greg Donovetsky
Sarah Francis
Burkhard Glaetzner
Brynjar Hoff
Heinz Hollinger
Vladamir Kurlin
John de Lancie
John Mack
Wayne Rapier
Ray Still
Marcel Tabuteau
Gregor Zubicky

CLARINET:

Burton Beerman
Eduard Brunner
James Campbell
Larry Combs
Detalmo Corneti
F. Gerard Errante
Laura Flax
Anthony Gigliotti
Benny Goodman
Alan Hacker
Michael Heitzler
Thea King
Dieter Klocker
Aage Oxenbad
Gervase dePeyer
Harry Sparnaay
Hans Rudolf Stadler
Suzanne Stephens
Richard Stoltzman
Frederick Thurston

BASSOON:

Carl Almenräder
Carl Baermann
Friedrich Baumann
Girolamo Besozzi
Georg Brandt
Frances Eustace
J. Walter Guetter
László Hara
James Holmes
Simon Kover
Luc Loubry
Christopher Millard
Wenzel Neukirchner
Jesse Read
Felix Rheiner
Georg Ritter
Sol Schoenbach
Daniel Smith
Knut Sonstevold
Masahito Tenaka

LIST 4.33 FAMOUS COMPOSERS OF WOODWIND MUSIC

FLUTE:

H.E. Apostel
Johann Sebastian Bach
Hank Badings
Rob duBois
Pierre Boulez
Claude Debussy
Wolfgang Fortner
Hans Werner Henze
Paul Hindemith
Arthur Honegger
Jacques Ibert
Otto Luening
Elisabeth Lutyens
Bruno Mederna
Frank Martin
Bohuslav Martinů
Darius Milhaud
Wolfgang Amadeus Mozart
George Perle
Goffredo Petrassi
Walter Piston
Sergei Prokofiev
Albert Roussel
Arnold Schoenberg
Humphrey Searle
Mátyás Sieber
Ralph Vaughn Williams
Edgar Varèse

OBOE:

Tomaso Albinoni
Johann Christoph Bach
Carl Philipp Emanuel Bach
Ludwig van Beethoven
Johannes Brahms
François Couperin
Georg Friedrich Händel
Ludwig August Lebrun
Jean-Baptiste Loeillet
Gustav Mahler
Wolfgang Amadeus Mozart
Franz Schubert
Richard Strauss
Ralph Vaughn Williams
Antonio Vivaldi

CLARINET:

Béla Bartók
Leonard Bernstein
Arthur Bliss
Aaron Copland
Paul Hindemith
Gustav Holst
Wolfgang Amadeus Mozart
Thea Musgrave
Carl Nielsen
Vincent Persichetti
Arnold Schoenberg
Igor Stravinsky
Carl Maria von Weber

BASSOON:

Johann Christoph Bach
Edward Elgar
Georg Friedrich Händel
Paul Hindemith
Sergei Prokofiev
Maurice Ravel
Camille Saint-Saëns
William Schumann
Igor Stravinsky
Georg Philipp Telemann
Heitor Villa-Lobos
Ermanno Wolf-Ferrari
Jan Dismas Zelenka

LIST 4.34   ORCHESTRAL COMPOSITIONS FEATURING THE VARIOUS WOODWIND INSTRUMENTS

E-Flat Clarinet

Berlioz:	*Symphonie Fantastique*
Ravel:	*Bolero*
Britten:	*Peter Grimes*

Alto Flute

Holst:	*The Planets*
Ravel:	*Daphnis et Chloé*
Stravinsky:	*The Rite of Spring*

Oboe d'amore

Ravel:	*Bolero*

Heckelphone

R. Strauss:	*Salomé* and *Elektra*

Saxophone

Bizet:	*L'Arlesienne* Suites
Berg:	Violin Concerto

Basset Horn

R. Strauss:	*Der Rosenkavalier*

Contrabass Clarinet

Schoenberg:	Five Pieces for Orchestra

Sarrusophone

Ravel:	*Rapsodie Espagnole*
Delius:	*Eventyr*

Flute

Bach:	Suite in B Minor
Bartók:	Concerto for Orchestra
Beethoven:	*Leonore* Overture no. 3; Symphony no. 6
Britten:	*Young Person's Guide to the Orchestra*
Debussy:	*Prelude à l'après-midi d'un faune*
Gluck:	"Dance of the Blessed Spirits" from *Orpheus and Eurydice*
Mendelssohn:	Overture to *A Midsummer Night's Dream*
Ravel:	*Daphnis et Chloé*
Rossini:	Overture to *William Tell*

List 4.34 (continued)

OBOE AND ENGLISH HORN

Menotti:	Dance Scene, from *Amhal and the Night Visitors*
Beethoven:	Symphony no. 6
Berlioz:	*Symphonie Fantastique*
Dvořák:	Symphony no. 9
Grieg:	*Peer Gynt* Suite no. 1
Haydn:	Symphony no. 22 *(Seasons)*
Prokofiev:	*Peter and the Wolf*
Schubert:	Symphony no. 9
Wagner:	*Tristan und Isolde*

B-FLAT CLARINET

Brahms:	Clarinet Quintet
Copland:	*El Salón Mexico*
Elgar:	*Enigma* Variations
Gershwin:	*Rhapsody in Blue*
Mendelssohn:	Overture to *A Midsummer Night's Dream*
Mozart:	Clarinet Concerto; Clarinet Quintet
Tchaikovsky:	"Dance of the Sugar Plum Fairy" from *The Nutcracker*
Weber:	Clarinet Concerto and Overture to *Der Freischutz*

SAXOPHONE

Britten:	"Dies Irae" from *Sinfonia da Requiem*
Mussorgsky-Ravel:	"The Old Castle" from *Pictures at an Exhibition*
Ravel:	*Bolero;* Rhapsody for Saxophone
Strauss:	*Symphonia Domestica*
Vaughn Williams:	*Job*

BASSOON

Bartók:	Concerto for Orchestra
Dukas:	*The Sorcerer's Apprentice*
Grieg:	"Anitra's Dance" from *Peer Gynt* Suite no. 1
Mendelssohn:	"Dance of the Clowns" from *A Midsummer Night's Dream*
Prokofiev:	*Peter and the Wolf*
Stravinsky:	*The Rite of Spring*
Tchaikovsky:	Symphony no. 5

PICCOLO

Shostakovich:	Symphony no. 7
Sousa:	"Stars and Stripes Forever"

LIST 4.35   BRASS INSTRUMENTS

bugle
cornet
French horn
sousaphone
trombone
trumpet
tuba

INFREQUENTLY USED BRASS

bass trumpet
D trumpet
euphonium
flugelhorn
tenor tuba
Wagner tuba

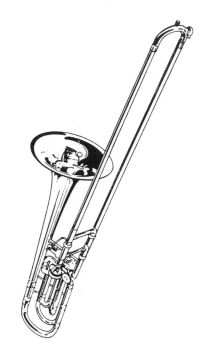

LIST 4.36   EARLY BRASS INSTRUMENTS

alphorn
hibernicon
long horn
ophimonocleide
posthorn
Russian bassoon
sackbut
serpent
serpentcleide
serpent froveille
serpent pieffault
trompettes di menestrels

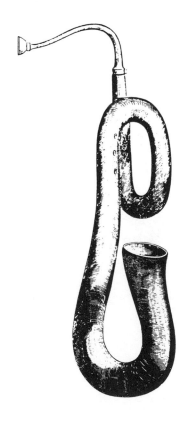

LIST 4.37 BRASS INSTRUMENT VIRTUOSI

TRUMPET

Maurice André
Ole Edvard Antonsen
Louis Armstrong
Eric Aubler
Wolfgang Basch
Andre Bernard
Dirceu Braz
William Camp
Edward Carroll
Herbert L. Clarke (cornet)
Miles Davis
Paul Falentin
Stanley Friedman
Ludwig Guttler
Hakan Hardenberger
David Hickman
Stephen Keavy
Samuel Krauss
Bernhard Laubin
Hannes Laubin
Wolfgang Laubin
Wynton Marsalis
Anthony Plog
Paul Plunkett (Baroque trumpet)
Gerard Schwartz
Thomas Stevens
Edward H. Tarr
Roger Voisin
John Wallace

FRENCH HORN

Kenneth Albrecht
Thomas Bacon
David Battey
Dennis Brain
John Cerminaro
Lowell Greer
Steve Gross
Soren Hermansson
Gregory Hustis
Mason Jones
Meir Rimon
William Scharnberg
Gunther Schuller

TROMBONE

Joseph Alessi
Ronald Barron
Dany Bonvin
Stanley Clark
Donald Knaub (bass trombone)
Christian Lindberg
Arthur Pryor
Armond Rosen
Armin Rosin
Paul Schreckenberger
Branimir Slocar
Benny Sluchin
Dennis Smith

TUBA

Roger Beherend (euphonium)
Roger Bobo
Brian Bowman (euphonium)
Jean-Pierre Chevailler (euphonium)
Floyd Cooley
Warren Deck
Eugene Dowling
Mark Nelson
Harvey Phillips
David Randolph
Jim Self

LIST 4.38 COMPOSITIONS FEATURING THE VARIOUS BRASS INSTRUMENTS

CORNET

Elgar:	*Cockaigne* Overture
Stravinsky:	*Petrushka*

FLUGELHORN

Vaughn Williams:	Symphony no. 9

TENOR TUBA (EUPHONIUM)

Holst:	*The Planets*
R. Strauss:	*Don Quixote*
R. Strauss:	*Ein Heldenlieben*

TRUMPET IN D

Stravinsky:	*The Rite of Spring*
Ravel:	*Bolero*

WAGNER TUBA

Bruckner:	Symphonies nos. 7,8 + 9
Janacek:	Synfonetta
R. Strauss:	*Elektra*
Wagner:	Operas from the *Ring of the Niebelungs*

FRENCH HORN

Berlioz:	"The Royal Hunt and Storm" from *Les Troyens*
Brahms:	Piano Concerto no. 2
Debussy:	*Prelude à l'après-midi d'un faune*
Handel:	*Water Music*
Mahler:	Symphony no. 3
Mendelssohn:	"Nocturne" from *A Midsummer Night's Dream*
Mozart:	Horn Concerti
Ravel:	*Pavane for a Dead Princess*
Tchaikovsky:	Symphony no. 5
Weber:	Overture to *Oberon*

TRUMPET

Bach:	Brandenburg Concerto no. 2
Beethoven:	*Leonore* Overture no. 3
Carter:	Symphony for 3 Orchestras
Clarke:	Trumpet Voluntary
Haydn:	Trumpet Concerto
Rossini:	Overture to *William Tell*
Verdi:	The Triumphal March from *Aida*

TROMBONE

Beethoven:	Symphony no. 5
Mozart:	*Don Giovanni*
Schubert:	Symphony no. 9
Wagner:	Overture to *Tannhäuser*
Weber:	Overture to *Der Freischutz*

TUBA

Berlioz:	Racoczy March from *The Damnation of Faust*
Berlioz:	*Symphonie Fantastique* 4th + 5th mvts.
Holst:	"Mars" from *The Planets*
Mussorgsky:	*A Night on Bald Mountain*
Mussorgsky-Ravel:	"Bylo" from *Pictures at an Exhibition*
Rimsky-Korsakov:	*Scheherazade*
Stravinsky:	Petruchka *Peasant with a Bear*
Vaughan Williams:	Tuba Concerto
Wagner:	Overture to *Die Meistersinger*
Wagner:	*Ride of the Valkyries*

© 1994 by Parker Publishing Company

LIST 4.39   PERCUSSION INSTRUMENTS

INSTRUMENTS OF DEFINITE PITCH

celesta	tubular bells
glockenspiel	vibraphone
marimba	xylophone
timpani (kettledrums)	

INSTRUMENTS OF INDEFINITE PITCH

anvil	rattle
bass drum	sleigh bells
bongos	snare drum
castanets	tambourine
claves	temple blocks
cymbals	timbales (tom-toms)
gong	triangle
güiro	whip
maracas	wind machine

LIST 4.40   COMPOSITIONS FEATURING PERCUSSION INSTRUMENTS

TIMPANI

Bartók:	Sonata for Two Pianos and Percussion
Beethoven:	Violin Concerto; Symphony no. 9
Berlioz:	"Tuba Mirum" from *Requiem*
Carter:	Piano Concerto

WIND MACHINE

Grofé:	*Grand Canyon* Suite
Ravel:	*Daphnis et Chloé*

PERCUSSION REPERTOIRE

Bartók:	Music for Strings, Percussion, and Celeste
Grieg:	*Peer Gynt* Suite
Haydn:	Symphony no. 100
Mozart:	*Die Zauberflöte* (glockenspiel)
Leopold Mozart:	*Toy* Symphony
Nielson:	Symphony no. 5
Ravel:	*Daphnis et Chloé*
Rimsky-Korsakov:	*Capriccio Espagnol*
Rossini:	Overture, *La Scala di Setta*
Saint-Saëns:	*Danse Macabre* (xylophone)
Shostokovich:	Symphony no. 15
Tippett:	Symphony no. 3
Tchaikovsky:	"Chinese Dance" and "Dance of the Sugar Plum Fairy" from *The Nutcracker; 1812 Overture*

117

List 4.40 (continued)

SLEIGH BELLS

Anderson	"Sleigh Ride"
Mahler	Symphony no. 4

RATTLE

R. Strauss	"Till Eulenspiegel"

WHIP

Anderson	"Sleigh Ride"
Milhaud	Symphonic Suite no. 2

LIST 4.41   ELECTRONIC INSTRUMENTS

analog synthesizer
computer (midi instruments)
digital synthesizer
electronic tape
guitar
Moog synthesizer
ondes martenot
organ
tape recorder
theremin
trautonium
wind controller
sampler

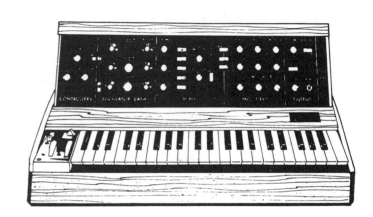

LIST 4.42   MECHANICAL INSTRUMENTS

barrel organ
carillon
flute clock
hurdy-gurdy
jack-in-the-box
music box
musical clock
phonograph
pianola
player piano
siren
wind machine

LIST 4.43   FOLK INSTRUMENTS AND THEIR COUNTRIES

accordion	France, Germany, Austria	koto	Japan
acoustic guitar	Spain	lung ti	China
alpenhorn	Switzerland	mandolin	Spain
bagpipes	Scotland, Ireland	maracas	South America
balalaika	Russia	mu-yus	China
bamboo pipe	China	nose flute	Fiji
bandura	Ukraine	nunga	Siberia
banjo	Africa	panpipes	Solomon Islands
bellows bagpipe	Hungary	Peruvian harp	Peru
bin	India	pipa	China
biniou	France	po-chung	China
biwa	Japan	qin	China
bouzouki	Greece	raft zither	Nigeria
cabaca	South America	rajao	Portugal
castanets	Spain	rattle drum	North American Indians
charango	Bolivia	san xian	Mongolia
chime gongs	Burma	sansa	West Africa
cimbal	Czechoslovakia	santouri	Greece
cimbalom	Hungary	sarangi	India
clappers	Egypt	shakuhachi	Japan
claves	Cuba, Latin America	shamisen	Japan
clay whistles	Portugal	sheng	China
crwdd	Wales	sihu	China
darabuka	Egypt	sitar	India
didgeridoo	Australia	steel guitar	Hawaii
dilruba	India	steel drum	West Indies
fiddle	Europe/U.S.A.	t'ao-ku	China
gamalon	Thailand	tabla	India
gamelans	Indonesia	tambura	India
gong	Southeast Asia	tiktiri	India
gourd whistle	Sudan	tsuzumi	Japan
hammer dulcimer	U.S.A.	tzeze	Uganda
harmonica	Germany	ud	Morocco
ilimba	Zimbabwe	ukelele	Hawaii
Irish whistles	Ireland	valiha	Madagascar
Jew's harp	U.S.A.	vina	India
kalengo	Nigeria	yang qin	China
kantele	Finland	zummara	Saudi Arabia

LIST 4.44 MUSICOLOGICAL CATEGORIES OF INSTRUMENTS

AEROPHONES

accordions
bagpipes
bassoons
bull-roarers
buzzers
clarinets
concertinas
end-blown flutes
flageolets
harmoniums
horns
mouth organs
multiple flutes
nose flutes
oboes
organs
panpipes
recorders
saxophones
shawms
side-blown flutes
trombones
trumpets
vessel flutes
whistle flutes
whistles

IDIOPHONES

clapper bells
concussion idiophones
metallophones
friction idiophones
gongs
jingles
lithophones
pellet bells
plucked idiophones
rattles
scraped idiophones
stamped idiophones
stamping idiophones
struck bells
vessels
xylophones

CHORDOPHONES

angle harps
bow harps
bowl lyres
box lyres
clavichords
dulcimer
fiddles
flat-backed lutes
frame harps
fretted lutes
ground zithers
harpsichords
long zithers
mouth bows
multiple bows
pianofortes
psalteries
raft zithers
resonated bows
round-backed lutes
simple bows
spinets
stick zithers
trough zithers
tube zithers
virginals

MEMBRANOPHONES

barrel drums
conical drums
cylindrical drums
footed drums
frame drums
friction drums
goblet drums
long drums
mirlitons
vessel drums
waisted drums

MECHANICAL AND ELECTRICAL

automatic pianos
carillons
chimes
electric guitars
electric organs
electro-mechanical instruments
mechanical music makers
mechanical organs
music boxes
radio-electric instruments

LIST 4.45   TOP AMERICAN AND CANADIAN ORCHESTRAS

ORCHESTRA	MUSIC HALL
American Symphony Orchestra	Carnegie Hall, New York
Atlanta Symphony Orchestra	Symphony Hall, Robert W. Woodruff Arts Center
Baltimore Symphony Orchestra	Joseph Meyerhoff Symphony Hall
Boston Symphony Orchestra	Symphony Hall
Buffalo Philharmonic Orchestra	Kleinhans Music Hall
Calgary Philharmonic Orchestra	Jack Singer Hall, Calgary Centre for Performing Arts
Chicago Symphony Orchestra	Orchestra Hall
Cincinnati Symphony Orchestra	Music Hall
Cleveland Orchestra	Severance Hall
Dallas Symphony Orchestra	Morton H. Meyerson Symphony Center
Detroit Symphony	Orchestra Hall
Edmunton Symphony Orchestra	Northern Alberta Jubilee Auditorium
Houston Symphony Orchestra	Jesse H. Jones Hall
Indianapolis Symphony Orchestra	Circle Theatre
Los Angeles Chamber Orchestra	Ambassador Auditorium, Pasadena
Los Angeles Philharmonic Orchestra	Dorothy Chandler Pavilion, Los Angeles
Louisville Orchestra	Whitney Hall
Milwaukee Symphony Orchestra	Vihlein Hall/Performing Arts Center
Minnesota Orchestra	Orchestra Hall, Minneapolis
Montréal Symphony Orchestra	Salle Wilfrid-Pelletier, Place des Arts
National Arts Centre Orchestra	Opera of National Arts Center
National Symphony Orchestra	Kennedy Center, Washington, D.C.
New Haven Symphony	Woolsey Hall
New Jersey Symphony Orchestra	Symphony Hall, Newark
	Monmouth Arts Center, Red Bank
	War Memorial Auditorium, Trenton
New World Symphony	Miami Beach
New York Philharmonic Orchestra	Avery Fisher Hall
Orchestre Symphonique de Québec	Grand Théâtre de Québec
The Philadelphia Orchestra	Academy of Music
Pittsburgh Symphony Orchestra	Heinz Hall
Rochester Philharmonic Orchestra	Eastman Theatre
St. Louis Symphony Orchestra	Powell Symphony Hall
St. Paul Chamber Orchestra	Ordway Music Theatre
San Francisco Symphony Orchestra	Davies Symphony Hall
Seattle Symphony Orchestra	Seattle Center Opera House
Toronto Symphony	Roy Thomson Hall
Utah Symphony Orchestra	Utah Symphony Hall
Vancouver Symphony	Orpheum

LIST 4.46 OTHER ORCHESTRAS

Academy of Ancient Music	London, Great Britain
Academy of St. Martin in the Fields	London, Great Britain
Berlin Philharmonic	Berlin, Germany
Berlin Symphony Orchestra	Berlin, Germany
Bournemouth Sinfonietta	Dorset, Great Britain
Gewandhausorchester	Leipzig, Germany
I Musici	Rome, Italy
Israel Philharmonic	Tel Aviv, Israel
London Symphony Orchestra	London, Great Britain
Orchestre de la Suisse Romande	Geneva, Switzerland
Orchestre National de France	Paris, France
Radio Symphony Orchestra of Berlin	Berlin, Germany
Royal Concertgebouw Orchestra	Amsterdam, Netherlands
The Royal Philharmonic Orchestra	London, Great Britain
The BBC Symphony Orchestra	London, Great Britain
Ulster Orchestra	Ulster, Ireland
Radio Symphony Orchestra of Berlin	Berlin, Germany

LIST 4.47 FAMOUS ORCHESTRA CONDUCTORS

Claudi Abbado	Italy
Gerd Albrecht	Germany
Ernst Ansemet	Switzerland
Vladimir Ashkenazy	Russia
Sir John Barbirolli	England
Daniel Barenboim	Argentina
Serge Baudo	France
Thomas Beecham	England
Leonard Bernstein	U.S.A.
Herbert Blomstedt	U.S.A.
Pierre Boulez	France
Iona Brown	England
Semyon Bychkov	Russia
Pablo Casals	Spain
Sergiu Celibidache	Rumania
Riccardo Chailly	Italy
Sergiu Comissiona	Rumania
Dennis Russell Davies	U.S.A.
Andrew Davis	Great Britain
Colin Davis	Great Britain
Edo de Waart	Holland
Dean Dixon	U.S.A.
Christoph von Dohnanyi	Germany
Charles Dutoit	Switzerland
Mark Elder	England
Christoph Eschenbach	Germany
Leon Fleischer	U.S.A.
Rafael Fruhbeck de Burgos	Spain
Gianluigi Gelmetti	Italy
Carlo Maria Giulini	Italy
Gunther Herbig	Germany
Christopher Hogwood	England
Neeme Jarvi	Estonia
Armin Jordan	Switzerland
Herbert von Karajan	Austria
Istvan Kertesz	Hungary
Otto Klemperer	Germany
Kiril Kondrashin	Russia
Serge Koussevitzky	Russia
Rafael Kubelik	Czechoslovakia
Erich Leindorf	Austria
Raymond Leppard	England
Yoel Levi	Rumania/U.S.A.
James Levine	U.S.A.
Jesus Lopez-Cobos	Spain
Lorin Maazel	France
Zdenek Macal	Czechoslovakia

List 4.47 (continued)

Charles Mackerras	U.S.A.
Neville Marriner	England
Kurt Masur	Germany
Eduardo Mata	Mexico
John Mauceri	U.S.A.
Zubin Mehta	India
Dimitri Mitropoulis	Greece
Riccardo Muti	Italy
Vaclav Neumann	Czechoslovakia
Roger Norrington	England
David Oistrakh	Russia
Eugene Ormandy	Hungary
Seiji Ozawa	Manchuria
Jean-François Paillard	France
Trevor Pinnock	England
André Previn	Germany
Fritz Reiner	Hungary
Mstislav Rostropovoch	Russia
Esa-Pekka Salonen	Finland
Jukka-Pekka Saraste	Finland
Thomas Schippers	U.S.A.
Gerard Schwartz	U.S.A.
Joseph Silverstein	U.S.A.
Giuseppe Sinopoli	Italy
Stanislaw Skrowaczewski	Poland
Leonard Slatkin	U.S.A.
Lawrence Leighton Smith	U.S.A.
Georg Solti	Hungary
Leopold Stokowski	England/U.S.A.
George Szell	Hungary
Yuri Temirkhanov	Russia
Klaus Tennstedt	Germany
Michael Tilson Thomas	U.S.A.
Yan Pascal Tortelier	France
Arturo Toscanini	Italy
Tamás Vásáry	Hungary/Switzerland
Bruno Walter	Germany
Hugh Wolff	France/U.S.A.
David Zinman	U.S.A.
Pinchas Zuckerman	Israel

See Also List 9.27, Famous African-American Symphonic Conductors

LIST 4.48 FOREIGN NAMES FOR THE INSTRUMENTS OF THE ORCHESTRA

ENGLISH	GERMAN	ITALIAN	FRENCH
piccolo	Kleine Flöte	flauto piccolo	petite flûte
flute	Flote	flauto	flûte
oboe	Hoboe	oboe	hautbois
English horn	Englisches Horn	corno inglese	cor anglais
clarinet	Klarinette	clarinetto	clarinette
bass clarinet	Bassklarinette	clarinetto basso (clarone)	clarinette basse
bassoon	Fagott	fagotto	basson
double-bassoon	Kontrafagott	contrafagotto	contre-basson
horn	Horn	corno	cor
trumpet	Trompete	tromba	trompette
trombone	Posaune	trombone	trombone
tuba	Tuba	tuba	tuba
timpani	Pauken	timpani	timbales
triangle	Triangel	triangolo	tambour de basque
cymbals	Becken	piatti	cymbales
bass drum	Grosse Trommel	gran cassa (tamburo)	grosse caisse
snare drum	Kliene Trommel	tamburo militare	tambour militaire
harp	Harfe	arpa	harpe
violin	Violine	violino	violon
viola	Bratche	viola	alto
cello	Violoncell	violoncello	violoncelle
double bass	Kontrabass	contrabassa	contrebasse

See Also List 1.10, Note Names in Various Languages; List 1.11, Rhythmic Words in Various Languages; and List 1.12, Other Musical Terms in Various Languages

LIST 4.49 TYPES OF BANDS

American symphonic wind band
Austrian brass band
brass band
concert band
dance band
horn band
jazz band
marching band
military band
one-man band
rehearsal band
stage band
steel band
swing band/touring band
symphonic band
wind band
wind ensemble

See Also List 4.51, Instrumentation of Various Types of Bands

LIST 4.50 BANDS OF HISTORICAL SIGNIFICANCE

Band of the Canadian Guards
Band of the National Guard of Paris
Boston Brigade Band
Goldman Band

Grand National Band
Grenadier Guards
Royal Horse Guards

Sousa Band
22nd Regiment Band
U.S. Marine Band

LIST 4.51 INSTRUMENTATION OF VARIOUS TYPES OF BANDS

MILITARY BAND

1 flute/piccolo
1 oboe
1 alto saxophone
1 tenor saxophone
1 bassoon
1 E-flat clarinet
8 B-flat clarinets
1 bass drum
2 horns
1 pair cymbals
1 euphonium
6 B-flat cornets
2 tenor trombones
1 bass trombone
2 tubas

DANCE BAND

Four to twenty members,
    including:
clarinet
saxophone
trumpet
trombone
xylophone
drum set
violin
double bass
piano

JAZZ BAND

Varies; may include:
clarinet
trumpet
trombone
drum set
banjo
double bass

JAZZ BAND (continued)

piano
saxophone
cornet
guitar
violin
flute

SYMPHONIC BAND

12 flutes (piccolo)
 4 oboes
 4 bassoons
20 clarinets
 4 alto clarinets
 4 bass clarinets
 4 alto saxophones
 2 tenor saxophones
 1 baritone saxophone
 8 French horns
14 cornets/trumpets
 9 trombones
 4 baritones
 4 tubas
 6 percussion

WIND ENSEMBLE

1 piccolo
1 first flute
1 second flute
2 oboes
1 English horn (optional)
2 bassoons
1 E-flat soprano clarinet
2 alto saxophones
1 tenor saxophone
1 baritone saxophone
4-5 French horns
3 cornets
2 trumpets

WIND ENSEMBLE (continued)

3 trombones
6 B-flat clarinets
1 alto clarinet
1 bass clarinet
1 contra alto clarinet
    (optional)
1 contra bass clarinet
    (optional)
1-2 baritones
1 double bass (optional)
1-2 tubas
1 harp (optional)
4 percussion

BIG BAND

Large number of brass and wind
    instruments, including:

clarinet
saxophone
trumpet
trombone
accordion
drum set
guitar
violin
cello
double bass
piano

MODERN POP/ROCK GROUPS

May include:

drum set
electric guitar
electric bass guitar
electric organ
electric piano
synthesizer

© 1994 by Parker Publishing Company

LIST 4.52 CHAMBER ENSEMBLES AND THEIR INSTRUMENTATION

STRING QUARTET

2 violins
1 viola
1 cello

BRASS QUINTET

2 trumpets
1 French horn
1 trombone
1 tuba

WOODWIND QUINTET

1 flute
1 oboe
1 clarinet
1 bassoon
1 French horn

TRIO SONATA

1 solo treble instrument
1 harpsichord (keyboard)
1 cello

SOLO SONATA

1 melody instrument
1 piano

PIANO TRIO

1 piano
1 violin
1 cello

PIANO QUARTET

1 piano
1 violin
1 viola
1 cello

STRING TRIO

1 violin
1 viola
1 cello

127

LIST 4.53 MUSIC FESTIVALS IN THE U.S.A.

FESTIVAL	LOCATION	TIME	SPECIALTY
Ann Arbor Festival	Ann Arbor, Michigan	May	symphony, choral works
Aspen Festival	Aspen, Colorado	summer	concerts, recitals, chamber music
Bethlehem Festival	Bethlehem, Pennsylvania	May	works of Bach
Casals Festival	Prades and Puerto Rico	April/May	music of Bach, Mozart, Schubert, and Brahms
Central City Opera Festival	Central City, Colorado	July/August	opera
Chautauqua Festival	Chautauqua, New York	July/August	opera, orchestra, chamber music, organ recitals
Coolidge Festival	Washington, D.C.		contemporary music
Marlboro Festival	Marlboro, Vermont	July/August	chamber music
May Music Festival	Cincinnati, Ohio	May	Cincinnati Symphony performances
Mostly Mozart	New York, New York	summer	orchestra, choral works, chamber music
Pacific Northwest Festival	Seattle, Washington	July	opera, music, drama
Ravinia Festival	Chicago, Illinois	summer	Chicago Symphony orchestra
Spoleto Festival (U.S. counterpart to Festival of Two Worlds)	Charleston, S. Carolina	spring	opera, concerts
Tanglewood Music	Lenox, Massachusetts	July/August	Boston Symphony Orchestra, concerts, recitals

LIST 4.54 EUROPEAN MUSIC FESTIVALS

FESTIVAL	LOCATION	TIME	SPECIALTY
Aldeburg Festival	London, England		English music, Britten's works
The Bayreuth Festival	Bayreuth, Germany	July/August	Wagner's operas
Edinburgh Festival	Edinburgh, Scotland	August	opera, drama, ballet, concerts
Florence Festival	Florence, Italy	May	opera, symphony, soloists, chamber groups
Glyndebourne Festival	Glyndebourne, England	May/June	opera
Holland Music Festival	Holland (several locations concurrently)	summer	orchestral and chamber music, solo recitals, choral works
International Society for Contemporary Music	varies		twentieth century music
Lucerne Festival	Lucerne, Switzerland	summer	orchestral, choral, and chamber music concerts
Royan Festival d'Art Contemporain	Royon, France	spring	contemporary music
The Salzburg Festival	Salzburg, Austria	July/August	music of Mozart
Festival of Two Worlds	Spoleto, Italy	summer	opera, ballet, chamber music, solo recitals, drama

Section V

OPERA AND VOCAL MUSIC

LIST 5.1 TYPES OF VOICES

MALE VOICES:

BASS
Basso Profundo
Basso Cantante

BARITONE

TENOR
Robust Tenor
Lyric Tenor

COUNTER-TENOR

UNBROKEN BOYS' VOICES

ALTO

TREBLE

FEMALE VOICES

CONTRALTO

MEZZO-SOPRANO

SOPRANO
Dramatic Soprano
Lyric Soprano
Coloratura Soprano

131

LIST 5.2   A HISTORY OF VOCAL GENRE

	SACRED	**SECULAR**
second century	hymns psalmody antiphon responsory old Roman chant	
sixth century	Gregorian chant	
tenth and eleventh centuries	cantus planus (plainsong) cantus mensuratus organum	Goliard songs chanson de geste
twelfth and thirteenth centuries	descant clausula conductus mass motet	trouvere song troubador song minneleider pastourelle cantilena hocket rota rondellus
fourteenth and fifteenth centuries	isorhythmic motet Fauxbourdon carol	tracento madrigal caccia ballade virelay rondeaux
sixteenth century	chorale motet anthem cantata chorale	lute ayres canzon villanesca opera madrigal art song early opera quodlibet lauda frottola lied
seventeenth century	oratorio	opera
eighteenth century	part songs	opera da capo aria comic opera
nineteenth century		art song ballad grand opera comic opera verismo opera lyric opera operetta
twentieth century		musical music videos

LIST 5.3 VOCAL MUSIC TERMS

a cappella	choral music sung without instrumental accompaniment
alto	the lowest unbroken boy's voice; lowest female voice
aria	elaborated song form of opera
aria da capo	aria with 3 sections: 1st section, contrasting middle section, first section again
ballad	song that tells a story
baritone	a male voice
bass	lowest male voice
cantata	vocal work for one or more voices with instrumental accompaniment
cantus firmus	an existing melody that becomes the basis of a polyphonic composition
choir	a body of church singers
choral	for chorus or choir
chorale	a hymn tune of the German Protestant Church
chorus	a group of people singing together—not connected with a church
counter-tenor	a high natural male voice that uses head resonances
Gregorian chant	great collection of plainsong used by Roman church since early Christian times
lyrics	words to a song
madrigal	vocal composition for several unaccompanied voices
motet	unaccompanied vocal setting of religious words
opera	a drama with scenery and acting which is generally sung throughout to accompaniment of an orchestra
oratorio	a setting of a religious libretto for soloists, chorus, and orchestra
plainsong	ancient tune to which Christian church services have been sung
recitative	vocal style which imitates natural speech inflections
refrain	a recurring section of music
song cycle	a set of related songs
soprano	highest female voice
spirituals	religious songs of African Americans, often based on Biblical stories
sprechstimme	speech song—halfway between song and speech

LIST 5.4   FAMOUS AMERICAN CHORAL GROUPS

All-American Boys Chorus	Costa Mesa, California
Boys Choir of Harlem	New York, New York
Chicago Children's Choir	Chicago, Illinois
Chicago Symphony Chorus	Chicago, Illinois
Choral Arts Society of Washington	Washington, D.C.
Colorado Children's Chorale	Denver, Colorado
Dale Warland Singers, Inc.	Minneapolis, Minnesota
Gloriae Dei Cantores	Orleans, Massachusetts
Handel and Haydn Society	Boston, Massachusetts
Los Angeles Master Chorale and Sinfonia	Los Angeles, California
The Mormon Tabernacle Choir	Salt Lake City, Utah
Musica Sacra	New York, New York
The National Chorale	New York, New York
Newark Boys' Chorus	Newark, New Jersey
New York Choral Society	New York, New York
Oratorio Society of New York	New York, New York
Paul Hill Chorale	Washington, D.C.
Philadelphia Boys' Choir and Men's Chorale	Philadelphia, Pennsylvania
Phoenix Boys Choir	Phoenix, Arizona
San Francisco Girls' Chorus	San Francisco, California
Tucson Arizona Boys Choir	Tucson, Arizona
The Washington Singers	Washington, D.C.
Westminster Choir	Princeton, New Jersey

LIST 5.5   OPERA TERMS

aria	the elaborated song form of opera
ballad opera	a form of eighteenth century entertainment with spoken dialogue alternating with music
basso buffo	a comic character in eighteenth century Italian opera
bel canto	an eighteenth century Italian vocal technique, emphasizing beauty of sound and brilliance of performance
chamber opera	small, intimate opera for a small orchestra
coloratura	rapid passage, trill or run in eighteenth or nineteenth century operatic arias
comic opera	light or sentimental opera with a happy ending
folk opera	an opera based on regional legends and tunes
grand opera	an opera with fully composed text
heldentenor	a tenor voice of great volume
leitmotif	method of opera composition with the representation of characters, situations, and themes by musical motifs
libretto	text of an opera
light opera	an opera that has a happy ending
lyric opera	general term used for serious opera, which usually has a sentimental story and melodious arias
musical	chief form of popular musical theater of the twentieth century
opera buffa	comic opera with an everyday comic character
opera comique	an opera which is light-hearted and comments on moral standards
opera seria	an opera with a high degree of formality and complexity
operetta	a play with an overture, songs, interludes, and dances
prima donna	leading female singer in an opera
recitative	a vocal style which imitates natural speech inflections
score	the written music for an opera used by the conductor
singspiel	German for a drama with music; usually applies to comic operas with spoken dialogue
verismo	an Italian operatic school of the late nineteenth century, utilizing realistic subjects from everyday life embellished with theatrical incidents
zarzuela	a type of Spanish opera with music intermingled with spoken dialogue

LIST 5.6   TYPES OF OPERAS

ballad opera	a form of eighteenth century entertainment with spoken dialogue alternating with music
Biblical opera	opera based on Biblical plots
chamber opera	small, intimate opera for a small orchestra
folk opera	an opera based on regional legends and tunes
grand opera	an opera with fully composed text
jazz opera	an opera with elements of jazz
light opera	an opera with a happy ending
masque	a form of entertainment in the sixteenth and seventeenth century containing poetry, music, and elaborate sets
nationalistic opera	opera based on folk music of a composer's region
opera buffa	comic opera with an everyday comic character
opera comique	an opera which is light-hearted and comments on moral standards
opera semiseria	a type of Italian opera of serious, melodramatic nature, with subsidiary comic material provided by servants
opera seria	an opera with a high degree of formality and complexity
operetta	a play with an overture, songs, interludes, and dances
romantic opera	opera from the romantic period, with a setting in nature and a theme based on folklore or the supernatural
singspiel	German for a drama with music; usually applies to a comic opera with spoken dialogue

LIST 5.7   EARLY OPERAS

Euridice	1600	Jacopo Peri
Orfeo (or La Favola d'Orfeo) (The Legend of Orpheus)	1607	Claudio Monteverdi
La Dafne	1608	Marco da Gagliano
Arianna (Ariadne)	1608	Claudio Monteverdi
Ballo delle Ingrate (The Dance of the Ungrateful Dead Souls)	1608	Claudio Monteverdi
Il Sant'Alessio (Saint Alessio)	1632	Stefano Landi
La Didone (Dido)	1641	Pier Francesco Cavalli
L'Incoronazione di Poppea (The Coronation of Poppea)	1642	Claudio Monteverdi
Il Pomo d'Oro (The Golden Apple)	1666	Antonio Cesti
Semiramide	1667	Antonio Cesti
Cadmus et Hermione (Cadmus and Harmonia)	1674	Jean-Baptiste Lully
Pomone	1671	Robert Cambert
Adam und Eva (Adam and Eve)	1678	Louis Theile
Venus and Adonis	1685	John Blow
Dido and Aeneas	1689	Henry Purcell
The Fairy Queen	1692	Henry Purcell
Almira	1705	Georg Friedrich Händel
Il Pastor Fido (The Faithful Shepherd)	1712	Georg Friedrich Händel
The Beggar's Opera	1728	John Gay
La Serva Padrona (The Maid Mistress)	1733	Giovanni Battista Pergolesi
L'Olimpiade (The Olympiad)	1735	Giovanni Battista Pergolesi

LIST 5.8   FAMOUS OPERAS BY CENTURY

17TH CENTURY

Euridice	1600	Jacopo Peri
L'Orfeo	1607	Claudio Monteverdi
Arianna (Ariadne)	1608	Claudio Monteverdi
L'Incoronazione di Poppea (The Coronation of Poppea)	1642	Claudio Monteverdi
Il Pomo d'Oro (The Golden Apple)	1666	Antonio Cesti
Dido and Aeneas	1689	Henry Purcell

18TH CENTURY

Giulio Cesare in Egitto (Julius Caesar in Egypt)	1724	Georg Friedrich Händel
The Beggar's Opera	1728	John Gay
La Serva Padrona (The Maid Mistress)	1733	Giovanni Battista Pergolesi
Orfeo e Euridice (Orpheus and Eurydice)	1762	Christoph Gluck
Le Nozze di Figaro (The Marriage of Figaro)	1786	Wolfgang Amadeus Mozart
Don Giovanni (Don Juan)	1787	Wolfgang Amadeus Mozart
Die Zauberflöte (The Magic Flute)	1791	Wolfgang Amadeus Mozart

19TH CENTURY

Il Barbiere di Siviglia (The Barber of Seville)	1816	Gioacchino Rossini
Norma	1831	Vincenzo Bellini
Lucia di Lammermoor (The Bride of Lammermoor)	1835	Gaetano Donizetti
Faust	1859	Charles François Gounod
Tristan und Isolde (Tristan and Isolde)	1865	Richard Wagner
Don Carlos	1867	Giuseppe Verdi
Die Meistersinger von Nürnberg (The Mastersingers of Nurenberg)	1868	Richard Wagner
Boris Godunov	1874	Modest Mussorgsky
Carmen	1875	Georges Bizet
Der Ring des Nibelungen (The Ring of the Nibelung) 　　*Das Rheingold (The Rheingold)* 　　*Die Walkure (The Valkurie)* 　　*Siegfried* 　　*Gotterdammerung (The Twilight of the Gods)*	1876	Richard Wagner
Otello	1887	Giuseppe Verdi
Falstaff	1893	Giuseppe Verdi

20TH CENTURY

Madama Butterfly (Madam Butterfly)	1904	Giacomo Puccini
Bluebeard's Castle	1911	Béla Bartók
Treemonisha	1911	Scott Joplin
Ariadne auf Naxos (Ariadne of Naxos)	1912	Richard Strauss
El Sombrero de Tres Picos (The Three-Cornered Hat)	1919	Manuel de Falla
The Cunning Little Vixen	1924	Leoš Janáček
Hárry János	1926	Zoltán Kodály
Oedipus Rex	1927	Igor Stravinsky
Threepenny Opera	1928	Kurt Weill

List 5.8 (continued)

Four Saints in Three Acts	1934	Virgil Thompson
Mathis der Maler (Matthias the Painter)	1934	Paul Hindemith
Peter Grimes	1945	Benjamin Britten
The Rape of Lucretia	1946	Benjamin Britten
Billy Budd	1951	Benjamin Britten
The Rake's Progress	1951	Igor Stravinsky
The Turn of the Screw	1954	Benjamin Britten
Wozzeck	1972	Alban Berg
Einstein on the Beach	1976	Philip Glass
Nixon in China	1987	John Adams

LIST 5.9   FAMOUS OPERAS AND THEIR COMPOSERS

OPERA	PREMIERE	COMPOSER
Aida	1871	Giuseppe Verdi
Amahl and the Night Visitors	1951	Gian Carlo Menotti
Andrea Chenier	1896	Umberto Giordino
Ariadne auf Naxos (Ariadne of Naxos)	1912	Richard Strauss
The Ballad of Baby Doe	1956	Douglas Moore
Un Ballo in Maschera (The Masked Ball)	1859	Giuseppe Verdi
Il Barbiere di Siviglia (The Barber of Seville)	1816	Gioacchino Rossini
The Bartered Bride	1866	Bedrich Smetana
The Beggar's Opera	1728	John Gay
La Bohème (The Bohemians)	1896	Giacomo Puccini
Boris Godunov	1874	Modest Mussorgsky
Carmen	1875	Georges Bizet
Cavalleria Rusticana (Rustic Chivalry)	1890	Pietro Mascagni
La Cenerentola (Cinderella)	1817	Gioacchino Rossini
Les Contes D'Hoffmann (The Tales of Hoffman)	1881	Jacques Offenbach
Così fan Tutte (So Do They All)	1790	Wolfgang Amadeus Mozart
The Cunning Little Vixen	1924	Leoš Janáček
Don Carlos	1867	Giuseppe Verdi
Don Giovanni (Don Juan)	1787	Wolfgang Amadeus Mozart
Einstein on the Beach	1976	Philip Glass
Eugene Onegin	1879	Peter Tchaikovsky
Falstaff	1893	Giuseppe Verdi
Faust	1859	Charles Gounod
Fidelio	1805	Ludwig van Beethoven
Der fliegende Holländer (The Flying Dutchman)	1843	Richard Wagner
La Forza del Destino (The Power of Destiny)	1862	Giuseppe Verdi

© 1994 by Parker Publishing Company

List 5.9 (continued)

© 1994 by Parker Publishing Company

Hänsel und Gretel (Hansel and Gretel)	1893	Englebert Humperdinck
L'Heure Espagnole (The Spanish Hour)	1911	Maurice Ravel
Lohengrin	1850	Richard Wagner
Lucia di Lammermoor (Lucia of Lammermoor)	1835	Gaetano Donizetti
Madama Butterfly (Madam Butterfly)	1904	Giacomo Pucchini
Manon	1884	Jules Massenet
Nixon in China	1987	John Adams
Le Nozze di Figaro (The Marriage of Figaro)	1786	Wolfgang Amadeus Mozart
Martha	1847	Friedrich von Flotow
Die Meistersinger von Nürnberg (The Mastersingers of Nurenberg)	1868	Richard Wagner
Norma	1831	Vincenzo Bellini
Orfeo ed Euridice (Orpheus and Eurydice)	1762	Christoph Gluck
Otello	1887	Giuseppe Verdi
I Pagliacci (The Players)	1892	Ruggiero Leoncavallo
Pelléas et Mélisande (Pelius and Melisande)	1902	Claude Debussy
Peter Grimes	1945	Benjamin Britten
Porgy and Bess	1935	George Gershwin
The Rake's Progress	1951	Igor Stravinsky
Rigoletto	1851	Giuseppe Verdi
Der Ring des Nibelungen (The Ring of the Nibelung)	1876	Richard Wagner
Der Rosenkavalier (Cavalier of the Rose)	1911	Richard Strauss
Samson et Dalila (Samson and Delilah)	1877	Camille Saint-Saëns
Tannhäuser	1845	Richard Wagner
Tosca	1900	Giacomo Puccini
La Traviata (The Wayward One)	1853	Giuseppe Verdi
Tristan und Isolde (Tristan and Isolde)	1865	Richard Wagner
Il Trovatore (The Troubador)	1853	Giuseppe Verdi
Turandot	1926	Giacomo Puccini
Wozzeck	1925	Alban Berg
Die Zauberflöte (The Magic Flute)	1791	Wolfgang Amadeus Mozart

See Also List 3.30, Famous Composers of Opera; List 5.7, Early Operas; and List 5.8, Famous Operas by Century

LIST 5.10   FAMOUS AMERICAN OPERAS

Amahl and the Night Visitors	Gian Carlo Menotti
Amelia Goes to the Ball	Gian Carlo Menotti
Anthony and Cleopatra	Samuel Barber
The Ballad of Baby Doe	Douglas Moore
The Devil and Daniel Webster	Douglas Moore
Four Saints in Three Acts	Virgil Thomson
Einstein on the Beach	Philip Glass
The King's Henchman	Deems Taylor
The Last Savage	Gian Carlo Menotti
The Medium	Gian Carlo Menotti
Merry Mount	Howard Hanson
Mona	Horatio Parker
The Mother of Us All	Virgil Thomson
Natoma	Victor Herbert
Nixon in China	John Adams
Peter Ibbetson	Deems Taylor
Porgy and Bess	George Gershwin
Susannah	Carlisle Floyd
Treemonisha	Scott Joplin
Vanessa	Samuel Barber

LIST 5.11   FAMOUS OPERA STARS PAST AND PRESENT

NAME	VOICE	COUNTRY
Licia Albanese	soprano	U.S.A.
Marietta Alboni	contralto	Italy
Marian Anderson	contralto	U.S.A.
Victoria de Los Angeles	soprano	Spain
Salvatore Baccaloni	bass	Italy
Cecilia Bartoli	mezzo-soprano	Italy
Kathleen Battle	soprano	U.S.A.
Francesco Benucci	bass	Italy
Bianca Bianchi	soprano	Germany
Elizabeth Billington	soprano	England
Jussi Björling	tenor	Sweden
Lucrezia Bori	soprano	Italy
Dorothea Bussani	soprano	Austria
Dame Clara Butt	contralto	England
Montserrat Caballé	soprano	Spain
Maria Callas	soprano	U.S.A.
Emma Calvé	soprano	France
José Carreras	tenor	Spain
Enrico Caruso	tenor	Italy
Feodor Chaliapin	bass	Russia
Boris Christoff	bass	Bulgaria
Isabella Colbran	soprano	Spain
Mario Del Monaco	tenor	Italy
Giuseppe De Luca	baritone	Italy
Emmy Destinn	soprano	Czechoslovakia

List 5.11 (continued)

Placido Domingo	tenor	Spain
Geraldine Ferrar	soprano	U.S.A.
Kathleen Ferrier	contralto	England
Dietrich Fischer-Dieskau	baritone	Germany
Kirsten Flagstad	soprano	Norway
Mary Garden	soprano	U.S.A.
Nicolai Gedda	tenor	Sweden
Giuditta Grisi	mezzo-soprano	Italy
Giulia Grisi	soprano	Italy
Sabina Heinefetter	soprano	Germany
Marilyn Horne	mezzo-soprano	U.S.A.
Dorothy Kirsten	soprano	U.S.A.
Luigi Lablache	bass	Italy
Lotte Lehmann	soprano	Germany
Nicolas Levasseur	bass	France
Jenny Lind	soprano	Sweden
George London	bass-baritone	Canada
Jean Madeira	contralto	U.S.A.
René Maison	tenor	Belgium
Maria Malibran	mezzo-soprano	Spain
Giovanni Martineli	tenor	Italy
John McCormack	tenor	Ireland
James McCracken	tenor	U.S.A.
Dame Nellie Melba	soprano	Australia
Lauritz Melchoir	tenor	Denmark
Robert Merrill	baritone	U.S.A.
Zinka Milanov	soprano	Yugoslavia
Sherrill Milnes	baritone	U.S.A.
Anna Moffo	soprano	U.S.A.
Birgit Niellson	soprano	Sweden
Jessye Norman	soprano	U.S.A.
Adolphe Nourrit	tenor	France
Adelina Patti	soprano	Spain
Luciano Pavarotti	tenor	Italy
Jan Peerce	tenor	U.S.A.
Roberta Peters	soprano	U.S.A.
Ezio Pinza	bass	Italy
Pol Plançon	bass	France
Lily Pons	soprano	France
Rosa Ponselle	soprano	U.S.A.
Leontyne Price	soprano	U.S.A.
Giovanni Rubini	tenor	Italy
Tito Schipa	tenor	Italy
Ernestine Schumann-Heink	contralto	Czechoslovakia
Elizabeth Schwarzkopf	soprano	Poland
Antonio Scotti	baritone	Italy
Renatta Scotto	soprano	Italy
Beverly Sills	soprano	U.S.A.
Giuseppi di Stefano	tenor	Italy
Risë Stevens	soprano	U.S.A.
Joan Sutherland	soprano	Australia
Kiri Te Kanawa	soprano	New Zealand
Renata Tebaldi	soprano	Italy
Lawrence Tibbett	baritone	U.S.A.
Helen Traubel	soprano	U.S.A.
Richard Tucker	tenor	U.S.A.
Leonard Warren	baritone	U.S.A.

See Also List 9.25, African-American Opera Stars

LIST 5.12   FAMOUS OPERA HOUSES

Bayreuth Festival Theatre	Bayreuth, Germany
Bolshoi Theatre	Moscow, Russia
Civic Opera Building	Chicago, U.S.A.
Covent Garden	London, England
Deutsche Oper	Berlin, Germany
Deutsche Staatsoper	Berlin, Germany
La Fenice	Venice, Italy
Hamburg Opera	Hamburg, Germany
Komische Oper	Berlin, Germany
Massimo Theatre	Palermo, Italy
Metropolitan Opera House	New York, U.S.A.
National Theatre	Munich, Germany
Opéra de La Bastille	Paris, France
Paris Opéra	Paris, France
Rome Opera	Rome, Italy
San Carlo	Naples, Italy
La Scala	Milan, Italy
Sydney Opera House	Sydney, Australia
Teatro Colon	Buenos Aires, Argentina
Vienna State Opera	Vienna, Austria
War Memorial Opera House	San Francisco, U.S.A.
Wortham Center	Houston, U.S.A.

LIST 5.13   FAMOUS OPERA COMPANIES

Australian Opera	Australia
Boshoi Theater	Russia
British National Opera	England
Canadian Opera	Canada
Cincinnati Opera Association	U.S.A.
Dallas Civic Opera	U.S.A.
Die Deutsche Oper	Germany
Die Komische Oper	Germany
Die Staatsoper	Austria, Germany
English National Opera	England
Houston Opera	U.S.A.
Lyric Opera of Chicago	U.S.A.
Metropolitan Opera	U.S.A.
Michigan Opera Theatre	U.S.A.
New Orleans Opera Association	U.S.A.
New York City Opera	U.S.A.
Opera Factory	Australia, Switzerland, England
Paris Opera	France
San Francisco Opera Co.	U.S.A.
Scottish Opera	Scotland
Vienna State Opera	Austria
Washington Opera	U.S.A.
Welsh National Opera	Wales

LIST 5.14 OPERAS WITH HISTORICAL THEMES

OPERA	COMPOSER	THEME
Aida	Giuseppe Verdi	Egyptian history
Amahl and the Night Visitors	Gian Carlo Menotti	birth of Christ
Andrea Chenier	Umberto Giordano	French Revolution
Anna Bolena (Anne Boleyn)	Gaetano Donizetti	Anne Boleyn
The Ballad of Baby Doe	Douglas Moore	turn of the century West
Boris Godunov	Modest Mussorgsky	Russian and Polish history, 1598–1605
Christophe Colomb (Christopher Columbus)	Darius Milhaud	Christopher Columbus
La Fanciulla del West (The Girl of the Golden West)	Giacomo Puccini	California Gold Rush
Giovanni d'Arco (Joan of Arc)	Giuseppe Verdi	Joan of Arc
Giulo Cesare in Egitto (Julius Caesar in Egypt)	Georg Friedrich Händel	Julius Caesar
L'Incoronazione di Poppea (The Coronation of Poppea)	Claudio Monteverdi	life of Nero, emperor of Rome
Maria Stuarda (Mary Stuart)	Gaetano Donizetti	Mary Queen of Scots
Mose in Egitto (Moses in Egypt)	Gioacchino Rossini	Moses in Egypt
Moses und Aron (Moses and Aaron)	Arnold Schoenberg	Moses and Aaron
Nixon in China	John Adams	Richard Nixon
Opera Flies	Halim El-Dabh	Kent State shootings
Porgy and Bess	George Gershwin	strife of African Americans
I Puritani	Vincenzo Bellini	the Puritans

LIST 5.15   OPERAS WITH ROMANTIC THEMES

OPERA	PREMIERE	COMPOSER
Anna Bolena	1830	Gaetano Donizetti
La Bohème	1896	Giacomo Puccini
Carmen	1875	Georges Bizet
Don Giovanni (Don Juan)	1787	Wolfgang Amadeus Mozart
La Donna del Lago (The Lady of the Lake)	1819	Gioacchino Rossini
Fidelio	1805	Ludwig van Beethoven
Genoveva	1850	Robert Schumann
Louise	1900	Gustave Charpentier
Lucia di Lammermoor (Lucia of Lammermoor)	1835	Gaetano Donazetti
Madama Butterfly (Madam Butterfly)	1904	Giacomo Puccini
Manon	1884	Jules Massenet
Manon Lescaut	1893	Giacomo Puccini
Norma	1831	Vincenzo Bellini
Le Nozze di Figaro (The Marriage of Figaro)	1786	Wolfgang Amadeus Mozart
I Pagliacci (The Players)	1892	Ruggiero Leoncavallo
Porgy and Bess	1935	George Gershwin
La Sonnambula (The Sleepwalker)	1831	Vincenzo Bellini
Tosca	1900	Giacomo Puccini
La Traviata (The Wayward One)	1853	Giuseppe Verdi
Tristan und Isolde (Tristan and Isolde)	1865	Richard Wagner
Turandot	1926	Giacomo Puccini

LIST 5.16   COMIC OPERAS

OPERA	PREMIERE	COMPOSER
Il Barbiere di Siviglia (The Barber of Seville)	1816	Gioacchino Rossini
The Bartered Bride	1866	Bedrich Smetana
La Cenerentola (Cinderella)	1817	Gioacchino Rossini
La Comte Ory (Count Ory)	1828	Gioacchino Rossini
Così fan Tutte (So Do They All)	1790	Wolfgang Amadeus Mozart
Don Pasquale	1843	Gaetano Donizetti
Falstaff	1893	Giuseppe Verdi
La Fille du Regiment (The Daughter of the Regiment)	1840	Gaetano Donizetti
Gianni Schicchi	1918	Giacomo Puccini
L'Heure Espagnole	1911	Maurice Ravel
L'Italiana in Algeri (The Italian in Algiers)	1813	Gioacchino Rossini
Lakme	1883	Léo Delibes
La Nozze di Figaro (The Marriage of Figaro)	1786	Wolfgang Amadeus Mozart
Die Meistersinger von Nürnberg	1868	Richard Wagner
Der Rosenkavalier (Cavalier of the Rose)	1911	Richard Strauss
Der Schauspieldirektor (The Impresario)	1786	Wolfgang Amadeus Mozart
La Serva Padrona (The Maid Mistress)	1733	Giovanni Battista Pergolesi
The Telephone	1947	Gian Carlo Menotti
Von Heute auf Morgen (From Day to Day)	1930	Arnold Schoenberg

LIST 5.17 OPERETTAS

Babes in Toyland	Victor Herbert
The Begum	Reginald De Koven
Blossom Time	Sigmund Romberg
The Blue Paradise	Sigmund Romberg
Boccaccio	Franz von Suppé
The Chocolate Soldier	Oscar Straus
Countess Maritza	Emmerich Kálmán
The Czar and Carpenter	Albert Lortzing
The Desert Song	Sigmund Romberg
Fatinitza	Franz von Suppé
The Firefly	Rudolf Friml
Die Fledermaus	Johann Strauss, Jr.
Galatea	Franz von Suppé
Gypsy Baron	Johann Strauss, Jr.
Gypsy Princess	Emmerich Kálmán
Kismet	music from Alexander Borodin
Maytime	Sigmund Romberg
Merry Widow	Franz Lehár
The Merry Wives of Windsor	Otto Nicolai
Naughty Marietta	Victor Herbert
The New Moon	Sigmund Romberg
Prince Ananias	Victor Herbert
The Red Mill	Victor Herbert
Robin Hood	Reginald De Koven
Rose Marie	Rudolf Friml
Song of Norway	music from Edvard Grieg
The Student Prince	Sigmund Romberg
The Vagabond King	Rudolf Friml
The Waltz Dream	Oscar Straus

See Also List 5.19, The Operettas of Gilbert and Sullivan

LIST 5.18 THE OPERAS OF GAETANO DONIZETTI

OPERA	DATE
Anna Bolena (Anne Boleyn)	1830
L'Élisir d'Amore (The Elixer of Love)	1832
Lucrezia Borgia	1833
Maria Stuarda (Mary Stewart)	1834
Lucia di Lammermoor (Lucia of Lammermoor)	1835
Roberto Devereux	1837
La Fille du Régiment (The Daughter of the Regiment)	1840
La Favorita (The Favorite)	1840
Linda di Chamounix (Linda of Chamounix)	1842
Don Pasquale	1843

LIST 5.19   THE OPERETTAS OF GILBERT AND SULLIVAN

Trial by Jury	1875
The Sorcerer	1877
H.M.S. Pinafore	1878
The Pirates of Penzance	1879
Patience	1881
Iolanthe	1882
Princess Ida	1884
The Mikado	1885
Ruddigore	1887
The Yeoman of the Guard	1888
The Gondoliers	1889
Utopia, Limited	1893
The Grand Duke	1896

LIST 5.20   THE OPERAS OF GIAN CARLO MENOTTI

OPERA	DATE	OPERA	DATE
Amelia Goes to the Ball	1937	*Amahl and the Night Visitors*	1951
The Old Maid and the Thief	1939	*The Saint of Bleecker Street*	1954
The Medium	1946	*Maria Golovin*	1958
The Telephone	1947	*The Last Savage*	1963
The Consul	1950	*Help, Help! The Globolinks*	1968

LIST 5.21   THE OPERAS OF WOLFGANG AMADEUS MOZART

OPERA	DATE
Opollo et Hyacinthus (Opollo and Hyacinthe)	1767
Bastien und Bastienne (Bastien and Bastienne)	1768
La Finta Semplice (The Pretended Simpleton)	1769
Mitridate rè di Ponto (Mithradates, King of Pontus)	1770
Ascanio in Alba (Ascanio of Alba)	1771
Lucio Silla (Lucius Silla)	1772
Il Sogno di Scipioni (The Dream of Scipio)	1772
Thamos, König in Aegypten (Thamos, King of Egypt)	1774
Il Re Pastore (The Shepherd King)	1775
Idomeneo, Re di Creta (Idomeneus, King of Crete)	1781
Die Entführung aus Dem Serail (The Abduction from Seraglio)	1782
Der Schauspieldirektor (The Impresario)	1786
Le nozze di Figaro (The Marriage of Figaro)	1786
Don Giovanni (Don Juan)	1787
Così fan tutte (So Do They All)	1790
La Clemenza di Tito (The Clemency of Titus)	1791
Die Zauberflöte (The Magic Flute)	1791

LIST 5.22   THE OPERAS OF GIACOMO PUCCINI

OPERA	DATE	OPERA	DATE
Edgar	1889	La Rondine (The Swallow)	1917
Manon Lescaut	1893	Trittico	1918
La Bohème (The Bohemians)	1894	Il Tabarro (The Cloak)	
Tosca	1900	Suor Angelica (Sister Angelica)	
Madama Butterfly (Madam Butterfly)	1904	Gianni Schicchi	
La Fanciulla del West		Turandot	1926
(The Girl of the Golden West)	1910		

LIST 5.23   THE OPERAS OF GIOACCHINO ROSSINI

OPERA	DATE
La Cambiale di matrimonio (The Bill of Marriage)	1810
La Pietra del Paragone (The Touchstone)	1812
Ciro in Babilonia (Cyrus in Babylon)	1812
L'Inganno Felice (The Happy Stratagem)	1812
La Scala di Seta (The Silken Ladder)	1812
Il Signor Bruschino (Mr. Bruschino)	1813
L'Italiana in Algeri (The Italian in Algiers)	1813
Tancredi	1813
Il Turco in Italia (The Turk in Italy)	1814
Elisabetta, Regina D'Inghilterra (Elizabeth, Queen of England)	1815
Il Barbiere di Siviglia (The Barber of Seville)	1816
La Cenerentola (Cinderella)	1817
La Gazza Ladra (The Thieving Magpie)	1817
Mosè in Egitto (Moses in Egypt)	1818
La Donna del Lago (The Lady of the Lake)	1819
Zelmira	1822
Semiramide	1823
Le Sieg de Corinthe (The Siege of Corinth)	1826
Le Comte Ory (Count Ory)	1828
Guillaume Tell (William Tell)	1829

LIST 5.24   THE OPERAS OF RICHARD STRAUSS

OPERA	DATE
Salomé	1905
Elektra	1909
Der Rosenkavalier (The Cavalier of the Rose)	1911
Ariadne auf Naxos (Ariadne of Naxos)	1912
Die Frau Ohne Schatten (The Woman Without a Shadow)	1919
Intermezzo	1924
Die Aegyptische Helena (The Egyptian Helen)	1928
Arabella	1933
Die Schweigsame Frau (The Silent Woman)	1935
Friedenstag (Peace Day)	1938
Daphne	1938
Die Liebe der Danaë (The Love of Danae)	1944
Capriccio	1944

LIST 5.25   THE OPERAS OF PETER TCHAIKOVSKY

OPERA	DATE	OPERA	DATE
Kusnetz Vakula (Vakula, the Smith)	1876	*Mazeppa*	1884
Yevgeny Onyegin (Eugene Onegin)	1879	*Pique Dame (The Queen of Spades)*	1890
Orleanskaya Dyeva (The Maid of Orleans)	1881	*Iolanta*	1892

LIST 5.26   THE OPERAS OF GIUSEPPE VERDI

OPERA	DATE	OPERA	DATE
Oberto, Conte di San Bonifacio (Oberto, Count of St. Boniface)	1839	*Stiffelio*	1850
Un Giorno di Regno (King for a Day)	1840	*Rigoletto*	1851
Nabucco (Nebuchadnezzar)	1842	*Il Trovatore (The Troubador)*	1853
I Lombardi alla Prima Crociata (The Lombards at the First Crusade)	1843	*La Traviata (The Wayward One)*	1853
Ernani	1844	*Les Vêpres Siciliennes (The Sicilian Vespers)*	1855
I Due Foscari (The Two Foscari)	1844	*Aroldo*	1857
Alzira	1845	*Simon Boccanegra*	1857
Giovanni d'Arco (Joan of Arc)	1845	*Un Ballo in Maschera (A Masked Ball)*	1859
Attila	1846	*La Forza del Destiny (The Power of Destiny)*	1862
Macbeth	1847	*Don Carlos*	1867
Il Corsaro (The Corsair)	1848	*Aida*	1871
La Battaglia di Legnano (The Battle of Legnano)	1849	*Otello*	1887
Luisa Miller	1849	*Falstaff*	1893

LIST 5.27 THE OPERAS OF RICHARD WAGNER

OPERA	DATE	OPERA	DATE
Die Feen (The Fairies)	1834	*Die Meistersinger von Nürnberg*	
Das Liebesverbot (Forbidden Love)	1836	*(The Mastersingers of Nurenburg)*	1868
Rienzi, der Letzte der Tribunen		*Der Ring des Nibelungen*	1876
(Rienzi, The Last of the Tribunes)	1842	*Das Rheingold (The Rhine Gold)*	
Der Fliegende Holländer		*Die Walkure (The Valkyrie)*	
(The Flying Dutchman)	1843	*Siegfried*	
Tannhäuser	1845	*Gotterdammerung (Twilight*	
Lohengrin	1850	*of the Gods)*	
Tristan und Isolde (Tristan and Isolde)	1865	*Parsifal*	1882

LIST 5.28 FAMOUS LIBRETTISTS

LIBRETTIST	REPRESENTATIVE WORK
Jules Barbier	*Tales of Hoffman; Faust*
Arrigo Boito	*Otello*
Michel Carré	*Tales of Hoffman; Faust*
Salvatore Commarano	*Lucia di Lammermoor*
Howard Dietz	*Die Fledermaus*
Jacopo Ferretti	*Cinderella*
Richard Genee	*Die Fledermaus*
Antonio Ghislanzoni	*Aida*
Giuseppe Giacosa	*La Bohème; Madama Butterfly*
Carl Haffner	*Die Fledermaus*
Ludovic Halevy	*Carmen*
DuBose Heyward	*Porgy and Bess*
Luigi Illica	*La Bohème; Madama Butterfly*
Hedwig Lachmann	*Salomé*
Ruggiero Leoncavallo	*I Pagliacci*
Henri Meilhac	*Carmen*
Gian Carlo Menotti	*all his operas*
Francesco Maria Piave	*La Traviata; Rigoletto; La Forza del Destino*
Lorenzo da Ponte	*Don Giovanni; Così fan Tutte; Marriage of Figaro*
Karel Sabina	*The Bartered Bride*
Emanual Schikaneder	*The Magic Flute*
Antonio Somma	*The Masked Ball*
Josef Sonnleithner	*Fidelio*
Cesare Sterbini	*The Barber of Seville*
Alessandro Striggio	*Orfeo*
Nahum Tate	*Dido and Aeneas*
Peter Tchaikovsky	*Eugene Onegin*
Richard Wagner	*The Ring of the Nibelung; The Flying Dutchman; Tannhäuser*
Adelheid Wette	*Hänsel and Gretel*

Section VI

MUSIC HISTORY

LIST 6.1 PERIODS AND MOVEMENTS IN WESTERN MUSICAL HISTORY

The history of music is a continuum. Division of music into periods is a somewhat arbitrary and artificial delineation. Each era acts as both a reaction to, as well as a summation and continuation of previous eras. Additionally, each era acts as a prologue to the next.

A.D. 600-850	**Early Middle Ages**	1750-1825	**Classical**
850-1150	**Romanesque**		Mannheim school
1150-1300	**Early Gothic**		Berlin School
	St. Martial		Viennese classic
	Notre Dame	1825-1900	**Romantic**
	Ars antiqua		Nationalism
1300-1450	**Late Gothic**		Impressionism
	Ars nova	1900-present	**Twentieth century**
	Burgundian school		Expressionism
1450-1600	**Renaissance**		Neoclassicism
	Flemish school		Serial techniques
	Venetian school		Musique concrete
	Roman school beginnings		Electronic music
1600-1750	**Baroque**		Aleatory music
	Nuove musiche		Minimalism
	Roman school		
	Bologna school		
	Neapolitan school		
	Rococo		

LIST 6.2 GENERAL CHARACTERISTICS OF RENAISSANCE MUSIC

GENERAL PRINCIPLES:

"ideal" sound, that of an a capella vocal
  ensemble or unbroken consort (similar
  instruments)
four or more voice lines of similar character
point of imitation as a compositional technique

TEXTURE:

similar contrapuntal voice parts
equality of lines
composers conceived of parts simultaneously,
  as a whole

MELODIES:

music develops as an independent entity, not
  needing text; and conversely, music attempts
  to express the images of the text; harmonies
  increasingly triadic

RHYTHMS:

two distinct tendencies:
fluid rhythm within a contrapuntal texture
or
strongly marked rhythmic patterns;
  predominantly chordal

INSTRUMENTATION:

music generally written for voices, not with
  specific instruments in mind
mean-tone system of tuning

153

LIST 6.3   MUSICAL FORMS DEVELOPED DURING THE RENAISSANCE

Forms introduced or developed during the Renaissance include:

anthem	caccia	frottola	opera	suite
aria	canzona	madrigal	prelude	toccata
ballade	chanson	mass	ricercar	variation
ballata	chorale	motet	rondeau	virelai

LIST 6.4   GENERAL CHARACTERISTICS OF BAROQUE MUSIC

No period of music can be summed up in list form. The following will give some guidelines to the beginning listener of Baroque music.

GENERAL PRINCIPLES:

unity of emotion
ornamentation
contrast
improvisation

TEXTURES:

more dense than Renaissance
thoroughbass technique: texture with two
   primary lines: melody and bass, with
   supporting harmonies
polyphony reaches the height of perfection
   in Bach

MELODIES:

Fortspinnung—the continuous "spinning
   out" of a single melodic idea; phrases not
   clearly delineated
use of ornamentation and variation; long
   coloraturas, moving recitatives
use of chromaticism; very expressive

DYNAMICS:

terrace—achieved by adding of subtracting
   players
dynamic tension

RHYTHMS:

from dance forms
rhythmic setting of text follows natural
   speech
continuous rhythmic drive, especially in the
   bass

INSTRUMENTATION:

writing becomes idiosyncratic for individual
   instruments and voices
equal-tempered tuning
use of instrumental forms
harpsichord
early orchestras include strings, flutes,
   oboes, trumpets, and timpani

See Also List 3.2, Representative Baroque Period Composers and Their Countries

LIST 6.5   MUSICAL FORMS DEVELOPED DURING THE BAROQUE PERIOD

Forms developed and/or established during the Baroque Period include:

cantata	French overture	organ prelude	sinfonia	suite
chorale prelude	fugue	ostinato forms	sonata	toccata
concerto	opera	recitative	sonata da camera	trio sonata
concerto grosso	oratorio	rondo	sonata da chiesa	variations
da capo aria				

LIST 6.6   GENERAL CHARACTERISTICS OF CLASSICAL PERIOD MUSIC

No period of music can be summed up in list form. The following will give some guidelines to the beginning listener of Classical period music.

GENERAL PRINCIPLES:

return to Greco-Roman ideals
variety of emotions within a single
    movement
clarity
elegance
intellectual
formalistic

TEXTURES:

less dense than either Baroque or Romantic
homophonic (melody with harmony)

MELODIES:

clearly defined musical phrases of differing
    lengths
contrasting themes

DYNAMICS:

used in a thematic way
crescendo and diminuendo, as opposed to
    terrace contrasts

STYLE:

strictly follows forms of the period
intended to please the society at large
mixture of comic and serious traits within a
    single work
variety of emotions, with control

INSTRUMENTATION:

new instruments
piano developing
clarinet
orchestra sections developing; strings taking
    precedence, woodwinds, brass, timpani

See Also List 3.3, Representative Classical Period Composers and Their Countries

LIST 6.7 MUSICAL FORMS DEVELOPED DURING THE CLASSICAL PERIOD

The following forms were introduced, developed, and widely used during the Classical period.

concerto (modern)

glee

lied

opera

rondo form

sonata form

sonata (modern)

string quartet

symphony

theme and variations

LIST 6.8 GENERAL CHARACTERISTICS OF ROMANTIC ERA MUSIC

No period of music can be summed up in list form. The following will give some guidelines to the beginning listener of Romantic music.

GENERAL PRINCIPLES:

emphasis on man's instincts and feelings,
   rather than intellect
intensity of emotion
individualism
greater freedom of form

TEXTURE:

mostly homophonic, with some return to
   contrapuntal writing

MELODIES:

longer, more lyrical
wide melodic leaps for expressive purposes
irregular phrase lengths
extensive use of chromaticism

HARMONIES:

use of the minor mode increases in
   popularity
extensive use of chromaticism
a steadily rising "dissonance threshold"
expansion of the tonal frame of reference

DYNAMICS:

extremes of dynamic gradations
abrupt changes for emotional effect

RHYTHMS:

freedom and flexibility
changes of rhythm, tempo, and meter
cross-rhythms

INSTRUMENTATION AND TONE COLOR:

great variety in tone color
special instrumental effects
large orchestrations, increased
   instrumentations
vast repertoire of solo piano music
tempo and other expression marks in the
   music increase in complexity

See Also List 3.4, Representative Romantic Period Composers and Their Countries

LIST 6.9 MUSICAL FORMS DEVELOPED DURING THE ROMANTIC ERA

The first three of these represent the most significant contribution of the Romantic era in the area of genre. The others had their beginnings in earlier periods.

character piece for piano	sonata	lied
art song for voice and piano	concerto	opera comique
symphonic poem (tone poem)	symphony	opera

See Also List 3.23, Composers of Symphonic Poems

LIST 6.10 GENERAL CHARACTERISTICS OF TWENTIETH CENTURY MUSIC

Music is usually classified and characterized long after its time; it still remains to be seen how the twentieth century will be viewed by the musicologists of the future. The following includes a variety of techniques used during the twentieth century.

MOVEMENTS DURING THE TWENTIETH CENTURY HAVE INCLUDED:

impressionism	neoclassicism	musique concrete	set theory
nationalism	serial techniques	aleatory music	eclecticism
expressionism	electronic music	minimalism	fusion

MOVES AWAY FROM TRADITIONAL HARMONIES INCLUDED:

serial (twelve-tone) music	atonal	non-tertian	microtones

DEVELOPMENTS IN INSTRUMENTATION HAVE INCLUDED:

non-conventional use of instruments and voices	computers in music
recording equipment	mixed- and inter-media
electronic instruments	

LIST 6.11 "LES SIX"

The name was given by Henri Collet to six French composers in 1919. Although their individual styles differed, they all opposed the vagueness of French impressionism and endorsed the characteristics of the just dawning neoclassical style. They all were admirers of composer Erik Satie and poet Jean Cocteau.

Georges Auric	1899–1983	Darius Milhaud	1892–1974
Louis Durey	1888–1979	Francis Poulenc	1899–1963
Arthur Honegger	1892–1955	Germaine Tailleferre	1892–1983

LIST 6.12   THE "MIGHTY HANDFUL"

The five principal Russian Nationalist composers of the late nineteenth/early twentieth centuries were known as the Mighty Handful.

Mily Balakirev	1837–1910	Modest Mussorgsky	1839–1881
Alexander Borodin	1833–1887	Nicolai Rimsky-Korsakov	1844–1908
Mikhail Glinka	1804–1857		

LIST 6.13   INSTRUMENTS THROUGHOUT WESTERN MUSIC HISTORY

MEDIEVAL INSTRUMENTS (1100–1600)

bagpipe
bells
bladder pipe
buisine
clappers
cymbals
fiddles
gittern
harp
horn
hurdy-gurdy
lyre
mandola
nakers
organ
pipe
psalteries
rebec
tabor

RENNAISSANCE (1400–1600)

baryton
bass cittern
bassanello
chiatarrone
cittern
clappers
clavichord
clavicytherium
colascione
cornemuse
cornetts

RENNAISSANCE (1400–1600) (continued)

courtaut
crumhorns
cuital
cymbals
deutsche schalmei
double bass
flute
guitar
handbell
harpsichord
horn
kettledrum
lira da braccio
lira da gamba
long drum
lute
mandola
musette
orpharion
pandora
penorcon
pipe
potative organ
psaltery
racket
rauschpfeife
regal
rennaissance recorders
serpent
shawms
side drum
soprano lute
sordine

RENNAISSANCE (1400–1600) (continued)

sordone
spinet
swallow's nest organ
theorbo
theorbo-lute
tromba marina
trombone
trumpet
vihuela
viola
viola d'amore
violin
violoncello
viols
virginal

BAROQUE AND CLASSICAL (1600–1825)

arpanetta
baroque recorders
basset horn
bassoon
chalumeaux
chamber organ
chitarra battente
cittern
clarinet d'amore
clarinet
clavichord
contrabassoon
cor anglais
cymbal
diatonic harp

158

List 6.13 (continued)

BAROQUE AND CLASSICAL (1400–1600) (continued)

diplo-kithara
double bass
flute
guitar
harpsichord
jingling johnny
kettledrum
kit
long drum
lute
mandolin
musical glasses
natural trumpet
natural horn
oboe
oboe da caccia
oboe d'amore
piano
piccolo
side drum
slide trombone
spinet
square piano
triangle
upright harpsichord
viola
violin
violoncello

ROMANTIC (1825–1900)

accordion
alto marching horn
alto horn
baritone oboe
bass clarinet
bass flute
bass drum
basshorn
bassoon
buccin trombone
bugle
castanets
celeste
clarinet
claves
clavicor

ROMANTIC (1825–1900) (continued)

concertina
contra bassoon
cor anglais
cornet
crook horn
cymbals
double bass
fife
flageolets
flute
glockenspiel
gongs
grand piano
guitar
hand horn
hand trumpet
harmonium
heckelclarina
kettledrum
keyed trumpet
konighorn
mouth organ
oboe
octavin
omnitonic horn
ophicleide
organ
orphica
parlour organ
pedal harp
piccolo
pyramid piano
sarrusophones
saxhorn
serpent
side drum
slide trombone
slide trumpet
symphonium
tambourine
tarogato
tenor trombone
tenor drum
triangle
tuba
tuba-dupré
tubular bells

ROMANTIC (1825–1900) (continued)

valved trumpet
viola
violin
violoncello
walking stick flute
walking stick guitar
walking stick violin
woodblock
xylophone
zither

MODERN (1900–present)

accordion
banjo
bass drum
bassoon
bugle
castanets
celeste
clarinets
claves
cocktail drums
concertina
contrabassoon
cor anglais
cornet
cymbals
double bass
electric guitar
electric organ
euphonium
flutes
glockenspiel
gong drum
gongs
grand piano
guitar
handbell
harp
Hawaiian guitar
horn
mandolin
maracas
melodeon
melodica
mouth organs

oboe
oboe d'amore
ondes Martenot
organ
recorder
saxophones
side drum
sousaphone
synthesizer

tambourine
tenor drum
timbales
timpani
triangle
trombone
trumpet
tuba
tubular bells

ukulele
upright piano
valve trombone
vibraphone
viola
violin
violoncello
xylophone
zither

LIST 6.14 COMPOSITION OF THE ORCHESTRA OVER THE CENTURIES

Baroque

2 oboes
1 oboe d'amore
1 oboe da caccia
1 bassoon
2 horns
2 trumpets
2 timpani
1 harpsichord
6 violins
3 violas
2 cellos
1 double bass

Classical

2 flutes
2 oboes
2 clarinets
2 bassoons
2 horns
2 trumpets
2 timpani
14 violins
6 violas
4 cellos
2 double basses

Romantic

1 piccolo
3 flutes
3 oboes
1 English horn
3 clarinets
1 bass clarinet
3 bassoons
1 contrabassoon
4 horns
4 Wagner tubas
4 trumpets
4 trombones
1 tuba
1 tam-tam
1 tubular bells
2 cymbals
1 glockenspiel
1 xylophone
1 bass drum
1 side drum
2 timpani
2 harps
30 violins
12 violas
10 cellos
8 double basses

Modern

3 flutes (third doubling piccolo)
3 oboes (third doubling English horn)
3 clarinets (third doubling bass clarinet)
3 bassoons (third doubling contrabassoon)
4 French horns
3 trumpets
3 trombones (2 tenor, 1 bass)
bass tuba
timpani
side drum
bass drum
cymbals
triangle
xylophone
glockenspiel, etc.
harp
18 first violins
16 second violins
14 violas
12 cellos
10 double basses

Section VII

POPULAR MUSIC

LIST 7.1   TYPES OF AMERICAN POPULAR MUSIC

big band	dance orchestras of the Swing Era, 1935–1945
bluegrass	a fast two-beat style that may be described as country & western or Dixieland
blues	twentieth century jazz song or dance song in 4/4 time
boogie-woogie	an eight to the bar piano style employing an ostinato bass with a blues chord structure
bebop	1940's jazz style with complex rhythm, intricate melodies, and adventurous harmony; features a soloist
country & western	music of Southeastern U.S.A. centered around Nashville, formerly known as hillbilly music
folk	music that is accepted in the community and usually is passed on by oral communication
folk revival	popular music based on revival of traditional folk songs and new compositions in a similar style
gospel	a type of religious popular song
honkey-tonk	a style of popular music which started in Texas in the 1930's and 40's. It was loud and had a heavy beat and dealt with problems associated with uprooted rural people
jazz	music mainly created by African Americans in the twentieth century; uses elements of European-American and tribal African music; characteristics include improvisation, bent pitches, swing, and polyrhythms
pop soul	a blend of the emotion of soul with the bright attractiveness of mainstream pop
ragtime	American popular music that features strongly syncopated melodies and steady beat accompaniment
rap	improvised rhyme performed to a rhythmic accompaniment
reggae	Jamaican popular music, heavily rhythmic and aggressive
rock and roll	music of the 1950's derived from rhythm and blues with heavy driving rhythm
rhythm and blues	1940's music which combines the elements of blues and jazz
soul	1960's music developed by African Americans, derived from blues and gospel singing mixed with rock rhythms
spiritual	religious songs of African Americans based on Bible stories
swing	1934–1945 music associated with big bands, more emphasis on solo improvisation, and equal weight given to each of the 4 beats of a measure
western swing	developed by Texas fiddler Bob Wills, a blend of bluegrass and big band

LIST 7.2   MOVEMENTS IN JAZZ

bebop	early 1940's style—with improvised, rapid melodies, full of asymmetrical phrases and accent patterns (Dizzy Gillespie, Thelonius Monk, Charlie Parker)
Chicago	subtler style of jazz which involved smaller orchestral combinations and freer play for improvisation (Bix Beiderbecke)
classic	a musical form, often improvisational, developed by African Americans and influenced by African rhythmic complexity, as well as European harmonic structure
cool	jazz that borrows advanced harmonies from twentieth century classical composers such as Stravinsky (The Modern Jazz Quartet)
Dixieland	a traditional style of jazz played by white musicians of the early New Orleans school
East Coast	a vigorous offshoot of bebop; also called hard bop
free form	spontaneous improvisation (Cecil Taylor)
fusion music	jazz with amplified instruments and rock-like beats (Miles Davis)
hard bop	see East Coast
hot	intense, purely improvisational jazz (Benny Goodman, Fletcher Henderson, Duke Ellington, Louis Armstrong)
jazz-rock	see fusion music
Latin	jazz influenced by Latin American rhythm
mainstream jazz	the modern form of swing
New Orleans	earliest form of jazz; evolved from the fusion of blues and ragtime, with various popular music
progressive	a 1940–1950's extension of jazz orchestral tradition (Stan Kenton)
straight	deliberately arranged and rehearsed jazz (Art Hickman)
sweet	see straight
West Coast	see cool

LIST 7.3   JAZZ TERMS

after hours	1920's and 30's term referring to jazz musicians performing after a gig
arrangement	a jazz composition
axe	a saxophone; or one's instrument
backline	the rhythm or percussion players in a jazz group
bad	good
bag	style, point of view, or way of behaving
ball	1930's term that meant a good time
book	term used to describe the library of a band; as a verb—to set up a paying job
bop	post World War II jazz style
box	piano
bread	money
changes	the chord progressions of a jazz composition
chops	lips, fingers; referring to being a very skilled player
clam	a wrong note
combo	a small group of instruments
cool	West Coast jazz style
dirty	hard, aggressive style of playing
down home	referring to one's ethnic roots; or playing with emotion
fluff	a wrong note
front line	melody instruments in a jazz group
frontman	bandleader
funky	distorted and wild sounds
gig	a playing job
horn	in jazz, any wind instrument
improvisation	spontaneous performance
jam session	informal gathering of jazz musicians
jazzwalk	sidewalks of New York City's 52nd Street, between 5th and 6th Ave.
later	goodbye
lick	a short passage or phrase
licorice stick	clarinet
scat singing	singing on nonsense syllables
shake	an extreme form of vibrato; like a trill, but with a bigger interval than a second
sideman	member of a jazz band who is not the leader
tag	coda
tailgate	a jazz trombone style using slides to and from long sustained notes
trad	New Orleans or Dixieland style
wail	give a great performance; play with deep feeling

LIST 7.4   JAZZ GREATS

Julian "Cannonball" Adderley
Laurindo Almeida
Louis "Satchmo" Armstrong
Mildred Bailey
William "Count" Basie
Leon "Bix" Beiderbecke
Roland "Bunny" Berigan
Alban "Barney" Bigard
Art Blakely
Jimmy Blanto
Charles "Buddy" Bolden
William "Big Bill" Broonzy
Clifford "Brownie" Brown
Ray Brown
Dave Brubeck
Bennett "Benny" Carter
Ron Carter
Sidney "Big Sid" Catlett
Ray Charles
Charlie Christian
Eric Clapton
Kenny "Klook" Clarke
Wilbur "Buck" Clayton
Al Cohn
William "Cozy" Cole
Nat "King" Cole
Ornette Coleman
John Coltrane
Eddie Condon
Armando "Chick" Corea
Tadley "Tadd" Dameron
Eddie "Lockjaw" Davis
Miles Davis
William "Wild Bill" Davison
Boniface "Buddy" De Franco
Paul Desmond
Vic Dickenson
Johnny Dodds
Warren "Baby" Dodds
Eric Dolphy
Jimmy Dorsey
Tommy "Georgia Tom" Dorsey
Roy "Little Jazz" Eldridge
Edward "Duke" Ellington
Bill Evans
Gil Evans
Ella Fitzgerald
Errol Garner
Stan Getz
John Birks "Dizzy" Gillespie·

Benjamin David "Benny" Goodman
Stephane Grappelli
Bobby Hackett
Lionel Hampton
Herbie Hancock
William Christopher "W.C." Handy
Coleman "Bean" Hawkins
Roy Haynes
James Fletcher "Smack" Henderson
Woodrow Charles "Woody" Herman
Jay Higgenbotham
Kenneth Earl "Fatha" Hines
John Cornelius "Rabbit" Hodges
Billie "Lady Day" Holiday
John Lee Hooker
Sam "Lightnin'" Hopkins
Mahalia Jackson
Milt "Bags" Jackson
Jean Baptiste "Illinois" Jacquet
Keith Jarrett
"Blind Lemon" Jefferson
Bunk Johnson William Geary
James Louis "J.J." Johnson
James Price Johnson
Elvin Ray Jones
Jonathan "Jo" Jones
Joseph Rudolph "Philly Joe" Jones
Quincy Delight Jones, Jr.
Thad Jones
Scott Joplin
Stan Kenton
B.B. King
Lee Konitz
Gene Krupa
Huddie "Leadbelly" Lebetter
John Lewis
Meade "Lux" Lewis
Jimmie Lunceford
Herbie Mann
Wynton Marsalis
Jimmy McPartland
Marian McPartland
Carmen McRae
Glenn Miller
Charles Mingus
Thelonius "Sphere" Monk
Wes Montogomery
Ferdinand Joseph LaMenthe
    "Jelly Roll" Morton
Bennie Moten

166

List 7.4 (continued)

Gerry Mulligan
Melvin "Turk" Murphy
Theodore "Fats" Navarro
Earnest "Red" Nichols
Kenneth "Red" Norvo
Anita O'Day
Joseph "King" Oliver
Edward "Kid" Ory
Jaco Pastorius
Charlie "Yardbird" Parker
Art Pepper
Oscar Peterson
Oscar Pettiford
Earl "Bud" Powell
Gertrude "Ma" Rainey
Don Redman
Jean Baptiste "Django" Reinhardt
Bernard "Buddy" Rich
Max Roach
Theodore "Sonny" Rollins
Jimmy Rushing
George Russell
Artie Shaw
George Shearing
Horace Silver
John "Zoot" Sims
Arthur "Zutty" Singleton

Elizabeth "Bessie" Smith
Clarence "Pine Top" Smith
Willie "The Lion" Smith
Francis "Muggsy" Spanier
Edward "Sonny" Stitt
Billy Strayhorn
Art Tatum
Billy Taylor
Percival "Cecil" Taylor
Weldon "Jack" Teagarden
Dave Tough
Lennie Tristano
Joseph "Big Joe" Turner
Alfred "McCoy" Tyner
Sarah Vaughan
Giuseppe "Joe" Venuti
Thomas "Fats" Waller
Ruth Lee "Dinah" Washington
William "Chick" Webb
Paul Whiteman
Charles "Cootie" Williams
MaryLou Williams
Teddy Wilson
Chresten "Kal" Winding
Jimmy Yancey
Lester "Prez" Young

LIST 7.5 1990'S JAZZ MUSICIANS

Geri Allen	clarinet	Christopher Hollyday	tenor saxophone
Woody Allen	piano	Keith Jarrett	piano
David Benoit	piano	Abbey Lincoln	vocal
George Benson	guitar	Branford Marsalis	tenor/soprano saxophone
Cindy Blackeman	drums	Wynton Marsalis	trumpet
Jane Ira Bloom	soprano saxophone	Jackie McLean	alto saxophone
Don Byron	clarinet	Myra Melford	piano
Michel Camilo	piano	Pat Metheny	guitar
James Carter	tenor saxophone	T.S. Monk	drums
Regina Carter	violin	Frank Morgan	alto saxophone
Steve Coleman	alto saxophone	David Murray	tenor saxophone
Ravi Coltrane	tenor saxophone	Joshua Redman	tenor saxophone
Harry Connick, Jr.	piano/vocal	David Sanbourn	alto saxophone
Eddie Daniels	clarinet	Diane Schuur	vocal
Miles Davis	trumpet	Horace Silver	piano
Joey De Francesco	organ	Nina Simone	vocal
Roy Hargrove	trumpet	Straight Ahead	female group
Joe Henderson	tenor saxophone	Cassandrea Wilson	vocal

LIST 7.6   BIG BAND LEADERS

Black bands of the late 1920's and early 1930's began to play in a style later known as "swing" The "Swing Era" actually started in 1936 when Benny Goodman, appearing on the NBC radio show "Let's Dance," was dubbed "The King of Swing." An international dance craze started that led to the formation of several hundred big bands.

Charlie Barnet (Charles Daly)
Count Basie (William)
Bunny Barigan (Roland)
Les Brown (Lester)
Cab Calloway (Cabell)
Benny Carter (Bennett)
Jimmy Dorsey
Tommy Dorsey (Georgia Tom)
Eddy Duchin
Duke Ellington (Edward)
Benny Goodman (Benjamin)
Lionel Hampton
Fletcher Henderson
Woody Herman
Earl Hines (Kenneth Earl "Fatha")
Harry James (Haag)
Thad Jones

Stan Kenton
Andy Kirk (Andrew)
Gene Krupa
Mel Lewis
Guy Lombardo (Gaetano)
Jimmie Lunceford
Glenn Miller (Alton)
Gerry Mulligan
Buddy Rich (Bernard)
Artie Shaw
Mel Torme
Rudy Vallee (Hubert)
Fred Waring
Chick Webb (William Henry)
Paul Whiteman
Teddy Wilson (Theodore)

168

LIST 7.7 BIG BAND HITS

"Alright, Okay, You Win"
"Among My Souvenirs"
"Angry"
"Artisty in Rhythm"
"At the Woodchopper's Ball"
"Ballin' the Jack"
"Basin Street Blues"
"Begin the Beguine"
"Besame Mucho"
"Blue Champagne"
"Boo-Hoo"
"Boogie Woogie Bugle Boy"
"Bugle Call Rag"
"Bye-Bye Blackbird"
"Caledonia"
"Candy"
"Chattanooga Choo Choo"
"The Continental"
"Daddy"
"Don't Get Around Much Anymore"
"Embraceable You"
"Five Foot Two, Eyes of Blue"
"For Sentimental Reasons"
"The Glow Worm"
"Goody Goody"
"Green Eyes"
"Harlem Nocturne"
"I Can't Give You Anything but Love"
"I Cried for You"
"I Won't Dance"
"I'm Looking over a Four Leaf Clover"
"I'm Sitting on Top of the World"
"In a Little Spanish Town"
"In a Sentimental Mood"
"In the Mood"
"Indiana"
"Indian Love Call"
"It's a Pity to Say 'Goodnight'"
"I've Got My Love to Keep Me Warm"
"June Night"
"Laura"
"Leap Frog"
"Let a Smile Be Your Umbrella"
"Let There Be Love"
"Let's Dance"
"Little Brown Jug"

"Long Ago and Far Away"
"Mairzy Doats"
"Mood Indigo"
"Moonglow"
"The Most Beautiful Girl in the World"
"A Nightingale Sang in Berkeley Square"
"Oh! You Beautiful Doll"
"The Old Lamplighter"
"On a Little Street in Singapore"
"One O'Clock Jump"
"On the Sunny Side of the Street"
"Opus 1"
"Satin Doll"
"Saturday Night Is the Loneliest Night of the Week"
"Seems Like Old Times"
"Sentimental Journey"
"The Sheik of Araby"
"Shoofly Pie and Apple Pan Dowdy"
"Side by Side"
"Solitude"
"Somebody Else Is Taking My Place"
"Somebody Loves You"
"Sometimes I'm Happy"
"The Song Is You"
"Stardust"
"A String of Pearls"
"Summertime"
"Sunrise Serenade"
"Sweet Someone"
"Take the A Train"
"Tangerine"
"Tenderly"
"Three O'Clock in the Morning"
"Tuxedo Junction"
"Twelfth Street Rag"
"The Way You Look Tonight"
"When My Baby Smiles at Me"
"When My Sugar Walks Down the Street"
"When the Red, Red Robin Comes Bob, Bob, Bobbin' Along"
"Whispering"
"Who?"
"Who's Sorry Now?"
"Wrap Your Troubles in Dreams"
"Yes, Indeed"
"Yesterdays"

LIST 7.8 TYPES OF ROCK MUSIC

acid	crusading	instrumental	raga
aleatory	dada	jazz	redneck
androgynous	destruction	Latin	rockabilly
art	downer	new wave	shock
attitude	electronic	no wave	sob
avant-garde	experimental	outlaw	soft
baroque	folk	poetic	southern
big band	fusion	pop	space
blues	glam	prepubescent	studio
bubble-gum	glitter	progressive	synth
christian	grunge	protest	theater
classical	hard	psychedelic	voodoo
country	heavy metal	punk	

LIST 7.9 ROCK AND ROLL NOTABLES

ARTISTS

Paula Abdul
Paul Anka
Frankie Avalon
Pat Benatar
Chuck Berry
Debby Boone
David Bowie
James Brown
Mariah Carey
Tracy Chapman
Ray Charles
Chubby Checker
Eric Clapton
Dick Clark
George Clinton
Phil Collins
Alice Cooper
Jim Croce
Bobby Darin
John Denver
Neil Diamond
Bo Diddley
Fats Domino

Bob Dylan
José Feliciano
Roberta Flack
Aretha Franklin
Peter Gabriel
Jerry Garcia
Art Garfunkel
Marvin Gaye
Gloria Gayner
Andy Gibb
M.C. Hammer
Jimi Hendrix
Buddy Holly
Whitney Houston
Janis Ian
Michael Jackson
Janet Jackson
Mick Jagger
Billy Joel
Elton John
Janis Joplin
B.B. King
Carole King

Cyndi Lauper
Brenda Lee
John Lennon
Jerry Lee Lewis
Little Richard
Frankie Lymon
Madonna
Paul McCartney
Meat Loaf
John Cougar Mellenkamp
George Michael
Guy Mitchell
Joni Mitchell
Van Morrison
Ricky Nelson
Olivia Newton-John
John Oates
Daryl Paul
Carl Perkins
Elvis Presley
Prince
Helen Reddy
Lionel Richie

Linda Ronstadt
Diana Ross
Neil Sedaka
Del Shannon
Silk
Paul Simon
Carly Simon
Dusty Springfield
Bruce Springsteen
Rod Stewart
Barbra Streisand
Donna Summer
James Taylor
Tina Turner
Luther Vandross
Eddie Van Halen
Bobby Vinton
Dionne Warwick
Mary Wells
Stevie Wonder
Neil Young
Frank Zappa

GROUPS

The Allman Brothers Band
The Animals
The Association
The Beach Boys
The Beatles
Bee Gees
Black Sabbath
Blind Faith
Blood, Sweat and Tears
Bon Jovi
Booker T. and the MGs
The Byrds
Canned Heat
The Cars
The Coasters
Credence Clearwater Revival
Crosby, Stills, Nash and Young
Danny and the Juniors
Spencer Davis Group
Dion and the Belmonts
Dire Straits

The Doobie Brothers
The Doors
The Drifters
Duran Duran
The Eagles
Earth, Wind and Fire
The Eurythmics
Everly Brothers
Fleetwood Mac
The Four Seasons
The Four Tops
The Grateful Dead
Bill Haley and the Comets
Hall and Oates
Buddy Holly and the Crickets
The Isley Brothers
The Jackson Five
Tommy James and the Shondells
Jay and the Americans
The Jefferson Airplane
    (Jefferson Starship)

The Kinks
Kiss
Gladys Knight and the Pips
Led Zepplin
Huey Lewis and the News
Little Anthony and the
    Imperials
Lovin' Spoonful
The Mamas and the Papas
10,000 Maniacs
Martha and the Vandellas
The Marvelettes
Steve Miller Band
The Monkees
Moody Blues
Nirvana
Pearl Jam
Tom Petty and the
    Heartbreakers
Pink Floyd
Police

GROUPS (continued)

Pretenders
The Young Rascals
Righteous Brothers
Smokey Robinson and the Miracles
The Rolling Stones
The Ronettes
Santana
The Shirelles
Simon and Garfunkel
Sly and the Family Stone
Sting

The Supremes
Talking Heads
The Temptations
Three Dog Night
U2
UB40
Steppenwolf
The Who
The Yardbirds
Yes

See Also List 7.10, Female Rock Groups

LIST 7.10 FEMALE ROCK GROUPS

Angels
The Bronx Jaynettes
The Chiffons
Chordettes
The Cookies
Crystals
Dixie Cups
The Go-Go's
Indigo Girls
The Jelly Beans
L7
Martha and the Vandellas

The Marvellettes
Paris Sisters
Patience and Prudence
Poni-Tails
The Ronettes
Salt 'n' Peppa
Shangri-Las
Shirelles
Shonen Knife
The Supremes
Shontels
Teen Queens

LIST 7.11   AMERICAN FOLK NOTABLES

Joan Baez
Harry Belafonte
Oscar Brand
The Brothers Four
  Bob Flick
  Michael Kirkland
  John Paine
  Richard Foley
Judy Collins
Bob Dylan
Steve Goodman
Nanci Griffith
Arlo Guthrie
Woody Guthrie
John Hartford
Burl Ives
The Kingston Trio
  Bob Shane
  Nick Reynolds
  Dave Guard
  John Stewart
    (replaced Guard)
Huddie "Leadbelly" Ledbetter
Gordon Lightfoot
McGarrigle Sisters
  Kate McGarrigle
  Anna McGarrigle
New Christy Minstrels (group formed)
  Randy Sparks, founder
John Jacob Niles
Phil Ochs

Odetta
New Lost City Ramblers
  Mike Seeger
  John Cohen
  Tom Paley
  Tracy Schwarz
    (replaced Paley)
Tom Paxton
Peter, Paul, and Mary
  Peter Yarrow
  Noel Paul Stookey
  Mary Ellen Travers
John Prine
Jean Ritchie
Paul Robeson
Earl Robinson
The Roches
  Maggie Roche
  Terre Roche
  Suzzy Roche
Peter Rowan
Tom Rush
Buffy Sainte-Marie
Pete Seeger
Taj Mahal
The Weavers
  Pete Seeger
  Lee Hays
  Ronnie Gilbert
  Fred Hellerman
Josh White

LIST 7.12   POP SINGERS

BLUES SINGERS

Mildred Bailey
Big Bill Broonzy
Leroy Carr
W.C. Handy
Alberta Hunter
Blind Lemon Jefferson
Louis Jordan
Brownie McGhee
Gertrude "Ma" Rainey
Jimmy Rushing
Bessie Smith
Al Terry
Joe Turner
Muddy Waters
Joe Williams
Howlin' Wolf

CABERET SINGERS

Mildred Bailey
Ruth Etting
Jane Froman
Libby Holman
Mabel Mercer
Helen Morgan
Harry Richman
Ethel Waters

CROONERS

Perry Como
Bing Crosby
Dean Martin
Frank Sinatra
Mel Torme
Rudy Vallee

GOSPEL SINGERS

Philip Bailey
Shirley Caesar
Ray Charles
James Cleveland
Sam Cooke
Andrae Crouch
Tennessee Ernie Ford
Aretha Franklin
Amy Grant
Larnelle Harris
Larry Hart
Mahalia Jackson
Clyde McPhatter
Sandi Patty
Wilson Pickett
Charley Pride
Lou Rawls
Della Reese
Michael W. Smith
Soeur Sourire
Russ Taff
Rosetta Tharpe
Alberta Walker
Clara Ward
Dionne Warwick
Deniece Williams

OTHERS

Harry Belafonte
Nat "King" Cole
Anita King
Ella Fitzgerald
Gladys Knight
Brenda Lee
"Jelly Roll" Morton
Kate Smith
Jack Teagarden
Sarah Vaughan
Thomas "Fats" Waller
Dinah Washington
Andy Williams

© 1994 by Parker Publishing Company

LIST 7.13   BLUES STYLES

Chicago	Jump	New Orleans Dance	Talking	Underground
Country	Mississippi Delta	Rhythm and Blues	Texas	

LIST 7.14 BLUES HALL OF FAME

Bill "Hoss" Allen
Chuck Berry
Blind Blake
Bobby "Blue" Bland
Big Bill Broozny
Charles Brown
Ray Brown
Leroy Carr
Ray Charles
Clifton Chenier
Albert Collins
Arthur "Big Boy" Crudup
Willie Dixon
Champion Jack Dupree
David "Honeyboy" Edwards
Sleepy John Estes
Lowell Fulson
Buddy Guy
Wynonie Harris
John Lee Hooker
Lightnin' Hopkins
Big Walter Horton
Son House
Howlin' Wolf
Mississippi John Hurt
J.B. Hutto
Elmore James
Skip James
Blind Lemon Jefferson
Lonnie Johnson
Robert Johnson
Tommy Johnson
Louis Jordan
Albert King
B.B. King
Freddie King
Leadbelly
Little Milton

Little Walter
Alan Lomax
John Lomax
Robert Jr. Lockwood
Magic Sam
Percy Mayfield
Fred McDowell
Jay McShann
Blind Willie McTell
Memphis Minnie
Memphis Slim
Johnny Minter
Muddy Waters
Robert Nighthawk
Gene Nobles
Charley Patton
Professor Longhair
Ma Rainey
Jimmy Reed
John "R" Richbourg
Jimmy Rogers
Otis Rush
Johnny Shines
Slim Harpo
Bessie Smith
Otis Spann
Tampa Red
Eddie Taylor
Hound Dog Taylor
Sonny Terry
Big Mama Thornton
Big Joe Turner
T-Bone Walker
Bukka White
Big Joe Williams
Sonny Boy Williamson I (John Lee Williamson)
Sonny Boy Williamson II (Rice Miller)
Johnny Winter

LIST 7.15 COUNTRY MUSIC ARTISTS

Roy Acuff
Alabama
Terry Allen
Bill Anderson
John Anderson
Liz Anderson
Eddie Arnold
Chet Atkins
Gene Autry
Moe Bandy
Clint Black
Suzie Bogguss
Debby Boone
Garth Brooks
Jim Ed Brown
Jimmy Buffett
Glen Campbell
Mary Chapin Carpenter
The Carter Family
Johnny Cash
Roy Clark
Patsy Cline
Billy Craddock
Billy Ray Cyrus
Charlie Daniels
John Denver
Holly Dunn
The Everly Brothers
Donna Fargo
Red Foley
Leftry Frizzell
Larry Gatlin
Crystal Gayle

Vince Gill
Mickey Gilley
Lee Greenwood
Woody Guthrie
Merle Haggard
Tom T. Hall
Emmylou Harris
Alan Jackson
Stonewall Jackson
Sonny James
Waylon Jennings
George Jones
Wynona Judd
The Kendalls
Kris Kristofferson
k. d. Lang
Patty Loveless
Lyle Lovett
Loretta Lynn
Barbara Mandrell
Reba McEntire
Roger Miller
Ronnie Milsap
The Monroe Brothers
Patsy Montana
Lorrie Morgan
Anne Murray
Willie Nelson
The Oak Ridge Boys
Roy Orbinson
Buck Owens
Dolly Parton
Johnny Paycheck

Webb Pierce
Elvis Presley
Ray Price
Charley Pride
Jim Reeves
Charlie Rich
Marty Robbins
Jimmie Rodgers
Kenny Rogers
Sawyer Brown
Ricky Skaggs
The Statler Brothers
George Strait
Mel Tillis
Randy Travis
Ernest Tubb
Tanya Tucker
Conway Twitty
Porter Wagoner
Jo Walker-Meador
Steve Wariner
Kitty Wells
Dottie West
Webb Wilder
Don Williams
Hank Williams, Jr.
Hank Williams, Sr.
Bob Wills
Tammy Wynette
Trisha Yearwood
Dwight Yoakam

LIST 7.16 THE COUNTRY MUSIC HALL OF FAME

Jimmie Rodgers, Fred Rose, Hank Williams	1961
Roy Acuff	1962
Elections held, but no one canidate had enough votes	1963
Tex Ritter	1964
Ernest Tubb	1965
James R. Denny, George D. Hay, Uncle Dave Macon, Eddy Arnold	1966
Red Foley, J.L. Frank, Jim Reeves, Stephen H. Sholes	1967
Bob Wills	1968
Gene Autry	1969
Original Carter Family, Bill Monroe	1970
Arthur Edward Satherley	1971
Jimmie Davis	1972
Patsy Cline, Chet Atkins	1973
Owen Bradley, Frank "Pee Wee" King	1974
Minnie Pearl	1975
Paul Cohen, Kitty Wells	1976
Merle Travis	1977
Grandpa Jones	1978
Hubert Long, Hank Snow	1979
Connie B. Gay, Original Sons of the Pioneers, Johnny Cash	1980
Vernon Dalhart, Grant Turner	1981
Lefty Frizzell, Marty Robbins, Roy Horton	1982
Little Jimmy Dickens	1983
Ralph Peer, Floyd Tillman	1984
Lester Flatt & Earl Scruggs	1985
Wesley Rose, The Duke of Paducah	1986
Rod Brasfield	1987
Roy Rogers, Loretta Lynn	1988
Jack Stapp, Hank Thompson, Cliffie Stone	1989
Tennessee Ernie Ford	1990
Boudleaux & Felice Bryant	1991
George Jones, Frances Preston	1992
Willie Nelson	1993
Merle Haggard	1994
Roger Miller, Jo Walker-Meador	1995
Patsy Montana, Buck Owens, Ray Price	1996

LIST 7.17 COUNTRY ENTERTAINER OF THE YEAR

Eddy Arnold	1967	Ronnie Milsap	1977	Hank Williams, Jr.	1987
Glen Campbell	1968	Dolly Parton/Janie Fricke	1978	Hank Williams, Jr.	1988
Johnny Cash	1969	Willie Nelson	1979	George Strait	1989
Merle Haggard	1970	Barbara Mandrell	1980	George Strait	1990
Carley Pride	1971	Barbara Mandrell	1981	Garth Brooks	1991
Loretta Lynn	1972	Alabama	1982	Garth Brooks	1992
Roy Clark	1973	Alabama	1983	Vince Gill	1993
Charlie Rich	1974	Alabama	1984	Vince Gill	1994
John Denver	1975	Ricky Skaggs	1985	Alan Jackson	1995
Mel Tillis	1976	Reba McEntire	1986	Brooks + Dunn	1996

LIST 7.18 BROADWAY MUSICALS

Ain't Misbehavin'	"Fats" Waller/Andy Razaf	1978
Annie	Charles Strouse/Martin Charnin	1977
Annie Get Your Gun	Irving Berlin	1946
Anything Goes	Cole Porter	1934
Applause	Charles Strouse/Lee Adams	1970
Babes in Arms	Richard Rodgers/Lorenz Hart	1937
Babes in Toyland	Victor Herbert/Glen MacDonough	1903
The Bandwagon	Arthur Schwartz/Howard Deitz	1931
Best Litte Whorehouse	Larry King/Peter Masterson	1978
Big	David Shire/Richard Maltby Jr.	1995
Big River	Roger Miller	1985
The Boys from Syracuse	Richard Rodgers/Lorenz Hart	1938
Brigadoon	Alan J. Lerner/Frederick Loewe	1947
By Jeeves	Andrew Lloyd Webber	1997
Bye Bye, Birdie	Charles Strouse/Lee Adams	1960
Cabaret	John Kander/Fred Ebb	1966
La Cage aux Folles	Jerry Herman	1983
Call Me Madam	Irving Berlin/Howard Linsay, Russel Crouse	1950
Camelot	Alan J. Lerner/Frederick Loewe	1960
Can-Can	Cole Porter	1953
Carnival	Bob Merill	1961
Carousel	Richard Rodgers/Oscar Hammerstein II	1945
Cats	Andrew Lloyd Webber	1981
A Chorus Line	Marvin Hamlisch/Michael Bennett	1975
Company	Stephen Sondheim	1970
Crazy for You	George Gershwin/Ira Gershwin/Ken Ludwig	1992
Damn Yankees	Richard Adler/Jerry Rose	1955
Dream Girls	Henry Krieger/Tom Eyen	1981
Evita	Andrew Lloyd Webber/Tim Rice	1979
Fanny	S.N. Behrman, Joshua Logan, Harold Rome	1956
The Fantastiks	Harvey Schmidt/Tom Jones	1960
Fiddler on the Roof	Jerry Bock/Sheldon Harnick	1964
Finian's Rainbow	Fred Saidy/E.Y. Harburg	1947

List 7.18 (continued)

TITLE	COMPOSER/LYRICIST	YEAR
Fiorello	Jerry Bock/Sheldon Harnick	1959
Flower Drum Song	Richard Rodgers/Oscar Hammerstein II	1958
42nd Street	Gower Champion	1980
Funny Girl	Bob Merrill/Jule Styne	1964
A Funny Thing Happened on the Way to the Forum	Stephen Sondheim	1962
Gentleman Prefer Blondes	Jule Styne/Leo Robin	1949
Girl Crazy	George Gershwin/Ira Gershwin	1930
Godspell	Stephen Schwartz	1971
Grease	Jim Jacobs/Warren Casey	1972
Guys and Dolls	Frank Lesser	1950
Gypsy	Jule Styne/Stephen Sondheim	1959
Hallelujah, Baby!	Jule Styne/Betty Comden, Adolph Green	1967
Hello, Dolly!	Jerry Herman	1964
Here's Love	Meredith Wilson	1963
How to Succeed in Business Without Really Trying	Frank Loesser	1961
110 in the Shade	Harvey Schmidt/Tom Jones	1963
Into the Woods	Stephen Sondheim	1987
Irma LaDouce	Margaret Monnot	1960
Jekyll + Hyde	Frank Wildhorn/Leslie Bricusse	1997
Jerome Robbins' Broadway	Andrew Lloyd Webber/Tim Rice	1980
Jesus Christ Superstar	Andrew Lloyd Webber/Tim Rice	1971
Joseph and the Amazing Technicolor Dream Coat	Andrew Lloyd Webber	1981
Jumbo	Richard Rodgers/Lorenz Hart	1935
The King and I	Richard Rodgers/Oscar Hammerstein II	1951
Kismet	Alexander Borodin, Robert Wright, George Forrest	1953
Kiss Me Kate	Cole Porter	1948
Kiss of the Spider Woman	John Kander/Fred Ebb	1993
Les Misérables	Claude-Michel Schönberg/Herbert Kretzmer	1985
The Life	Cy Coleman/Ira Gasman	1997
Little Mary Sunshine	Rick Besoyan	1959
Little Me	Cy Coleman/Carolyn Leigh	1962
A Little Night Music	Stephen Sondheim	1973
Little Shop of Horrors	Alan Menkin/Howard Ashman	1991
Mame	Jerry Herman	1966
Man of La Mancha	Mitch Leigh/Joe Darion	1965
Me and My Girl	Noel Gay/L. Arthur Rose, Douglas Furber	1986
Milk and Honey	Gerry Harman	1961
Miss Saigon	Claude-Michel Schönberg/Richard Maltby, Jr. from the original French lyrics by Alain Boublil	1991
Most Happy Fella	Frank Loesser	1956
Mr. President	Irving Berlin	1962
Music Man	Meredith Wilson	1957
My Fair Lady	Alan J. Lerner/Frederick Loewe	1956
My Favorite Year	Steven Flaherty/Lynn Ahrens	1992

List 7.18 (continued)

TITLE	COMPOSER/LYRICIST	YEAR
The Mystery of Edwin Drood	Rupert Holmes	1985
The New Moon	Sigmund Romberg/Oscar Hammerstein II	1928
No Strings	Richard Rodgers	1962
Oh Kay!	George Gershwin/Ira Gershwin	1926
Oklahoma	Richard Rodgers/Oscar Hammerstein II	1943
Oliver	Lionel Bart	1963
On the Town	Leonard Bernstein/Betty Comden, Adolph Green	1944
On Your Toes	Richard Rodgers/Lorenz Hart	1936
Paint Your Wagon	Alan J. Lerner/Frederick Loewe	1951
Pajama Game	Richard Adler/Jerry Ross	1954
Pal Joey	Richard Rodgers/Lorenz Hart	1940
Passion	Stephen Sondheim/James Lapine	1994
Phantom of the Opera	Andrew Lloyd Webber, Charles Hart, Richard Stilgoe	1986
Pippin	Roger O. Hirson/Stephen Schwartz	1972
Raisin	Judd Woldin/Robert Brittan	1973
Redhead	Albert Hague	1959
Rent	Jonathan Larson	1996
Roberta	Otto Harbach/Jerome Kern	1933
Rocky Horror Picture Show	Richard O'Brien	1975
The Secret Garden	Lucy Simon/Marsha Norman	1991
1776	Sherman Edwards/Peter Stone	1969
She Loves Me	Jerry Bock/Sheldon Harnick	1963
Show Boat	Oscar Hammerstein II/Jermome Kern	1927
Side by Side	Stephen Sondheim (et al.)	1977
Silk Stockings	Cole Porter	1955
Sophisticated Ladies	Duke Ellington (et al.)	1981
The Sound of Music	Richard Rodgers/Oscar Hammerstein II	1959
South Pacific	Richard Rodgers/Oscar Hammerstein II	1949
Starlight Express	Andrew Lloyd Webber/Richard Stilgoe	1987
St. Louis Woman	Harold Arlen/Johnny Mercer	1946
Sunday in the Park with George	Stephen Sondheim	1984
Sunset Boulevard	Andrew Lloyd Webber	1995
Sweeny Todd	Stephen Sondheim	1979
The Who's Tommy	Pete Townshend	1993
Titanic	Maury Yeston/Peter Stone	1997
Top Banana	Johnny Mercer	1951
A Tree Grows in Brooklyn	Dorothy Fields/Arthur Schwartz	1951
Two Gentleman of Verona	Galt MacDermot/John Guare	1971
The Unsinkable Molly Brown	Meredith Wilson	1960
The Vagabond King	Rudolf Friml/Brian Hook, W.H. Post	1925
West Side Story	Leonard Bernstein/Stephen Sondheim	1957
Wild Cat	Cy Coleman/Carolyn Leigh	1960
The Will Rogers Follies	Cy Coleman/Betty Comden, Adolph Green	1991
The Wiz	Charlie Small/William Brown	1975
Wonderful Town	Leonard Bernstein/Betty Comden, Adolph Green	1953
Zorba	John Kander/Fred Ebb	1968

See Also List 7.19, Tony Awards for Best Musical

LIST 7.19 TONY AWARDS FOR BEST MUSICAL

Kiss Me Kate	1949	*A Little Night Music*	1973
South Pacific	1950	*Raisin*	1974
Guys and Dolls	1951	*The Wiz*	1975
The King and I	1952	*A Chorus Line*	1976
Wonderful Town	1953	*Annie*	1977
Kismet	1954	*Ain't Misbehavin*	1978
The Pajama Game	1955	*Sweeny Todd*	1979
Damn Yankees	1956	*Evita*	1980
My Fair Lady	1957	*42nd Street*	1981
The Music Man	1958	*Dream Girls*	1982
Redhead	1959	*Cats*	1983
Fiorello	1960	*La Cage aux Folles*	1984
Bye Bye, Birdie	1961	*Big River*	1985
How to Succeed in Business		*The Mystery of Edwin Drood*	1986
Without Really Trying	1962	*Les Misérables*	1987
A Funny Thing Happened		*The Phantom of the Opera*	1988
on the Way to the Forum	1963	*Jerome Robbin's Broadway*	1989
Hello Dolly!	1964	*City of Angels*	1990
Fiddler on the Roof	1965	*The Will Rogers Follies*	1991
Man of La Mancha	1966	*Crazy for You*	1992
Cabaret	1967	*Kiss of the Spider Woman*	1993
Hallelujah, Baby!	1968	*Passion*	1994
1776	1969	*Sunset Boulevard*	1995
Applause	1970	*Rent*	1996
Company	1971	*Titanic*	1997
Two Gentlemen of Verona	1972		

LIST 7.20 COMPOSERS AND LYRICISTS OF MUSICALS

COMPOSERS

Richard Adler	Andrew Lloyd Webber
Harold Arlen	Frank Loesser
Irving Berlin	Bob Merrill
Leonard Bernstein	Richard Rodgers
Leonard Bock	Seigmund Romberg
Warren Casey	Harold Rome
George M. Cohan	Harvey Schmidt
Cy Coleman	Stephen Schwartz
Noel Coward	Charles Strouse
George Gershwin	Jule Styne
Marvin Hamlisch	Harry Warren
Jerry Herman	Kurt Weill
Jim Jacobs	Judd Woldin
John Kander	Vincent Youmans
Jerome Kern	Meredith Wilson
Burton Lane	
Mitch Leigh	

LYRICISTS

Lee Adams	Oscar Hammerstein II
Richard Adler	E.Y. Harburg
Irving Berlin	Sheldon Harnick
Marc Blitzstein	Lorenz Hart
Jerry Bock	Jerry Herman
Guy Bolton	Jim Jacobs
Robert Britton	Tom Jones
Martin Charnin	Carolyn Leigh
Betty Comden	Alan J. Lerner
Noel Coward	Frank Loesser
Joe Darion	Joseph McCarthy
Warren Casey	Cole Porter
Howard Dietz	Richard Rodgers
Fred Ebb	Harold Rome
Dorothy Fields	Leonard Sillman
Ira Gershwin	Stephen Soldheim
Adolph Green	Harry Warren
	Meredith Wilson

LIST 7.21 LONGEST RUNNING BROADWAY MUSICALS

A Chorus Line	1977–1983	*La Cage aux Folles*	1983–1987
Annie	1975–1990	*Les Misérables*	1987–
Cats	1982–	*Man of La Mancha*	1965–1971
Dancin'	1978–1982	*My Fair Lady*	1956–1962
Fiddler on the Roof	1964–1972	*Oh, Calcutta*	1976–1989
42nd Street	1980–1989	*Oklahoma*	1943–1948
Grease	1972–1980	*Pippin*	1971–1977
Hair	1968–1972	*South Pacific*	1949–1954
Hello, Dolly!	1964–1971	*The Wiz*	1975–1979

LIST 7.22 TOP TUNES OF THE 1920'S

"Ain't Misbehavin'"	1928	Louis Armstrong
"Among My Souvenirs"	1927	Jack Hylton & orchestra
"April Showers"	1921	Al Jolson
"Baby Face"	1926	Jan Garber & orchestra
"Back in Your Own Back Yard"	1928	Al Jolson
"The Best Things in Life Are Free"	1927	George Olsen & orchestra
"Button Up Your Overcoat"	1928	Helen Kane, Fred Waring's Pennsylvanians
"California, Here I Come"	1924	Al Jolson
"Collegiate"	1926	Fred Waring's Pennsylvanians
"Crazy Rhythm"	1928	Ben Bernie
"'Deed I Do"	1926	Ben Bernie & orchestra
"Everybody Loves My Baby"	1924	Clarence Williams' Blue Five
"Five Foot Two, Eyes of Blue"	1925	Gene Austin
"Hallelujah"	1927	Nat Shilkret & orchestra
"Honeysuckle Rose"	1929	Paul Whiteman & orchestra
"I Can't Believe That You're in Love with Me"	1927	Roger Wolfe Kahn & orchestra
"I Can't Give You Anything but Love"	1928	Cliff Edwards
"I Cried for You"	1923	Cliff Edwards
"If You Knew Susie"	1925	Eddie Cantor
"If You Were the Only Girl in the World"	1929	Rudy Vallee & his Connecticut Yankees
"I'm Sitting on Top of the World"	1925	Al Jolson
"In a Little Spanish Town"	1926	Paul Whiteman & orchestra
"It All Depends on You"	1926	Paul Whiteman & orchestra
"Jealous"	1924	Little Jack Little
"Let a Smile Be Your Umbrella"	1927	Roger Wolfe Kahn
"Look for the Silver Lining"	1920	Marion Harris
"Make Believe"	1927	Howard Marsh & Norma Terris
"Manhattan"	1925	Ben Selvin & orchestra
"Me and My Shadow"	1927	Ted Lewis
"Mean to Me"	1929	Helen Morgan
"Miss You"	1929	Rudy Vallee
"Mississippi Mud"	1927	Paul Whiteman & orchestra

List 7.22 (continued)

Song	Year	Artist
"Moonlight and Roses"	1925	Lanny Ross
"More Than You Know"	1929	Jane Froman
"Ol' Man River"	1927	Paul Robeson with Paul Whiteman & orchestra
"Paddlin' Madelin' Home"	1925	Cliff "Ukelele Ike" Edwards
"Second Hand Rose"	1921	Fanny Brice
"Sentimental Me"	1925	June Cochrane
"Stardust"	1929	Isham Jones & orchestra
"Sugar Blues"	1923	Sara Martin
"There'll Be Some Changes Made"	1921	Billy Higgins, Ethel Waters
"Together"	1928	Paul Whiteman & orchestra
"The Wang Wang Blues"	1921	Paul Whiteman & orchestra
"'Way Down Yonder in New Orleans"	1922	Creamer & Layton
"Wedding Bells Are Breaking Up That Old Gang of Mine"	1929	Gene Austin
"When My Sugar Walks Down the Street"	1924	Phil Harris & orchestra
"When the Red, Red Robin Comes Bob, Bob Bobbin' Along"	1926	Al Jolson
"Who's Sorry Now"	1923	Van & Schenck
"Yearning"	1925	Gene Austin
"Yes! We Have No Bananas"	1923	Frank Silver's Music Masters
"You're the Cream in My Coffee"	1928	Jack Whiting & Ona Munson

LIST 7.23   TOP TUNES OF THE 1930'S

"All of Me"	1931	Paul Whiteman, Louis Armstrong
"Blue Prelude"	1933	Isham Jones & orchestra (theme of Woody Herman & orchestra)
"Boo Hoo"	1937	Guy Lombardo & Royal Canadians
"Bye Bye Blues"	1930	Theme of Bert Lown & orchestra
"Caravan"	1937	Duke Ellington & orchestra
"The Continental"	1934	Leo Reisman & orchestra
"East of the Sun"	1934	Tom Coakley & orchestra
"Easy to Love"	1936	James Stewart
"Falling in Love with Love"	1938	Frances Langford
"A Foggy Day"	1937	Bob Crosby & orchestra
"For All We Know"	1934	Morton Downey
"Have You Ever Been Lonely?"	1933	Paul Whiteman & orchestra
"Heartaches"	1931	Guy Lombardo & Royal Canadians
"I Can't Get Started with You"	1935	Hal Kemp & orchestra
"I Don't Know Why (I Just Do)"	1931	Wayne King & orchestra
"I'll Never Smile Again"	1939	Tommy Dorsey & orchestra
"I'm Gettin' Sentimental over You"	1932	Tommy Dorsey & orchestra (theme)
"I'm Gonna Sit Right Down and Write Myself a Letter"	1935	Fats Waller
"In a Shanty in Old Shanty Town"	1932	Ted Lewis & orchestra
"In the Mood"	1938	Edgar Hayes & orchestra
"In the Still of the Night"	1937	Tommy Dorsey & orchestra
"It Ain't Necessarily So"	1935	John Bubbles
"It's a Blue World"	1939	Tony Martin
"It's De-Lovely"	1936	Ethel Merman
"It's Only a Paper Moon"	1933	Nat "King" Cole
"It's the Talk of the Town"	1933	Glen Gray & the Casa Loma orchestra
"I've Got the World on a String"	1932	Cab Calloway
"I've Got You under My Skin"	1936	Hal Kemp & orchestra
"The Lady Is a Tramp"	1937	Sophie Tucker
"Let's Dance"	1935	Benny Goodman & orchestra (theme)
"Love Is Here to Stay"	1938	Kenny Baker
"Love Letters in the Sand"	1931	Russ Columbo
"Lullaby of the Leaves"	1932	George Olsen & orchestra
"Memories of You"	1930	Louis Armstrong
"Mood Indigo"	1931	Duke Ellington & orchestra
"Moon over Miami"	1935	Eddy Duchin & orchestra
"Moonlight Serenade"	1939	Glenn Miller & orchestra (theme)
"My Funny Valentine"	1937	Frank Sinatra
"My Prayer"	1939	Sammy Kaye & orchestra
"Nevertheless"	1931	Jack Denny & orchestra
"Nice Work If You Can Get It"	1937	Jan Duggan
"On the Sunny Side of the Street"	1930	Harry Richman
"Paper Doll"	1930	Tommy Lyman
"Pennies from Heaven"	1936	Bing Crosby
"Red Sails in the Sunset"	1935	Bing Crosby
"September Song"	1938	Bing Crosby
"Smoke Gets in Your Eyes"	1933	Irene Dunne
"Stars Fell on Alabama"	1934	Jack Teagarden
"Summertime"	1935	Abbie Mitchell

List 7.23 (continued)

"That's My Desire"	1931	Lanny Ross
"These Foolish Things (Remind Me of You)"	1936	Benny Goodman & orchestra
"They Can't Take That Away from Me"	1937	Fred Astaire
"This Can't Be Love"	1938	Eddie Albert & Marcy Westcott
"Under a Blanket of Blue"	1933	Glen Gray & the Casa Loma orchestra
"What a Diff'rence a Day Made"	1934	Dorsey Bros. orchestra
"Where or When"	1939	Judy Garland
"Where the Blue of the Night (Meets the Gold of the Day)"	1931	Bing Crosby
"You're My Everything"	1931	Dan Dailey
"Yours"	1931	Tito Schipa

LIST 7.24   TOP TUNES OF THE 1940'S

"All or Nothing at All"	1940	Harry James & orchestra (Frank Sinatra, vocal)
"Almost Like Being in Love"	1947	David Brooks & Marion Bell
"Anniversary Song"	1946	Al Jolson
"As Time Goes By"	1942	Dooley Wilson
"Bewitched"	1941	Bill Snyder & orchestra
"Blueberry Hill"	1940	Gene Autry, Glenn Miller & orchestra
"Boogie Woogie Bugle Boy"	1941	The Andrews Sisters
"The Breeze and I"	1940	Jimmy Dorsey & orchestra
"Cabin in the Sky"	1940	Ethel Waters & Dooley Wilson
"Candy"	1944	Jo Stafford, Johnny Mercer & the Pied Pipers
"Chattanooga Choo Choo"	1941	Glenn Miller & orchestra
"Come Rain or Come Shine"	1946	Frank Sinatra
"Cruising Down the River"	1949	Blue Barron & orchestra
"Daddy"	1941	Sammy Kaye & orchestra
"Don't Fence Me In"	1944	Roy Rogers
"Don't Sit under the Apple Tree"	1942	The Andrews Sisters
"Fools Rush In"	1940	Glenn Miller & orchestra
"For Sentimental Reasons"	1947	Nat "King" Cole
"God Bless' the Child"	1941	Billie Holiday
"Green Eyes"	1941	Jimmy Dorsey
"Harbor Lights"	1940	Rudy Vallee
"Harlem Nocturne"	1940	Ray Noble & orchestra
"Have I Told You Lately That I Love You"	1945	Gene Autry, Bing Crosby
"How Are Things in Glocca Morra"	1946	Dick Haymes
"How High the Moon"	1940	Benny Goodman & orchestra
"I Could Write a Book"	1940	Eddy Duchin & orchestra
"I Don't Want to Set the World on Fire"	1941	The Ink Spots
"If I Loved You"	1945	Perry Como

185

List 7.24 (continued)

"I'll Be Around"	1942	Cab Calloway & orchestra
"I'll Remember April"	1941	Woody Herman & orchestra
"I'm Beginning to See the Light"	1944	Duke Ellington & orchestra; Harry James & orchestra
"Imagination"	1940	Glenn Miller & orchestra
"In the Mood"	1940	Glenn Miller & orchestra
"It's a Grand Night for Singing"	1945	Dick Haymes
"It's a Most Unusual Day"	1948	Ray Noble & orchestra
"Juke Box Saturday Night"	1942	Glenn Miller & orchestra
"June Is Bustin' Out All Over"	1945	Christine Johnson
"The Last Time I Saw Paris"	1940	Kate Smith
"Lilli Marlene"	1940	Marlene Dietrich
"Mairzy Doats"	1943	The Merry Macs
"Managua, Nicaragua"	1947	Freddy Martin & orchestra
"Moonlight in Vermont"	1945	Billy Butterfield & orchestra
"A Nightingale Sang in Berkeley Square"	1940	Glenn Miller & orchestra
"Oh, What a Beautiful Mornin'"	1943	Bing Crosby
"Oklahoma"	1943	Alfred Drake
"Old Devil Moon"	1947	Ella Logan & Donald Richards
"The Old Lamplighter"	1946	Sammy Kaye & orchestra
"Opus One"	1945	Tommy Dorsey
"Peg O' My Heart"	1947	The Harmonicats
"People Will Say We're in Love"	1943	Alfred Drake & Joan Roberts
"Poinciana"	1943	David Rose & orchestra
"Polka Dots and Moonbeams"	1940	Tommy Dorsey & orchestra
"Red Roses for a Blue Lady"	1948	Guy Lombardo & Royal Canadians
"Saturday Night Is the Loneliest Night of the Week"	1944	Frank Sinatra
"Say Si Si"	1940	Xavier Cugat & orchestra
"Seems Like Old Times"	1946	Guy Lombardo & Royal Canadians
"Sentimental Journey"	1944	Les Brown & orchestra
"Shoo Fly Pie and Apple Pan Dowdy"	1946	Dinah Shore
"Speak Low"	1943	Guy Lombardo & Royal Canadians
"A String of Pearls"	1942	Glenn Miller & orchestra
"A Sunday Kind of Love"	1946	Claude Thornhill & orchestra
"The Surrey with the Fringe on Top"	1943	Alfred Drake & Joan Roberts
"Swinging on a Star"	1944	Bing Crosby
"Tangerine"	1942	Jimmy Dorsey
"Tenderly"	1946	Sarah Vaughan
"Tennessee Waltz"	1948	Patti Page
"That Old Black Magic"	1942	Billy Daniels
"There Must Be a Way"	1945	Charlie Spirak & orchestra vocal Jimmy Saunders
"The Things We Did Last Summer"	1946	Sinatra
"Tuxedo Junction"	1940	Erskine Hawkins & orchestra
"When You Wish upon a Star"	1940	Cliff Edwards (as Jiminy Cricket)
"Wunderbar"	1949	Alfred Drake & Patricia Morrison
"You Can't Be True Dear"	1948	Ken Griffin & Jerry Wayne
"You'd Be So Nice to Come Home To"	1942	Don Ameche & Janet Blair
"You'll Never Walk Alone"	1945	Christine Johnson
"You Made Me Love You—I Didn't Want to Do It"	1941	Harry James & orchestra
"Younger Than Springtime"	1949	William Tabbert
"Zip-A-Dee-Doo-Dah"	1945	Johnny Mercer & the Pied Pipers

LIST 7.25 TOP TUNES OF THE 1950'S

"Ain't That a Shame"	1955	Fats Domino
"All I Have to Do Is Dream"	1958	Everly Brothers
"All Shook Up"	1957	Elvis Presley
"April Love"	1957	Pat Boone
"Around the World"	1956	Victor Young & orchestra
"Arrivederci, Roma"	1954	Georgia Gibbs
"At the Hop"	1957	Danny & the Jrs.
"Autumn Leaves"	1950	Roger Williams & orchestra
"Ballad of Davy Crocket"	1955	Bill Hayes
"Banana Boat Song"	1956	Harry Belafonte
"Blue Suede Shoes"	1955	Elvis Presley
"Blue Tango"	1951	Leroy Anderson & orchestra
"Blue Velvet"	1951	Tony Bennett
"Bye Bye, Love"	1957	Everly Brothers
"Canadian Sunset"	1956	Hugo Winterhalter & orchestra
"Cara Mia"	1954	David Whitfield
"C'est Si Bon"	1950	Johnny Desmond
"Chain Gang"	1956	Bobby Scott
"Chantilly Lace"	1958	Jerry Lee Lewis
"Cherry Pink and Apple Blossom White"	1951	Perez Prado & orchestra
"Climb Every Mountain"	1959	Patricia Neway
"Cry"	1951	Johnny Ray
"Crying in the Chapel"	1953	The Orioles
"Don't Be Cruel"	1956	Elvis Presley
"Earth Angel"	1955	The Crew Cuts
"Ebb Tide"	1953	Frank Chacksfield & orchestra
"Enjoy Yourself"	1950	Guy Lombardo & Royal Canadians
"Everything's Coming Up Roses"	1959	Ethel Merman
"Fever"	1956	Peggy Lee
"Frosty the Snowman"	1951	Gene Autry
"The Glow Worm"	1952	Mills Brothers
"Goodnight, Irene"	1950	The Weavers
"Great Balls of Fire"	1957	Jerry Lee Lewis
"The Green Door"	1956	Jim Lowe
"Heartbreak Hotel"	1956	Elvis Presley
"Here's That Rainy Day"	1953	John Raitt
"Hound Dog"	1956	Elvis Presley
"I Believe"	1953	Frankie Lane
"I Love Paris"	1953	Les Baxter & orchestra
"I'm Yours"	1952	The Four Aces
"It's All in the Game"	1951	Tommy Edwards
"It's Just a Matter of Time"	1959	Brook Benton
"Itsy Bitsy Teenie Weenie Yellow Polka Dot Bikini"	1960	Brian Hyland
"Jailhouse Rock"	1957	Elvis Presley
"Just in Time"	1956	Judy Holliday
"Kisses Sweeter than Wine"	1957	Jimmie Rodgers
"Lady of Spain"	1952	Eddie Fisher
"Let Me Go, Lover"	1954	Joan Weber
"Love Is a Many Splendored Thing"	1955	The Four Aces
"Love Letters in the Sand"	1957	Pat Boone
"Love Me Tender"	1956	Elvis Presley

List 7.25 (continued)

Song	Year	Artist
"Mack the Knife"	1959	Bobby Darin
"Misty"	1959	Johnny Mathis
"Mona Lisa"	1959	Nat "King" Cole
"Mr. Wonderful"	1956	Olga James
"Music! Music! Music!"	1950	Teresa Brewer
"Oh! My Pa-pa"	1953	Eddie Fisher
"Old Cape Cod"	1956	Patti Page
"Only You"	1955	The Platters
"On the Street Where You Live"	1956	Vic Damone
"The Party's Over"	1956	Judy Holliday
"The Poor People of Paris"	1956	Les Baxter
"Rag Mop"	1950	The Ames Brothers
"Rock and Roll Waltz"	1956	Kay Starr
"Rock Around the Clock"	1953	Bill Haley & the Comets
"Satin Doll"	1958	Ella Fitzgerald
"Shake, Rattle and Roll"	1954	Elvis Presley
"Sh-Boom"	1954	The Crew Cuts
"Shrimp Boats"	1951	Jo Stafford
"Sincerely"	1955	McGuire Sisters
"Singing the Blues"	1956	Guy Mitchell
"Sixteen Tons"	1959	Tennessee Ernie Ford
"Smile"	1959	Tony Bennett
"Stranger in Paradise"	1953	The Four Aces
"Tammy"	1957	Debbie Reynolds
"Teddy Bear"	1957	Elvis Presley
"That's All"	1952	Nat "King" Cole
"That's Amore"	1954	Dean Martin
"They Call the Wind Maria"	1954	Rufus Smith
"Three Coins in the Fountain"	1954	Frank Sinatra
"Tom Dooley"	1958	Kingston Trio
"True Love"	1956	Bing Crosby & Grace Kelly
"Tutti-Frutti"	1955	Little Richard
"Unchained Melody"	1955	Les Baxter & orchestra
"Unforgettable"	1951	Nat "King" Cole
"Vaya Con Dios"	1953	Les Paul & Mary Ford
"Venus"	1959	Frankie Avalon
"Wake Up Little Susie"	1957	Everly Brothers
"The Wayward Wind"	1956	Gogi Grant
"Wheel of Fortune"	1952	Kay Starr
"When I Fall in Love"	1951	Nat "King" Cole
"Wonderful! Wonderful!"	1957	Johnny Mathis
"Yellow Rose of Texas"	1955	Mitch Miller
"Young at Heart"	1954	Frank Sinatra

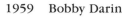

LIST 7.26   TOP TUNES OF THE 1960'S

Song	Year	Artist
"Alley Cat Song"	1962	Bent Fabric
"Alley Oop"	1960	The Hollywood Argyles
"Aquarius"	1967	The Fifth Dimension
"As Long as He Needs Me"	1960	Shirley Bassey
"As Tears Go By"	1966	The Rolling Stones
"Blowin' in the Wind"	1963	Peter, Paul & Mary
"By The Time I Get to Phoenix"	1967	Glen Campbell
"Cabaret"	1966	Herb Alpert & the Tijuana Brass
"California Dreamin'"	1965	The Mamas & the Papas
"Can't Help Falling in Love"	1961	Elvis Presley
"Chapel of Love"	1964	The Dixie Cups
"Cherish"	1965	The Association
"Cathy's Clown"	1960	Everly Brothers
"Daydream"	1966	The Lovin' Spoonful
"Daydream Believer"	1967	The Monkees
"The Days of Wine and Roses"	1962	Henry Mancini & orchestra, vocal Andy Williams
"Dominique"	1963	The Singing Nun
"Downtown"	1964	Petula Clark
"Duke of Earl"	1962	Gene Chandler
"The Exodus Song"	1960	Ferrante & Teicher
"Ferry Cross the Mersey"	1964	Gerry & the Pacemakers
"Fly Me to The Moon"	1965	Tony Bennett
"Georgy Girl"	1966	The Seekers
"The Girl from Ipanema"	1964	Stan Getz, Joao Gilberto, Astrud Gilberto
"Go Away Little Girl"	1963	The Happenings
"Goin' Out of My Head"	1964	Little Anthony & the Imperials
"Green Green Grass Of Home"	1965	Tom Jones
"Green Tambourine"	1967	The Lemon Pipers
"Groovin'"	1967	Young Rascals
"Guantanamera"	1963	The Sandpipers
"Hang on Sloopy"	1964	The McCoys
"Happy Together"	1967	The Turtles
"A Hard Day's Night"	1964	The Beatles
"Hello Mary Lou"	1961	Ricky Nelson
"Help!"	1965	The Beatles
"Hey Jude"	1968	John Lennon & Paul McCartney
"Hit the Road, Jack"	1961	Ray Charles
"Honey"	1968	Bobby Goldsboro
"If Ever I Would Leave You"	1960	Robert Goulet
"If I Had a Hammer"	1962	Peter, Paul & Mary
"If I Were a Carpenter"	1966	Bobby Darin
"I Heard It Through the Grapevine"	1968	Marvin Gaye
"I Left My Heart in San Francisco"	1962	Tony Bennett
"I'm a Believer"	1967	The Monkees
"It's My Party"	1963	Leslie Gore
"It's Not Unusual"	1965	Tom Jones
"I Want to Hold Your Hand"	1964	The Beatles
"King of the Road"	1964	Roger Miller
"Light My Fire"	1967	The Doors
"Little Green Apples"	1968	O.C. Smith
"Louie, Louie"	1963	The Kingsmen

"Love Is Blue"	1968	Paul Mauriat & orchestra
"Monday, Monday"	1966	The Mamas & the Papas
"Monster Mash"	1962	Bobby Pickett & the Crypt-Kickers
"Moody River"	1961	Pat Boone
"More"	1963	Kai Winding & orchestra
"My Coloring Book"	1962	Sandy Stewart
"My Cup Runneth Over"	1966	Ed Ames
"Na Na Hey Hey Kiss Him Goodbye"	1969	Steam
"Never on Sunday"	1960	Don Costa & orchestra
"One Tin Soldier"	1969	Original Caste
"Only the Lonely"	1960	Roy Orbison
"Our Day Will Come"	1963	Ruby & the Romantics
"Paper Roses"	1960	Anita Bryant
"People"	1964	Barbra Streisand
"Please, Please Me"	1964	The Beatles
"Proud Mary"	1969	Creedence Clearwater Revival
"Raindrops"	1961	Dee Clark
"Raindrops Keep Fallin' on My Head"	1969	B.J. Thomas
"Return to Sender"	1962	Elvis Presley
"Runaround Sue"	1961	Dion
"San Francisco"	1967	Scott McKenzie
"Satisfaction"	1965	The Rolling Stones
"She Loves You"	1964	The Beatles
"Sherry"	1962	The Four Seasons
"Soldier Boy"	1962	The Shirelles
"So Much in Love"	1963	The Tymes
"The Sounds of Silence"	1965	Simon & Garfunkel
"Spanish Harlem"	1961	Ben E. King
"Strangers in the Night"	1966	Bert Kaempfert & orchestra, vocal Frank Sinatra
"Sunrise, Sunset"	1964	Roger Williams & orchestra
"Teen Angel"	1960	Mark Dinning
"That's Life"	1964	Ocie Smith; 1966, Frank Sinatra
"The Twist"	1960	Chubby Checker
"Things"	1962	Bobby Darin
"Those Were the Days"	1968	Mary Hopkin
"Travelin' Man"	1961	Ricky Nelson
"Try to Remember"	1960	The Brothers Four
"Turn! Turn! Turn!"	1965	The Byrds
"Up, Up and Away"	1967	The Fifth Dimension
"Watch What Happens"	1964	Jean-Paul Vignon
"What Kind of Fool Am I?"	1962	Sammy Davis, Jr.
"Where Have All the Flowers Gone?"	1961	The Kingston Trio
"Where the Boys Are"	1961	Connie Francis
"A Whiter Shade of Pale"	1967	Procol Harum
"Who Can I Turn To"	1964	Tony Bennett
"Windy"	1967	The Association
"Wooden Heart"	1961	Joe Dowell
"Yesterday, When I Was Young"	1969	Roy Clark
"You've Made Me So Very Happy"	1969	Blood, Sweat and Tears

LIST 7.27   TOP TUNES OF THE 1970'S

"Afternoon Delight"	1976	Starland Vocal Band
"After The Love Has Gone"	1979	Earth Wind & Fire
"American Pie"	1971	Don McLean
"American Woman"	1970	Guess Who
"Annie's Song"	1974	John Denver
"Baby, Come Back"	1978	Player
"Bad Bad Leroy Brown"	1973	Jim Croce
"Brandy"	1972	Looking Glass
"Candy Man"	1971	Sammy Davis, Jr.
"Cat's in the Cradle"	1974	Harry Chapin
"Cracklin' Rosie"	1970	Neil Diamond
"Crocodile Rock"	1973	Elton John
"Delta Dawn"	1972	Helen Reddy
"Dreams"	1977	Fleetwood Mac
"Dream Weaver"	1976	Gary Wright
"Ease on Down the Road"	1975	Consumer Rapport
"Evergreen"	1976	Barbra Streisand
"Fly Like an Eagle"	1977	Steve Miller Band
"Heartache Tonight"	1979	The Eagles
"Hooked on a Feeling"	1974	The Blue Suede
"Hot Child in the City"	1978	Nick Gilder
"How Deep Is Your Love"	1977	Bee Gees
"I Am Woman"	1972	Helen Reddy
"I Feel the Earth Move"	1971	Carole King
"I Just Want to Be Your Everything"	1977	Andy Gibb
"I Think I Love You"	1970	Partridge Family
"I Wish"	1977	Stevie Wonder
"I Write the Songs"	1976	Barry Manilow
"Jazzman"	1974	Carole King
"Jive Talkin'"	1975	Bee Gees
"Joy to the World"	1971	Three Dog Night
"Killing Me Softly with His Song"	1973	Roberta Flack
"Knock Three Times"	1971	Tony Orlando & Dawn
"Last Dance"	1978	Donna Summer
"Lean on Me"	1972	Bill Withers
"Let It Be"	1970	The Beatles
"Let Your Love Flow"	1976	Bellamy Brothers
"Listen to What the Man Said"	1975	Paul McCartney & Wings
"Loves Me Like a Rock"	1973	Paul Simon
"Lyin' Eyes"	1975	The Eagles
"Mandy"	1975	Barry Manilow
"Midnight Train to Georgia"	1973	Gladys Knight & the Pips
"My Sweet Lord"	1970	George Harrison
"Night Fever"	1977	Bee Gees
"Ramblin' Man"	1973	The Allman Brothers
"Rhinestone Cowboy"	1974	Glen Campbell
"Rock with You"	1979	Michael Jackson

"Shadow Dancing"	1978	Andy Gibb
"Shake Your Booty"	1979	The Jacksons
"Southern Nights"	1977	Glenn Campbell
"Stayin' Alive"	1977	Bee Gees
"Sunshine on My Shoulders"	1974	John Denver
"Thank God I'm a Country Boy"	1975	John Denver
"The First Time Ever I Saw Your Face"		Roberta Flack
"The Tears of a Clown"	1970	The Miracles
"The Way We Were"	1973	Barbra Streisand
"Tie a Yellow Ribbon Round the Ole Oak Tree"	1973	Tony Orlando & Dawn
"Time In A Bottle"	1974	Jim Croce
"Tonight's the Night"	1976	Rod Stewart
"Torn Between Two Lovers"	1977	Mary MacGregor
"You Are the Sunshine of My Life"	1973	Stevie Wonder
"You Decorated My Life"	1979	Kenny Rogers
"You Don't Bring Me Flowers"	1978	Neil Diamond & Barbra Streisand
"You Light Up My Life"	1977	Debby Boone

LIST 7.28   TOP TUNES OF THE 1980'S

"Abracadabra"	1982	Steve Miller Band
"Addicted to Love"	1986	Robert Palmer
"All Out of Love"	1980	Air Supply
"Always on My Mind"	1982	Willie Nelson
"Another One Bites the Dust"	1980	Queen
"Beat It"	1982	Michael Jackson
"Betty Davis Eyes"	1981	Kim Carnes
"Billie Jean"	1983	Michael Jackson
"Blessed Are the Believers"	1981	Anne Murray
"Borderline"	1983	Madonna
"Born in the U.S.A."	1985	Bruce Springsteen
"Breakdance"	1984	Irene Cara
"Call Me"	1980	Blondie
"Celebration"	1981	Kool & the Gang
"Cool Love"	1981	Pablo Cruise
"Could I Have This Dance"	1980	Anne Murray
"Crazy Little Thing Called Love"	1980	Queen
"Do That to Me One More Time"	1980	The Captain & Tennille
"Down Under"	1982	Men at Work
"Ebony and Ivory"	1982	Stevie Wonder & Paul McCartney
"Elvira"	1981	Oakridge Boys

List 7.28 (continued)

"Endless Love"	1981	Diana Ross
"Every Breath You Take"	1983	The Police
"Eye of the Tiger"	1982	Survivor
"Faith"	1987	George Michael
"Feels So Right"	1981	Alabama
"Games People Play"	1981	Alan Parsons Project
"Glory Days"	1984	Bruce Springsteen
"Got My Mind Set on You"	1987	George Harrison
"Graceland"	1986	Paul Simon
"Heaven Is a Place on Earth"	1987	Belinda Carlisle
"Hold on to the Nights"	1988	Richard Marx
"If You Don't Know Me by Now"	1989	Simply Red
"I Just Called to Say I Love You"	1984	Stevie Wonder
"In America"	1980	Charlie Daniels Band
"Islands in the Stream"	1983	Kenny Rogers & Dolly Parton
"I Wouldn't Have Missed It for the World"	1982	Ronnie Milsap
"Jump"	1983	Van Halen
"Key Largo"	1982	Bertie Higgins
"Kyrie"	1986	Mr. Mister
"Like a Virgin"	1984	Madonna
"Livin' on a Prayer"	1987	Bon Jovi
"Make It Real"	1988	The Jets
"My Prerogative"	1989	Bobby Brown
"Need You Tonight"	1987	Inxs
"Never Knew Love Like This Before"	1980	Stephanie Mills
"9-5"	1981	Dolly Parton
"One More Night"	1985	Phil Collins
"On My Own"	1986	Patti LaBelle & Michael McDonald
"On the Road Again"	1980	Willie Nelson
"Open Your Heart"	1987	Madonna
"Physical"	1981	Olivia Newton-John
"Right Here Waiting"	1989	Richard Marx
"Saving All My Love for You"	1985	Whitney Houston
"Say You, Say Me"	1985	Lionel Richie
"Shake You Down"	1987	Gregory Abbott
"Should've Known Better"	1987	Richard Marx
"Straight Up"	1989	Paula Abdul
"Take My Breath Away"	1986	Berlin
"The Greatest Love of All"	1986	Whitney Houston
"The Look"	1989	Roxette
"Toy Soldiers"	1989	Martika
"True Colors"	1986	Cyndi Lauper
"Upside Down"	1980	Diana Ross
"We Built This City"	1985	Starship
"What's Love Got to Do with It"	1984	Tina Turner
"When I See You Smile"	1989	Big English
"Where Do Broken Hearts Go?"	1987	Whitney Houston

LIST 7.29 TOP TUNES OF THE 1990'S

"Achy Breaky Heart"	1992	Billy Ray Cyrus
"All For Love"	1994	Bryan Adams/Rod Stewart/Sting
"All 4 Love"	1992	Color Me Badd
"All Around the World"	1990	Lisa Stansfield
"All That She Wants"	1994	Ace of Base
"All the Man That I Need"	1991	Whitney Houston
"Always Be My Baby"	1996	Mariah Carey
"Another Day in Paradise"	1990	Phil Collins
"A Whole New World"	1993	Peabo Bryson & Regina Belle
"Baby Baby"	1991	Amy Grant
"Baby Got Back"	1992	Sir Mix-A-Lot
"Because You Loved Me"	1996	Celine Dion
"Beauty and the Beast"	1992	Celine Dion & Peabo Bryson
"Because I Love You"	1990	Stevie B.
"Black Cat"	1990	Janet Jackson
"Black Velvet"	1990	Allanah Myles
"Blaze of Glory"	1990	Jon Bon Jovi
"Breathe Again"	1994	Toni Braxton
"Can't Help Falling in Love"	1993	UB40
"Close to You"	1990	Maxi Priest
"Cradle of Love"	1990	Billy Idol
"Dazzey Duks"	1993	Duice
"Do Me!"	1990	Bell Biv DeVoe
"Don't Let Go"	1997	En Vogue
"Don't Speak"	1994	No Doubt
"Don't Turn Around"	1994	Ace of Base
"Don't Want to Fall in Love"	1990	Jane Child
"Downtown Train"	1990	Rod Stewart
"Dreamlover"	1993	Mariah Carey
"Emotions"	1991	Mariah Carey
"End of the Road" (From "Boomerang")	1992	Boyz II Men
"Escapade"	1990	Janet Jackson
"Everything I Do I Do It for You"	1991	Bryan Adams
"Fantasy"	1996	Mariah Carey
"First Time"	1991	Surface
"Freak Me"	1993	Silk
"From a Distance"	1990	Bette Midler
"Give Me One Reason"	1996	Tracy Chapman
"Gonna Make You Sweat"	1991	C&C Music Factory
"Head Over Feet"	1997	Alanis Morissette
"Hero"	1994	Mariah Carey
"High Enough"	1991	Damn Yankees
"Hold On"	1990	Wilson Phillips
"How Am I Supposed to Live"	1990	Michael Bolton
"I Believe"	1995	Blessed Union of Souls
"Ice Ice Baby"	1990	Vanilla Ice
"I'd Do Anything for Love"	1993	Meat Loaf
"I Don't Have the Heart"	1990	James Ingram
"If I Ever Fall in Love"	1993	Shai
"If Wishes Come True"	1990	Sweet Sensation
"I Know"	1995	Dionne Farris
"I'll Be There for You"	1995	The Rembrandts
"I'll Be Your Everything"	1990	Tommy Page
"I'll Make Love to You"	1994	Boyz II Men
"I Love Your Smile"	1992	Shanice

List 7.29 (continued)

Title	Year	Artist
"I'm Too Sexy"	1992	Right Said Fred
"Informer"	1993	Snow
"I Swear"	1994	All-4-One
"Ironic"	1996	Alanis Morissette
"I the Way"	1991	High-Five
"It Must Have Been Love"	1990	Roxette
"I Wanna Sex You Up"	1991	Color Me Badd
"I Will Always Love You"	1993	Whitney Houston
"Jump"	1992	Kris Kross
"Jump Around"	1992	House of Pain
"Killing Me Softly"	1996	Fugees
"Kiss from a Rose"	1995	Seal
"Knockin' Da Boots"	1993	H-Town
"Let Her Cry"	1995	Hootie & the Blowfish
"Lovefool"	1997	Cardigans
"Love Is A Wonderful Thing"	1991	Michael Bolton
"Love Takes Time"	1990	Mariah Carey
"Love Will Lead You Back"	1990	Taylor Dayne
"Love Will Never Do"	1991	Janet Jackson
"Macarena"	1996	Los Del Rio/Bayside Boys Mix
"Missing"	1996	Everything But the Girl
"More Than Words"	1991	Extreme
"Nothing Compares 2 U"	1990	Sinead O'Connor
"November Rain"	1992	Guns N' Roses
"Nuthin' But A G Thang"	1993	Dr. Dre
"One More Try"	1991	Timmy T
"One Sweet Day"	1996	Mariah Carey with Boyz II Men
"Opposites Attract"	1990	Paula Abdul with the Wild Pair
"Poison"	1990	Bell Biv DeVoe
"Praying for Time"	1990	George Michael
"Pump Up the Jam"	1990	Technotronic
"Release Me"	1990	Wilson Phillips
"Roam"	1990	The B-52s
"Rump Shaker"	1993	Wreckx-N-Effect
"Run Around"	1995	Blues Traveler
"Rush Rush"	1991	Paula Abdul
"The Sign"	1994	Ace of Base
"Smells Like Teen Spirit"	1992	Nirvana
"Someday"	1991	Mariah Carey
"Stay (I Missed You)"	1992	Lisa Loeb & Nine Stories
"Step by Step"	1990	New Kids on the Block
"Take a Bow"	1995	Madonna
"Tears in Heaven"	1992	Eric Clapton
"Tha Crossroads"	1996	Bone Thugs-N-Harmony
"The Power of Love"	1994	Celine Dion
"To Be With You"	1992	Mr. Big
"Unbelievable"	1991	Natalie Cole/Nat "King" Cole
"Under the Bridge"	1992	Red Hot Chili Peppers
"Unskinny Bop"	1990	Poison
"Vision of Love"	1990	Mariah Carey
"Vogue"	1990	Madonna
"Waterfalls"	1995	TLC
"Water Runs Dry"	1995	Boyz II Men
"When a Man Loves a Woman"	1991	Michael Bolton
"When I Come Around"	1995	Green Day
"Whoomp! (There It Is)"	1993	Tag Team
"You Learn"	1996	Alanis Morissette
"You're Makin' Me High"	1996	Toni Braxton

LIST 7.30 POP MUSIC ORGANIZATIONS

Academy of Country Western Music
6255 Sunset Blvd., Suite 923
Hollywood, CA 90028

American Federation of Musicians
Paramount Bldg.
1501 Broadway, Suite 600
New York, NY 10036

American Guild of Music
5354 Washington St.
Downers Grove, IL 60515

American Guild of Musical Artists
1727 Broadway
New York, NY 10019

American Society of Composers, Authors,
  and Publishers
1 Lincoln Plaza
New York, NY 10023

The Blues Foundation
PO Box 241546
Memphis, TN 38124

Country Music Association
7 Music Circle N.
PO Box 22299
Nashville, TN 37202

National Academy of Popular Music
875 3rd Ave., 8th Floor
New York, NY 10022

National Academy of Recording Arts
  and Sciences
303 North Glenoaks Blvd., Suite 140
Burbank, CA 91502-1178

National Music Council
Box 5551
Englewood, NJ 07631-5551

National Music Publishers Association
205 East 42nd St., 18th Floor
New York, NY 10017

Recording Industry Association of America
1020 19th St. NW, Suite 200
Washington, DC 20036

Songwriters' Guild of America
276 5th Ave.
New York, NY 10001

LIST 7.31 AMERICAN MUSIC FESTIVALS WHICH INCLUDE POPULAR MUSIC

American Folksong Festival	Olive Hill, KY	Summer
Annual National Ragtime Festival	St. Louis, MO	June
Artpack	Lewiston, NY	Summer
Asheville Mountain Dance and Folk Festival	Asheville, NC	August
Aspen Music Festival	Aspen, CO	Summer
Britt Festivals	Jacksonville, FL	Summer
Concord Summer Jazz Festival	Concord, CA	July
Festival of American Folklife	Washington, DC	Summer
Flagstaff Festival of the Arts	Flagstaff, AZ	Summer
Florida Folk Festival	White Springs, FL	May
Interarts Summer Festival	Honolulu, HI	June–July
Interlochen Arts Festival	Interlochen, MI	Summer
Kool Jazz Festival	Newport, RI	Summer
Mississippi River Festival	Edwardsville, IL	Summer
Monterey Jazz Festival	Monterey, CA	September
National Folk Festival	Washington, DC	Summer
New England Folk Festival	Natick, MA	April
New Orleans Jazz and Heritage Festival	New Orleans, LA	April
Ozark Folk Festival	Eureka Springs, AR	October
Philadelphia Folk Festival	Philadelphia, PA	August
Ravinia Festival	Chicago, IL	Summer
Singing on the Mountain	Linville, NC	June
Summerfest	Milwaukee, WI	Summer
Tanglewood Music Festival	Lenox, MA	Summer
Waterloo Music Festival	Stanhope, NJ	Summer

LIST 7.32 FAMOUS "FATHERS"

"THE FATHER OF . . ."	NAME
Bluegrass Music	Bill Monroe
The Blues	William C. Handy
Boogie-Woogie	Jimmy Yancey
British Blues	John Mayall
Country Music	Jimmie Rodgers
Delta Blues	Robert Johnson
Folk Rock	Bob Dylan
Gospel Music	Thomas A. Dorsey
Rhythm & Blues	Louis Jordan
Rock & Roll	Arthur "Big Boy" Crudup/Bill Haley
Soul	Ray Charles
The Daddy of Western Swing	Bob Wills
Grandfather of British Rock	Joh Mayall

LIST 7.33 FAMOUS "MISTERS"

Mr. C	Perry Como	Mr. Personality	Lloyd Price
Mr. Dynamite	James Brown	Mr. Pitiful	Otis Redding
Mr. Guitar	Chet Atkins		

LIST 7.34 "ROYAL" COGNOMENS

Empress of the Blues	Bessie Smith
High Priestess of Soul	Nina Simone
King Freak of New York	Lou Reed
King of Calypso	Harry Belafonte
King of the Crooners	Bing Crosby
King of Delta Blues	Robert Johnson
King of Hillbilly Piano Players	Moon Mullican
King of Jazz	Paul Whiteman
King of the Mambo	Perez Prado & Tito Puente
King of Mountain Music	Roy Acuff
King of Progressive Country	Willie Nelson
King of Ragtime	Scott Joplin
King of the Road	Roger Miller
King of Rock & Soul	Solomon Burke
King of the Stroll	Chuck Willis
King of the Surf	Trini Lopez
King of Swing	Benny Goodman
King of the 12-String Guitar	Huddie Ledbetter
King of Western Pop	Elvis Presley
King of Western Swing	Spade Cooley
Kings of Rhythm	Ike Turner's Band
Kings of Rock Comedy	Cheech & Chong
Lady	Billie Holiday
Lady Soul	Aretha Franklin
March King	John Philip Sousa
Queen of the Blues	Dinah Washington
Queen of Country Music	Mother Maybelle Carter
Queen of Folk	Joan Baez
Queen of Gospel Singers	Mahalia Jackson
Queen of the Jukeboxes	Dinah Washington
Queen of Ragtime Pianists	Del Wood
Queen of Rock	Janis Joplin, Carly Simon, Carole King, Rita Coolidge
Sheik of the Shake	Chuck Willis
Uncrowned Queen of the Blues	Ida Cox

LIST 7.35 MUSICIAN COGNOMENS

Bear Cat	Rufus Thomas	Guitar Man	Jerry Reed
Big Bill	William Lee Conley Broonzy	Hillbilly Cat	Elvis Presley
Big Bopper	J.P. Richardson	Iceman	Jerry Butler
Big Mama	Willie Mae Thornton	Killer	Jerry Lee Lewis
Bird	Charlie Parker	Leadbelly	Huddie Ledbetter
The Birdman	Pete Townshend	Lizard King	Jim Morrison
Bix	Leon Bismarck Beiderbecke	Midnight Idol	Wayne Newton
Black Elvis	Jimi Hendrix	Ol' Blue Eyes	Frank Sinatra
Black Moses	Isaac Hayes	Paris's Black Pearl	Dionne Warwick
The Black Swan	Elizabeth Taylor Greenfield	Pearl	Janis Joplin
Boss of the Blues	Joe Turner	Professor Longhair	Roy Byrd
Cadillac Jack	Shakey Harris	Rabbit	Johnny Hodges
The Divine Miss M	Bette Midler	Satchmo	Louis Armstrong
The Divine Sarah	Sarah Vaughan	Silver Fox	Charlie Rich
Diz	John Birks Gillespie	Slowhand	Eric Clapton
Duke	Edward Kennedy Ellington	Sweet Mama Stringbean	Ethel Waters
The Fab Four	The Beatles	Tennessee Plowboy	Eddy Arnold
Fatha	Earl Hines	Tiny Tim	Herbert Khoury
First Tycoon of Teen	Phil Spector	Willie the Lion	William Henry Smith
Frogman	Clarence Henry	Wonder Boy Preacher	Solomon Burke
The Groaner	Bing Crosby	Yardbird	Charlie Parker

LIST 7.36 DRUG RELATED ROCK AND ROLL DEATHS

1967	Brian Epstein	manager of The Beatles
1968	Frankie Lymon	of The Teenagers
1969	Brian Jones	of The Rolling Stones
1970	Alan Wilson	of Canned Heat
	Janis Joplin	
	Jimi Hendrix	
1971	Jim Morrison	of The Doors
1972	Danny Whitten	of Crazy Horse
	Brian Cole	of the Association
	Clyde McPhatter	
	Billy Murcia	of The New York Dolls
1973	Graham Parsons	of The Byrds
1974	Robbie McIntosh	of The Average White Band
	Nick Drake	
1975	Tim Buckley	
	Tommy Bolin	
1976	Florence Ballard	of The Supremes
1977	Elvis Presley	
1978	Keith Moon	of The Who
1979	Sid Vicious	of The Sex Pistols
	Jimmy McCullogh	
	Lowell George	of Little Feat
1980	John Bonham	of Led Zepplin
	Bon Scott	of AC/DC
1981	Tim Hardin	
	Michael Bloomfield	

Section VIII

DANCE

LIST 8.1   KINDS OF DANCING

abstract ballet	a ballet without a plot
ballet	theatrical dance
ballroom	social dances
barn	rural American dance in 4/4 time
clog dance	a rustic dance done in wooden-soled shoes
cotillion	popular ballroom dance in which the lead couple chooses the figures, and the partners constantly change
country (contradanse)	a social dance derived from a folk dance
folk	a dance that has connection to traditional life of the people
jazz	dance developed by African Americans, using African dance techniques
modern	a variety of contemporary theatrical dance styles
soft shoe	a dance related to tap, but done with soft-soled shoes
square	American folk dance in which an even number of couples are arranged in a square
stage	a dance performed primarily for the entertainment of an audience
tap	a dance that has rapid tapping of toes and heels on the floor, using shoes with metal "taps"

LIST 8.2   BALLET TERMS

adagio	*côté, de*	*en bas*	*piqué*
allegro	*cou de pied*	*en face*	*pirouette*
allongé	*coupé*	*en haut*	*plié*
arabesque	*croisé*	*en l'air*	*point*
assemblé	*danse terre-à-terre*	*entrechat*	*port de bras*
attitude	*danseur*	extension	*premier danseur*
balance	*degagé*	*fondu*	*relevé*
ballerina	*demi bras*	*fouetté*	*révérance*
ballet blanc	*demi-plié*	*glissade*	*rond de jambe*
ballet romantique	*demipointes*	*grand*	*royale*
barre	*demipointes*	*jeté*	*sauté*
basse	*derrière*	*léotard*	*serré*
battement	*devant*	notation	*sissone*
batterie	*dévelopé*	*pas de bourée*	*soubresant*
bravura	*écarté*	*pas de chat*	syllabus
chainé	*échappé*	*pas de deux*	*tendu*
changement-de-pied	*éffacé*	*pas de quatre*	turnout
chassé	*emboîté*	*pas de trois*	tights
choreography	*en arrière*	*passé*	variation
corps de ballet	*en avant*	*penché*	

LIST 8.3   FAMOUS MALE BALLET DANCERS

Robert Barnett
Mikhail Baryshnikov
Robert Blankshine
Anthony Blum
Todd Bolender
Adolphe Bolm
Erik Bruhn
Lew Christensen
Jaques D'Amboise
Anton Dolin
William Dollar
Anthony Dowell
Kaleria Fedicheva
Michel Fokine
Robert Helpmann
John Kriza
Nicholas Magallanes
Robert Maiorano
Bruce Marks

Peter Martins
Leonide Massine
Michael Maule
Arthur Mitchell
Vaslav Nijinsky
Rudolf Nureyev
Roland Petie
Marius Petipa
Derek Rencher
Lawrence Rhodes
Jerome Robbins
Yuri Soloviev
Filippo Taglioni
Vladimir Tikhonov
Anthony Tudor
Sergei Vikulov
Edward Villela
Johnathan Watts

LIST 8.4 FAMOUS FEMALE BALLET DANCERS

Diana Adams
Angele Albrecht
Lucette Aldous
Alicia Alonzo
Elena Andreyanova
Irina Baranova
Tania Bari
Deanna Bergsma
Marietta Bonfanti
June Brae
Carlotta Brianza
Karena Brock
Marilyn Burr
Hilda Butsova
Marie Camargo
Jean Coralli
Joyce Cuoco
Starr Danias
Natalia Dudinskaya
Suzanne Farrell
Olga Ferri
Dame Margo Fonteyn
Carla Fracci
Catherine Geltzer
Nana Gollner
Lucile Grahn
Cynthia Gregory
Carlotta Grisi
Melissa Hayden
Tamara Karsavina
Nora Kaye
Allegra Kent
Toni Lander
Sara Leland
Maris Liepa

Catherine Littlefield
Natalia Makarova
Alicia Markova
Monica Mason
Yekaterina Maximova
Pamela May
Kay Mazzo
Patricia McBride
Agnes de Mille
Marnee Morris
Bronislava Nijinsky
Alice Nikitina
Nadia Nurina
Mimi Paul
Anna Pavlova
Maya Plisetskaya
Olga Preobrajenska
Marie Rambert
Ida Rubinstein
Lynn Seymour
Moira Shearer
Antoinette Sibley
Lydia Sokolova
Marie Tagglioni
Maria Tallchief
Veronica Tennant
Nina Timofeyeva
Helgi Tomasson
Tamara Toumanova
Galina Ulanova
Nina Vyroubova
Dame Ninette de Valois
Sallie Wilson
Rebecca Wright

LIST 8.5 FAMOUS MALE CHOREOGRAPHERS

Alvin Ailey
Gerald Arpino
Frederick Ashton
George Balanchine
Maurice Béjart
Todd Bolender
John Butler
Jean Coralli
John Cranko
Merce Cunningham
Jean Dauberval
Anton Dolin
Eliot Feld
Michel Fokine
Yuri Grigorovich
Lev Ivanov
Robert Joffrey
Kurt Jooss
Leonid Lavrovsky

José Limón
Eugene Loring
Kenneth MacMillan
Leonide Massine
Arthur Mitchell
Dennis Nahat
Vaslav Nijinsky
Jean-Georges Noverre
Jules Perrot
Marius Petipa
Roland Petit
Wenzel Reisinger
Jerome Robbins
Arthur Saint-Léon
Filippo Taglioni
Paul Taylor
Anthony Tudor
Rotislav Zakharov

See Also List 9.23, Famous African-American Choreographers

LIST 8.6 FAMOUS FEMALE CHOREOGRAPHERS

Isadora Duncan
Katherine Dunham
Martha Graham
Hanya Holm
Doris Humphrey
Agnes de Mille
Bronislava Nijinsky

Lynn Seymour
Sybil Shearer
Anna Sokolow
Marie Taglioni
Helen Tamiris
Twyla Tharp
Dame Ninette de Valois

See Also List 9.23, Famous African-American American Choreographers

LIST 8.7 GREAT BALLETS

BALLET	COMPOSER	CHOREOGRAPHER
Appalachian Spring	Aaron Copland	Martha Graham
L'après-midi d'un faune	Claude Debussy	Jerome Robbins
Billy the Kid	Aaron Copland	Eugene Loring
Cinderella	Sergei Prokofiev	Rotislav Zakaharov
Coppelia	Léo Delibes	Arthur Saint-Leon
Eugene Onegin	Peter Tchaikovsky	John Cranko
Fancy Free	Leonard Bernstein	Jerome Robbins
Giselle	Aldophe Adam	Jules Perrot and Jean Coralli
La fille mal gardee		
(The Unchaperoned Daughter)	Ferdinand Herold	Jean Dauberval
A Midsummer Night's Dream	Felix Mendelssohn	George Balanchine
The Nutcracker	Peter Tchaikovsky	Lev Ivanov
L'Oiseau de feu		
(The Firebird)	Igor Stravinsky	Michel Fokine
Ondine	Hans Werner Henze	Frederick Ashton
Orpheus	Igor Stravinsky	George Balanchine
Petrushka	Igor Stravinsky	Michel Fokine
Rodeo	Aaron Copland	Agnes de Mille
Romeo and Juliet	Sergei Prokofiev	Leonid Lavrovsky
Le Sacre du printemps		
(The Rite of Spring)	Igor Stravinsky	Vaslav Nijinsky
Scheherazade	Nicolai Rimsky-Korsakov	Michel Fokine
Sleeping Beauty	Peter Tchaikovsky	Marius Petipa
Spartacus	Aram Khachaturian	Yuri Grigorovich
Swan Lake	Peter Tchaikovsky	Julius Reisinger
La Sylphide	Jean Schneitzhoeffer	Filippo Taglioni
The Three-Cornered Hat	Manuel de Falla	Leonid Messine

207

LIST 8.8 U.S. DANCE COMPANIES

African American Dance Ensemble
Alvin Ailey Dance Theater
Aman Folk Ensemble
American Ballet Theatre
Atlanta Ballet
Avaz International Dance Theatre
Ballet Arizona
Ballet Chicago
Ballet Hispanico of New York
BalletMet
Ballet Omaha
Ballet West
Tandy Beal and Company
Boston Ballet
Trisha Brown Company
Donald Byrd/The Group
Caribbean Dance Company
Chen and Dancers
Lucinda Childs Dance Company
The Cincinnati Ballet Company
Cleveland/San Jose Ballet
Colorado Ballet
Cunningham Dance Foundation
Dance Alloy
Dance Exchange
Danceteller
Dance Theatre of Harlem
Dayton Ballet Association
Dayton Contemporary Dance Company
Laura Dean Musicians and Dancers
Garth Fagan's Bucket Dance Theatre
Feld Ballet
Fort Worth Ballet
Joe Goode Performance Group
David Gordon Pickup Company
Martha Graham Dance Company
Hartford Ballet
Erick Hawkins Dance Company
Joseph Holmes Dance Theater
Houston Ballet
Hubbard Street Dance Company
Jazz Tap Ensemble
Margaret Jenkins Dance Company
Joffrey Ballet
Bill T. Jones/Arnie Zane Company
Rebecca Kelly Dance Company
KHADRA International Folk Ballet
Zivili Koko Ensemble
Lewitzky Dance Foundation

José Limón Dance Company
Loretta Livingson and Dancers
Los Angeles Chamber Ballet
Louisville Ballet
Lar Lubovitch Dance Company
Miami City Ballet
Bebe Miller and Company
Milwaukee Ballet
Monnaie Dance Group
Elisa Monte Dance Company
Mordine and Company
Jennifer Muller/The Works
Muntu Dance Theater
New Dance Ensemble
Rosalind Newman and Dancers
New York City Ballet
North Carolina Dance Theater
Oakland Ballet
ODC/San Francisco
Ohio Ballet
Pacific Northwest Ballet
Parsons Ballet Company
Pennsylvania Ballet
Philadanco
Pittsburgh Ballet Theatre
Pilobolus Dance Theater
Stuart Pimsler Dance and Theater
Pittsburgh Dance Alloy
Repertory Dance Theatre
Richmond Ballet
Ririe-Woodbury Dance Company
Nicholas Rodriguez/Dance Compass
San Francisco Ballet
Santana Spanish Dance Arts Company
Sarasota Ballet
Solomons Company/Dance
Southern Ballet Theater
State Ballet of Missouri
Paul Taylor Dance Company
Joyce Trisler Danscompany
Tulsa Ballet Theatre
Dan Wagoner and Dancers
Washington Ballet
Nina Wiener Dance Company
Zenon Dance Company
Zeromoving Dance Company

LIST 8.9   INTERNATIONAL DANCE COMPANIES

African Dance Company of Ghana	Ghana
Australian Ballet Company	Australia
Ballet Folklorico de Mexico	Mexico
Le Ballet National Juenesses Musicales de France	France
Ballet of Flanders	Belgium
Ballet Rambert	England
Ballet Russe de Monte Carlo	Monaco
Ballets Africans de la Republique de Guinee	Guinea
Ballets de Paris	France
Ballets des Champs-Elysees	France
Ballets Etorki	France
Ballets Modernes de Paris	France
Ballets Sopianae	Hungary
Ballet-Theatre Contemporain	France
Bat-Dor Dance Company	Israel
Batsheva Dance Company	Israel
Bayanihan Dance Company	Philippines
Berlin Ballet	Germany
Bolshoi Ballet	Russia
Dutch National Ballet	Netherlands
Gulbenkian Ballet	Portugal
Iranian National Ballet	Iran
The Israel Ballet	Israel
Kirov Ballet	Russia
Komaki Ballet	Japan
Les Grands Ballets Canadiens	Canada
London City Ballet	England
Metropolitan Ballet	England
National Ballet of Canada	Canada
National Ballet of Cuba	Cuba
The National Ballet of Finland	Finland
National Ballet of Mexico	Mexico
Netherlands Dance Theater	Netherlands
New London Ballet	England
Norwegian National Ballet	Norway
Prague Ballet	Czech Republic
The Royal Ballet	England
Royal Danish Ballet	Denmark
Royal New Zealand Ballet	New Zealand
Royal Swedish Ballet	Sweden
Royal Winnipeg Ballet	Canada
The Scottish Ballet	Scotland
University of Cape Town Ballet	South Africa

LIST 8.10   MODERN BALLROOM DANCES

cha-cha   jitterbug   mambo   rumba   tango
Charleston   lindy   polka   samba   waltz
foxtrot

LIST 8.11   FAMOUS STAGE DANCERS

Paula Abdul   Mick Jagger
Adele Astaire   Danny Kaye
Fred Astaire   Gene Kelly
Ray Bolger   Madonna
Jimmy Cagney   Ann Miller
Gower Champion   The Nicholas Brothers
Marge Champion   Donald O'Connor
Cyd Charisse   Juliet Prowse
George M. Cohan   Bill Robinson ("Bojangles")
M.C. Hammer   Ginger Rogers
Rita Hayworth   The Step Brothers
Gregory Hines   Shirley Temple
Michael Jackson   Ben Vereen

LIST 8.12   "DANCE" SONGS

These 20th century pop songs were created to be used with unique dances of the same name.

"Achy Breaky Heart"   "The Hustle"
"The Alley Cat"   "La Paloma Twist"
"Beer Barrel Polka"   "Let's do the Freddie"
"The Breakdown"   "Limbo Rock"
"Bristol Stomp"   "Macarena"
"Bugaloo"   "Mashed Potato Time"
"The Cha-Cha-Cha"   "Monkey"
"The Continental"   "Ponytime"
"Dance the Mess Around"   "Push and Pull"
"The Dipsey Doodle"   "Shimmy Shimmy"
"Do the Funky Chicken"   "Skate"
"Do the Funky Penguin"   "The Stroll"
"Frug"   "The Twist"
"Hitch Hike"   "The Wah-Watusi"
"The Hokey Pokey"   "Walking the Dog"
"The Hucklebuck"

LIST 8.13 REPRESENTATIVE DANCES OF VARIOUS NATIONS

aino kchume	Syria
ais ge	Greece
bakmaas	Finland
bao	Philippines
baroigestanz	Eastern European Jewish cultures
barong	Indonesia
berde oyun havasi	Turkey
böhmischer landler	Austria
bolero	Spain
cachucha	Spain
čiocarlanul	Rumania
conga	Cuba
debki	Syria
delilo	Turkey
doud lebska polka	Czech Republic
dubke	Arab countries
el baile bel palo	Guam
fandango	Spain
flamenco	Spain
gae Gordon	Scotland
gopak	Ukraine
guaracha	Cuba
hambo	Sweden
haplik	Philippines
harmonica	Israel
hasapiko	Greece
highland fling	Scotland
horah	Israel
horehronsky	Slovenia
horo	Rumania
ibo	Africa
iste hendek	Turkey
jarabe de la botella	Mexico
jig arglwydd caernkrfon	Wales
Jo Jon	Armenia
kalamatianos	Greece
kak-pol-lugu	Georgia
kapuvari verbunk	Hungary
karapyet	Russia
kartuli	Armenia
kecak	Indonesia
klumpakojis	Lithuania
kochari	Armenia
kohanuchka	Russia
kor csardas	Hungary
kreuz koenig	Germany

List 8.13   (continued)

krici krici tiček	Croatia
la bastringue	French Canada
la raspa	Mexico
lauterbach	Switzerland
legong	Indonesia
lesnoto	Bulgaria
mambo	Latin America
mazulinka	Slovenia
mazurka	Poland
merengue	Dominican Republic
Morris dance	England
nebesko	Serbia
oro	Bulgaria
pajduska	Bulgaria
pata pata	Nigeria
patchtanz	Eastern European Jewish cultures
polka	Bohemia
poskakuša	Bosnia
prite puti	Bulgaria
raaksi jaak	Estonia
ranchera	Argentina
reel/jig	Scotland/Ireland
Robin Ddiogg	Wales
rorospols	Norway
ruha	Finland
rumba	Cuba
samba	Brazil
sardana	Spain
savilla se bele loza	Bosnia
sheikhani	Syria
sher	Eastern European Jewish cultures
siebenschritt	Germany
siemsa berte	Ireland
sonföderhonig	Denmark
srpkinja kolo	Serbia
sword dance	Scotland
syrto	Greece
tango	Argentina
tankobushi	Japan
tantoli	Norway
tarantella	Italy
tinikling	Philippines
totur	Denmark
troika	Russia
weggis dance	Switzerland
zaroura	Syria
zhurawei	Lithuania
ziogelis	Lithuania
zweifacher	Austria

LIST 8.14   TYPES OF PRE-CLASSICAL DANCE

allemande	17th–18th century moderate striding dance of formal character with simple steps and leaping
ballo	a popular lively Italian dance of the 15th and 16th centuries, with a regular beat and song-like melodies
bassadanza	15th century sedate court dance in duple metre
basse danse	graceful 15th–16th century court dance
brando	16th century Italian equivalent of the branle
branles	collective term for French folk dances of the 16th century
calata	15th century Italian dance in triple and compound meter
canary	dance in 3/8 or 6/8, similar to a jig
carole	line or circular dance of the 12th–13th century Western Europe
chaconne	sensuous couple dance in triple time from Spain or Arabia
courante	16th century French court dance in compound time
estampie	medieval instrumental dance which consists of repeated versicles
gagliarda	lively German round dance in 2/4 time developed in the mid 1820's
galliard	17th century court dance in triple time with complicated steps
gavotte	dance in 4/4 time with steady rhythm and complicated steps; originally a court dance under Marie Antoinette
gigue	French form of the jig
jig	ancient folk dance of the British Isles; usually in 6/8 or 12/8 time
minuet	a popular French court dance with small steps and in triple time
moresca	Renaissance dance of exotic character
passacaglia	16th century Spanish dance performed in 3/4 time; popular in the court of Louis XIV of France
passamezzo	16th century Italian promenading dance
pavan	Italian court dance of the 16th–17th century, similar to the bassadanza
rigaudon	lively 15th century couples dance accompanied by singing
saltarello	14th–15th century Italian dance with rapid steps and leaps
sarabande	a dance from the Middle Ages done in triple time; it spread widely in the 17th through 18th centuries

Section IX

INTEGRATING MUSIC WITH THE CONTENT AREAS

LIST 9.1 COLONIAL AMERICAN SONGS, GAMES, AND DANCES

"Come, My Love"
"The Death of General Wolfe"
"Green Gravel"
"Jenny Jenkins"
"Johnny Has Gone for a Soldier"
"Katie Cruel"
"The Lazy Man"
"London Bridge"
"Malbrouk Cotillion"
"Milking Pails"
"Oats and Beans and Barley Grow"
"The Old Man Who Lived in the Woods"
"Old Roger Is Dead"
"Scottish Reel"
"Six-Hand Reel"
"Soldier, Soldier, Won't You Marry Me?"
"Springfield Mountain"
"Sweet William"

LIST 9.2 SONGS OF THE AMERICAN REVOLUTION

"Adams and Liberty"
"An American Frigate"
"American Hero"
"The Anacreontic Song"
"Ballad of Donald Monroe"
"Ballad of Major André"
"Ballad of Trenton"
"Barbara Allen"
"The Battle of the Kegs"
"Beneath a Weeping Willow's Shade"
"The Bennington Riflemen"
"Billy Broke Locks"
"Brandywine Quick-Step"
"Chester"
"Come Out You Continentalers"
"Cornwallis Burgoyned"
"Cornwallis Country Dance"
"David's Lamentation"
"The Deserter"
"The Dying Redcoats"
"Fare Thee Well, You Sweethearts"
"The Fate of John Burgoyne"

"Fish and Tea"
"Free America"
"The Girl I Left Behind Me"
"The Green Mountaineer"
"How Stands the Glass"
"In Good Old Colony Days"
"Johnny Has Gone for a Soldier"
"The Liberty Son"
"Marion's Men"
"My Days Have Been So Wondrous"
"Old Soldiers of the King"
"The Rebels"
"Revolutionary Tea"
"Shule Aroon"
"The Star Spangled Banner"
"A Toast"
"To the Commons"
"Washington's March"
"What a Court Hath Old England"
"Yankee Doodle"
"The Yankee Privateer"

LIST 9.3   SONGS OF THE EARLY NATIONAL PERIOD

"The Bonny Bunch of Roses"
"The Chesapeake and the Shannon"
"The Constitution and Guerriere"
"Green Grow the Rushes"
"The Hunters of Kentucky"

"Jefferson and Liberty"
"Johnny Bull, My Jo, John"
"Mrs. McGrath"
"Napolean Bonaparte"

LIST 9.4   SONGS OF THE WAR OF 1812

"The American Star"
"The Battle of Stonington"
"Benjamin Beall"
"The Boys of Ohio"
"The Dragoon Bold"
"Hey, Betty Martin"
"The Hunters of Kentucky"

"The Indian Yell"
"The New Yankee Doodle Dandy"
"Parliament of England"
"Patriotic Diggers"
"The Star Spangled Banner"
"The Yankee Girls"
"The Yankee Volunteers"

LIST 9.5   SONGS OF THE SEA AND IMMIGRATION

"Across the Western Ocean"
"The Banks of Newfoundland"
"Blood-Red Roses"
"Blow the Man Down"
"Blow Ye Winds"
"Cape Cod Chanty"
"The Castle of Dormore"
"The Erie Canal"
"The Farmer's Curst Wife"
"The Golden Vanity"
"The Greenland Whale Fishery"
"Haul on the Bowline"
"Leave Her, Johnny, Leave Her"
"Off to the Sea Once More"
"The Pesky Sarpent"
"The Praties, They Grow Small"

LIST 9.6 SONGS OF THE PIONEERS AND WESTWARD EXPANSION

"Buckskin Buddies"
"Buckskin Buddies' Reprise"
"Buffalo Gals"
"Canaan Land"
"Chinquapin's Soliloquy"
"Daniel and Rebecca's Wedding Song"
"Daniel! Daniel!"
"The Dying Californian"
"The Fools of Forty-Nine"
"Good Gun, Good Horse, Good Wife"
"Hush, Little Baby"
"I Am the Cumberland Gap"
"Jamie's Song"
"Kentucky, My Home, Sweet Home"
"Let's Go a-Huntin'"

"Life Here on the Yadkin"
"The Lumberman's Alphabet"
"My Darling Clementine"
"Oh, Susannah"
"Old Settler's Song"
"The Riddle Song"
"Sacramento"
"Santy Anno"
"The Single Girl"
"Skip to My Lou"
"Sweet Betsy from Pike"
"When I Was Single"
"Wilderness Road"
"The Wisconsin Emigrant"

220

LIST 9.7 SONGS OF THE MEXICAN WAR

"The Battle Call"
"The Bayonet Boys"
"Buck and Gag Him"
"Buena Vista"
"Come Raise Aloft the Red, White, and Blue"
"The Death of Crockett"
"Fair Land of Texas"
"Female Volunteer for Mexico"
"Fire Away"
"Join the Hickory Blues"
"The Leg I Left Behind Me"
"Love and Battle"

"New York Volunteers' Camp Song"
"Remember the Alamo"
"Rio Bravo"
"The Song of Texas"
"Texan Rangers' Song"
"The Texas War Cry"
"Two Arms"
"Uncle Sam to Texas"
"The Union Call"
"'Way Down in Mexico"
"We're the Boys for Mexico"
"Zachary Taylor"

LIST 9.8 COWBOY SONGS

"Billy the Kid"
"The Brazos River"
"Down in the Valley"
"Dreary Black Hills"
"Get Along Little Dogies"
"Good-By, Old Paint"
"Hangman, Hangman"
"Hell in Texas"
"Independence"
"I Ride an Old Paint"
"Jesse James"
"Let the Wagon Roll"
"Little Joe the Wrangler"
"My Home's in Montana"
"Night-Herding Song"
"The Old Chisholm Trail"

"Old Paint"
"Old Texas"
"Oregon Painted Faces"
"Pioneer Trail"
"Ramblin' Shoes"
"Red River Valley"
"Sacramento"
"Shenandoah"
"The Streets of Laredo"
"Think Twice Before You Go"
"Trusty Lariat"
"Wayfarin' Stranger"
"Westward Ho!"
"Windy Bill"
"Zebra Dun"

LIST 9.9   SONGS OF SLAVERY

"Bound to Go"
"Follow the Drinking Gourd"
"Hangman, Slack on the Line"
"Hush-A-Bye" ("All the Pretty Little Horses")
"Jimmy Rose"
"Lay This Body Down"
"Poor Rosy"
"Roll, Jordan, Roll"
"The Rose of Alabama"
"Sail O Believer"
"Sold off to Georgy"
"T'aint Gonna Rain No Mo!"

LIST 9.10   NEGRO SPIRITUALS

"Beyond That Star"
"By and By"
"Do Lord Remember Me"
"Every Time I Feel the Spirit"
"Father Abraham"
"Go Down, Moses"
"The Gospel Train"
"Go Tell It on the Mountain"
"Hail! Hail! Hail!"
"I Know the Lord"
"I'm a-Rolling"
"I'm Going to Sing"
"I'm So Glad"
"In-a That Morning"
"It's Me, O Lord"
"Joshua Fit the Battle"
"Many Thousands Gone"
"Mary Had a Baby"
"Motherless Child"
"My Lord, What a Morning!"
"Old Time Religion"
"O Mary, Don't You Weep"
"Rise Up Shepherd and Follow"
"Shine, Shine"
"Sister Mary Had-a But One Child"
"Somebody's Knocking"

"Steal Away"
"Study War No More"
"Swing Low, Sweet Chariot"
"Weary Traveler"
"When Moses Smote the Water"
"When the Saints"
"You Got a Right"
"You Shall Reap"
"Zion's Children"

222

LIST 9.11   CIVIL WAR SONGS

"Abe Lincoln"
"Abide with Me"
"Abolitionist Hymn"
"All Quiet on the Potomac"
"Aura Lee"
"Battle Cry of Freedom"
"Battle Hymn of the Republic"
"The Battle of Shiloh"
"Beautiful Dreamer"
"The Bonnie Blue Flag"
"Day of Drums"
"Dixie"
"Farewell, Mother"
"Flag of Columbia"
"Goober Peas"
"Holy! Holy! Holy! Lord God Almighty"
"The Homespun Dress"
"In Charleston Jail"
"I've Been in the Storm So Long"
"John Brown's Body"
"Just Before the Battle, Mother"
"Kingdom Coming"
"La Paloma"
"Lincoln and Liberty"

"Longstreet's Rangers"
"Lorena"
"Marching Through Georgia"
"Maryland, My Maryland"
"Old Black Joe"
"Old Rebel"
"The Rebel Soldier"
"Richmond Is a Hard Road to Travel"
"Roll, Alabama Roll"
"Shenandoah"
"The Southern Soldier Boy"
"Sweet and Low"
"Tenting on the Old Camp Ground"
   ("Tenting Tonight")
"There Was an Old Soldier"
"Tramp, Tramp, Tramp"
"Twilight at Appomattox"
"The Vacant Chair"
"Wait for the Wagon"
"Weeping Sad and Lonely"
"When Johnny Comes Marching Home"
"When This Cruel War Is Over"
"Year of Jubilo"

LIST 9.12   SONGS OF THE SPANISH-AMERICAN WAR

"Bacon on the Rind"
"By Old Fort San Felipe"
"The Caraboa"
"Down by Old Manila Bay"
"A Dream"
"The Emancipated Race"
"The Filipino Hombre"
"The Governor General's Song"

"If a Lady's Wearin' Pantaloons"
"In Mindanao"
"Little Brown Brothers"
"On the Road to Old Luzon"
"A Rookie"
"El Soldado Americano"
"The Soldiers' Song"
"Transport Song"

LIST 9.13 AMERICAN WORK SONGS

"The Boll Weevil"
"Cotton Needs Pickin'"
"Drill, Ye Tarriers"
"Erie Canal"
"I've Been Workin' on the Railroad"
"Joe Hill"
"John Henry"
"Paddy Works on the Railroad"
"Pick a Bale of Cotton"

LIST 9.14   WORLD WAR I SONGS

"The Caissons Go Rolling Along"
"Down Among the Sheltering Palms"
"Goodbye Broadway, Hello France!"
"Hail! Hail! The Gang's All Here"
"It's a Long Way to Tipperary"
"Keep the Home Fires Burning"
"K-K-K-Katy" ("The Stammering Song")

"Oh, How I Hate to Get Up in the Morning"
"Oh, Johnny Oh"
"Oui, Oui Marie"
"Over There"
"Pack Up Your Troubles in Your Old Kit Bag"
"Smiles"
"There's a Long, Long Trail"

LIST 9.15   WORLD WAR II SONGS

"Air Corps Lament"
"Barnacle Bill the Pilot"
"Bless 'Em All"
"Coming in on a Wing and a Prayer"
"Don't Sit Under the Apple Tree"
"God Bless America"
"Goodnight"
"Heave To, My Lads, Heave Ho!"
"I Am an American"
"I Lost My Heart at the Stage Door Canteen"
"I've Got Sixpence"
"The Last Time I Saw Paris"
"Marines' Hymn"
"My Sister and I"
"Navy Hymn"
"No Love, No Nuthin', Till My Baby Comes Home"
"Praise the Lord and Pass the Ammunition"
"Remember Pearl Harbor"
"Song of the Navy"
"There'll Always Be an England"

"This Is the Army, Mr. Jones"
"The U.S. Air Force Song"
"Wherever You Are"
"White Christmas"
"The White Cliffs of Dover"

LIST 9.16   CIVIL RIGHTS AND PROTEST SONGS

"Ain't Gonna Let Nobody Turn Me 'Round"
"Ain't You Got a Right to the Tree of Life"
"Calypso Freedom"
"The Eve of Destruction"
"Everybody Says Freedom"
"Free at Last"
"Get on Board, Children"
"Guide My Feet"
"Hallelujah, I'm a Travellin'"
"Hold On"
"If You Miss Me from the Back of the Bus"

"I'm Gonna Sit at the Welcome Table"
"I'm on My Way"
"Oh, Freedom"
"One Little Step Toward Freedom"
"Sing Mandela Free"
"This Little Light"
"Up Over My Head"
"We Shall Not Be Moved"
"We Shall Overcome"
"Woke up This Morning with My Mind on Freedom"

LIST 9.17   PATRIOTIC SONGS

"The Battle Cry of Freedom"
"America"
"America, America"
"America the Beautiful"
"Anchors Aweigh"
"Assembly"
"Columbia, Gem of the Ocean"
"Fifty Nifty United States"
"God Bless America"
"God Bless the U.S.A."
"Hail, Columbia"
"Home, Sweet Home"
"I'm a Yankee Doodle Dandy"
"Seventy-Six Trombones"
"The Spice of America"
"The Star Spangled Banner"
"Stars and Stripes Forever"
"Texas, Our Texas"
"There Are Many Flags"
"This Is My Country"
"This Land Is Your Land"
"Three Cheers for the Red, White, and Blue"
"The United States"
"We Love the U.S.A."
"Yankee Doodle Boy"
"You're a Grand Old Flag"

LIST 9.18   NATIONAL ANTHEMS OF VARIOUS COUNTRIES

Australia	"Advance Australia Fair"
Austria	"Oesterreichische Bundeshymne" (National Hymn)
Bahamas	"March On, Bahamaland!"
Belgium	"La Brabanconne"
Bolivia	"Himno Nacional" (National Hymn)
Brazil	"Hino Nacional Brasileiro" (National Hymn)
Bulgaria	"Natsionalniyat Khim" (National Hymn)
Cambodia	"Democratic Kampuchea" (National Hymn)
Cameroon	"O Cameroun" ("Oh, Cameroon")
Canada	"Oh Canada"
China	"March of the Volunteers"
Denmark	"Kong Christian stod ved hojen mast" ("King Christian Stood by the "Lofty Mast")
Ecuador	"Salve, O patria" ("Hail, Oh Fatherland")

List 9.18   (continued)

Egypt	"Bilady, Bilady, Bilady" ("My Country, My Country")
England	"God Save the Queen"/King (depending upon ruler's gender)
Ethiopia	"Ityopia, Ityopia Kidemi" ("Ethiopia, Ethiopia, Go Forward")
Fiji	"Good Bless Fiji"
Finland	"Maamme" ("Our Land")
France	"La Marseillaise"
Germany	"Deutschlandlied"
Ghana	"Hail the Name of Ghana"
Greece	"Hymnos pros tin Elephtherian" ("Hymn to Liberty")
Guatemala	"Himno Nacional de Guatemala" (National Hymn)
Haiti	"La Dessalinienne" ("The Song of Dessalines")
Hungary	"Isten áldd meg a magyart" ("God Bless the Hungarians")
Iceland	"O Gud vors lands" ("Oh God of Our Land")
India	"Jana gana mana" ("Thou Art the Ruler")
Indonesia	"Indonesia Raya"("Greater Indonesia")
Iraq	"Al-Salaam al Jumhuriya" ("Salute of the Republic")
Ireland	"Amhran na bhFiann" ("The Soldier's Song")
Israel	"Hatikvah" ("The Hope")
Italy	"Inno de mameli" ("Mameli's Hymn")
Jamaica	"Jamaica National Anthem"
Japan	"Kimi ga yo" ("The Reign of Our Emperor")
Kenya	"Ed Mungu Nguvu Yetu" ("Oh God of Our Creation")
Lebanon	"Kulluna lil-watan" ("All for the Fatherland")
Luxembourg	"Ons hémecht" ("Our Fatherland")
Mexico	"Mexicanos, al grito de guerra" ("Mexicans, to the Cry of War")
Netherlands	"Wilhelmus van Nassouwe" ("William of Nassau")
New Zealand	"God Save the Queen"
Nicaragua	"Salve a ti, Nicaragua" ("Hail to Thee, Nicaragua")
Norway	"Ja, vi elsker dette Landet" ("Yes, We Love This Land")
Poland	"Jeszcze Polska nie zginela" ("Poland Is Not Yet Forsaken")
Portugal	"A' Portugesa" ("In the Portuguese Way")
South Africa	"The Call of South Africa"
Spain	"Marcha Real" ("Royal March")
Switzerland	"Schweizer Psalm" ("Swiss Hymn")
Turkey	"Istiklal marsi" ("Independence March")
United States of America	"The Star Spangled Banner"
Vietnam	"Tien Quan Ca" ("Forward Soldiers")

LIST 9.19   NATIONAL ANTHEMS USED IN LARGER COMPOSITIONS

"Czar's Anthem"	Russia	*Marche Slave*	Tchaikovsky
		Danish Overture	Tchaikovsky
		1812 Overture	Tchaikovsky
"Emperor's Hymn"	Austria	String Quartet op. 76, no. 3	Haydn
"God Save the King"	England	*Battle and Victory*	Weber
		Occasional Oratorio	Händel
		"Battle Symphony" from *Wellington's Victory*	Beethoven
"La Marseillaise"	France	*1812 Overture*	Tchaikovsky
		The Two Grenadiers	R. Schumann
"Our Land"	Finland	*Finlandia*	Sibelius
"Rule, Britannia"	Great Britain	*Occasional* Oratorio	Händel
		Alfred	Arne
		"Battle Symphony" from *Wellington's Victory*	Beethoven
"The Star Spangled Banner"	U.S.A.	*Madama Butterfly*	Puccini

LIST 9.20   HOLIDAY SONGS

New Year's Day January 1	"Auld Lang Syne" "The Bells on New Year's Day"
Dr. Martin Luther King January 15	"Get Aboard, Little Children" "He's Got the Whole World in His Hands" "Michael, Row the Boat Ashore" "We Shall Overcome"
Abraham Lincoln February 12	"Abraham, Martin, and John" "Battle Hymn of the Republic" "Lincoln and Liberty" "Old Abe Lincoln" "Out from the Wilderness"
Valentine's Day February 14	"Mister Frog Went a-Courting" "A Paper of Pins" "You Are My Sunshine"
George Washington February 22	"Hail, Columbia!" "Washington, the Great" "Yankee Doodle"
St. Patrick's Day March 17	"Cockles and Mussels" "Michael Finnegan" "Saint Patrick Was a Gentleman" "When Irish Eyes Are Smiling"

List 9.20 (continued)

April Fool's Day April 1	"The Animal Fair" "There's a Hole in the Bucket" "There Was an Old Lady Who Swallowed a Fly" "This Old Man"
Earth Day April 22	"Woodsman, Spare That Tree"
Memorial Day Last Monday in May	"Taps" "Tramp! Tramp! Tramp!" "When Johnny Comes Marching Home Again" "Battle Hymn of the Republic"
Flag Day June 14	"Battle Cry of Freedom" "The Red, White, and Blue" "The Star Spangled Banner" "There Are Many Flags from Many Lands" "You're a Grand Old Flag"
Independence Day July 4	"America" "America, the Beautiful" "Hail, Columbia" "Yankee Doodle"
Labor Day First Monday in September	"John Henry" "Erie Canal" "Drill, Ye Tarriers" "I've Been Working on the Railroad"
Columbus Day October 12	"He Knew the Earth Was Round-O" "In 1492" "It's All Wrong" "Sailing, Sailing"
Halloween October 31	"Them Bones" "Ten Little Goblins"
Election Day First Tuesday in November	"For He's a Jolly Good Fellow" "Hail to the Chief" "Happy Days Are Here Again"
Veteran's Day November 11	"The Caissons Go Rolling Along" "God Bless America" "The Marine's Hymn" "Over There" "You're in the Army Now"
Thanksgiving Fourth Thursday in November	"Over the River and Through the Woods" "Turkey in the Straw" "We Gather Together"

LIST 9.21 SEASONAL MUSIC

Autumn

"Autumn" from *Four Seasons*	Vivaldi
Automne, op. 18	Fauré
"A Song of Autumn"	Elgar
Autumn Concertino	Thompson
In Autumn Overture	Grieg
Autumn Legend	Alwyn

Winter

Winter Holiday	Prokofiev
Winter Bonfire Suite	Prokofiev
"Skater's Waltz"	Waldteufel
Winterliebe, op. 48, no. 5	Strauss
"Winter Was Hard"	Sallinen
"Blow, Blow Thou Winter's Wind"	Arne
Winternacht, op. 15, no. 2	Strauss
"Winter" from *Four Seasons*	Vivaldi
"The Winter Garden Rag"	Oleman
"Winter Wonderland"	Bernard
Etude, op. 25, no. 11	Chopin
Winter Waters	Bax
A Mind of Winter	Benjamin
"Wintersturme Waltz," op. 1	Fucik
Winter Concertino	LaMarque-Ponf
Winter Words, op. 52	Britten
Winter Pages	Rorem
Winter Legends	Bax
Die Winterreise	Schubert

List 9.21 (continued)

Spring

"On Hearing the First Cuckoo in Spring"	Delius
"Spring" from *Four Seasons*	Vivaldi
"The Last Spring"	Grieg
"Spring" (Vesna)	Glazunov
Violin Sonata no. 5	Beethoven
Symphony no. 1	Schumann
Symphony no. 6 (*Pastoral*)	Beethoven
The Rite of Spring	Stravinsky
Spring Symphony, op. 44	Britten
"Wir Beide Wollen Springen"	Strauss
"Vaaren Springtime" op. 3	Grieg
"Le Primtemps"	Hahn
Songs without Words	Mendelssohn
"Rustle of Spring," op. 32	Sinding
"Love and Spring Waltz"	Waldteufel
"Spring Came Early"	Gulda
"Am Springbrunnen," op. 23	Zabel
"Voices of Spring," op. 410	J. Strauss, Jr.
"Spring Song," op. 16	Sibelius
"Spring Morning"	Delius

Summer

Summer Day Suite	Prokofiev
"Summer" from *Four Seasons*	Vivaldi
The Seasons	Glazunov
"Summertime"	Gershwin
"To Be Sung of a Summer Night"	Delius
"Summer Evening"	Kodály
"The Last Rose of Summer"	Britten
"Summerland"	Still
"Summer Night on the River"	Delius
"Summer Night"	Hoover
"A Song of Summer"	Delius
"Summer Music"	Bax
"The Midsummer Marriage"	Tippett
"Summer"	Bridge
Summer Music, op. 31	Barber

LIST 9.22 SIGNIFICANT AFRICAN-AMERICAN MUSICIANS

Marian Anderson	opera singer	Earl Hines	jazz pianist
Louis Armstrong	trumpeter, band leader	Billie Holiday	singer
Pearl Bailey	singer, comedienne	Lena Horne	singer
Josephine Baker	singer, dancer	Whitney Houston	singer
Hank Ballard	rhythm and blues	Mahalia Jackson	singer
Count Basie	jazz pianist, band leader	Michael Jackson	singer
Kathleen Battle	singer	James P. Johnson	composer
Sidney Bechet	clarinetist	J. Rosamond Johnson	pianist
Harry Belafonte	calypso style singer	Scott Joplin	composer
Chuck Berry	rhythm and blues	Ulysses Kay	composer
Thomas Bethune	pianist	B.B. King	guitarist, singer
James Bland	song writer	Huddie Ledbetter	singer, song writer
James Brown	singer	Henry Lewis	conductor
Ray Brown	bassist	Jimmie Lunceford	orchestra leader
Grace Bumbry	concert vocalist	Branford Marsalis	saxophonist
Harry Burleigh	composer	Wynton Marsalis	trumpeter
Cab Calloway	singer, band leader	Johnny Mathis	singer
Diahann Carroll	singer	Dorothy Maynor	singer
Ron Carter	bassist	Florence Mills	singer
Ray Charles	pianist, singer	Charles Mingus	bassist, composer
Nat "King" Cole	singer	Thelonius Monk	pianist, composer
Ornette Coleman	saxophonist	Wes Montgomery	guitarist
John Coltrane	saxophonist, band leader	Jelly Roll Morton	pianist, composer
Arthur Cunningham	composer	Odetta	singer
Miles Davis	trumpeter, band leader	King Oliver	cornetist, band leader
Sammy Davis, Jr.	singer, dancer	Charlie Parker	saxophonist
William Dawson	composer, conductor	Leontyne Price	singer
James DePriest	conductor	Max Roach	drummer
Robert Dett	composer	Paul Robeson	singer
Dean Dixon	orchestra conductor	Nina Simone	singer
Mattiwilda Dobbs	opera singer	Bessie Smith	singer
Todd Duncan	actor, singer	William Still	composer, conductor
Duke Ellington	composer	Art Tatum	pianist
Ella Fitzgerald	singer	Sarah Vaughan	singer
Aretha Franklin	singer	Shirley Verrett	singer
Paul Freeman	conductor	Fats Waller	pianist
Erroll Garner	jazz pianist	William Warfield	singer
Dizzy Gillespie	trumpeter, band leader	Dionne Warwick	singer
Elizabeth Greenfield	soprano	Ethel Waters	singer
Lionel Hampton	vibraphonist	Andre Watts	pianist, conductor
W.C. Handy	cornetist, composer	Clarence White	composer
Coleman Hawkins	saxophonist	Tony Williams	drummer
Roland Hayes	tenor	Lester Young	saxophonist
Nathalie Hinderas	concert pianist		

LIST 9.23 FAMOUS AFRICAN-AMERICAN CHOREOGRAPHERS

Alvin Ailey   Katherine Dunham   Geoffrey Holder

LIST 9.24 FAMOUS AFRICAN-AMERICAN DANCERS

Carolyn Adams   Gregory Hines
Alvin Ailey   Maurice Hines
Hinton Battle   Mary Hinkson
John Bubbles   Geoffrey Holder
Greg Burge   Judith Jamison
Sammy Davis, Jr.   Carmen de Lavallade
Arthur Duncan   Avon Long
Katherine Dunham   Bill (Bojangles) Robinson
Mercedes Ellington   Ben Vereen

LIST 9.25 AFRICAN-AMERICAN OPERA STARS

Adele Addison	soprano	Hilda Harris	mezzo-soprano
Roberta Alexander	soprano	Roland Hayes	tenor
Betty Lou Allen	mezzo-soprano	Barbara Hendricks	mezzo-soprano
Marian Anderson	contralto	Ben Holt	baritone
Martina Arroyo	soprano	Isole Jones	mezzo-soprano
Priscilla Baskerville	lyric soprano	Dorothy Maynor	soprano
Kathleen Battle	soprano	Robert McFerrin	baritone
Gwendolyn Bradley	soprano	Myra Merritt	soprano
Grace Bumbrey	mezzo-soprano	Leona Mitchell	soprano
Steven Cole	tenor	Jessye Norman	soprano
Vincent Cole	tenor	Leontyne Price	lyric soprano
Philip Creech	tenor	Florence Quivar	mezzo-soprano
Osceola Davis	soprano	George Shirley	tenor
Mattiwalda Dobbs	coloratura soprano	Andrew Smith	baritone
Todd Duncan	baritone	Arthur Thompson	baritone
Simon Estes	bass-baritone	Shirley Verrett	mezzo-soprano
Denyce Graves	mezzo-soprano	William Warfield	baritone
Reri Grist	coloratura soprano		

233

LIST 9.26 FAMOUS AFRICAN-AMERICAN SINGERS

Pearl Bailey
Josephine Baker
Shirley Bassey
PegLeg Bates
Harry Belafonte
George Benson
Chuck Berry
Billy Bowen
James Brown
Oscar Brown, Jr.
Anita Bush
Jerry Butler
Cab Calloway
Diahann Carroll
Ray Charles
James Cleveland
Nat "King" Cole
Sam Cooke
Dorothy Dandridge
Billy Daniels
Sammy Davis, Jr.
Fats Domino
Billy Eckstine
Lola Falana

Ella Fitzgerald
Roberta Flack
Aretha Franklin
Charlie Fuqua
Marvin Gaye
Elizabeth Taylor Greenfield
Isaac Hayes
Roland Hayes
Jimi Hendrix
Billie Holiday
Lena Horne
Alberta Hunter
Mahalia Jackson
Michael Jackson
B.B. King
Eartha Kitt
Gladys Knight
Huddie Ledbetter
Little Richard
Johnny Mathis
Carmen McRae
Donald Mills
Florence Mills
Abbie Mitchell

Melba Moore
Leontyne Price
Charley Pride
Lou Rawls
Otis Redding
Little Richard
Lionel Richie
Paul Robeson
Smokey Robinson
Diana Ross
Nina Simone
Bessie Smith
Tina Turner
Leslie Uggams
Sarah Vaughan
Adam Wade
Dionne Warwick
Dinah Washington
Ethel Waters
Joe Williams
Tony Williams
Jackie Wilson
Nancy Wilson
Stevie Wonder

See Also List 9.25, African-American Opera Stars

LIST 9.27   FAMOUS AFRICAN-AMERICAN SYMPHONIC CONDUCTORS

William Levi Dawson
James DePreist
Dean Dixon
Isaiah Jackson

Henry Lewis
Michael Morgan
Karl Hampton Porter

LIST 9.28   THE AFRO-AMERICAN FIVE

These African-American composers made great contributions in the area of symphonic music.

Harry T. Burleigh	1866–1949	William Grant Still	1895–1978
Clarence Cameron White	1880–1960	William Levi Dawson	1898–1990
R. Nathaniel Dett	1882–1943		

234

LIST 9.29 CHILDREN'S LITERATURE RELATED TO ELEMENTARY MUSIC

Abiyoyo	Pete Seeger	Pre-K–4
Always Room for One More	Sorche Nic Leodhas	K–3
Busy Monday Morning	Janina Domanska	Pre-K–1
Count Me In	Chris Conover	Pre-K–2
A Different Tune	Barbara Gregorich	K–2
The Donkey Cart	Clyde Bulla	Pre-K–2
Eye Winker, Tom Tinker, Chin Hopper	John Glazer	Pre-K–3
The Fisherman's Song	Carly Simon	Pre-K–3
The Fox Went Out on a Chilly Night	Peter Spier	Pre-K–3
Frog Went a-Courting	Wendy Watson	Pre-K–3
Frederick	Leo Lionni	Pre-K–3
Geraldine, the Music Mouse	Leo Lionni	Pre-K–3
Go Tell Aunt Rhody	Aliki	Pre-K–2
Hush Little Baby	Aliki	Pre-K–1
I Know an Old Lady Who Swallowed a Fly	Rose Bonne	Pre-K–3
I Like the Music	Leah Komaiko	Pre-K–3
I Make Music	Eloise Greenfield	Pre-K–1
I'm a Little Teapot	Shelagh McGee	Pre-K–2
In a Cabin in the Woods	McNally and Michael	Pre-K–2
I See a Song	Eric Carle	Pre-K–3
The Jolly Mon	Jimmy Buffet	4–8
Mama Don't Allow	Thacher Hurd	Pre-K–3
Mary Had a Little Lamb	Hale/de Paola	Pre-K–2
Mary Wore Her Red Dress	Merle Peek	Pre-K–2
Mister King	Raija Siekkinen	1–3
Mommy, Buy Me a China Doll	Harve Zemach	K–2
The Most Beautiful Song	Max Bollinger	K–3
Music, Music for Everyone	Vera B. Williams	K–3
Old MacDonald Had a Farm	Abner Graboff	Pre-K–3
Piggies	Don and Audrey Wood	Pre-K–2
Play Rhymes	Marc Brown	Pre-K–1
Possum Come a Knockin'	Nancy Van' Laan	Pre-K–3
Really Rosie	Maurice Sendak	K–4
Rise and Shine	Fiona French	Pre-K–2
Roland, the Minstrel Pig	William Steig	K–3
Sally Go Round the Moon	Nancy and John Langstaff	K–4
Six Little Ducks	Chris Conover	K–3
There's a Hole in the Bucket	Nadine Bernard	Pre-K–3
The Troll Music	Anita Lobel	Pre-K–2
This Old Man	Robin Koontz	Pre-K–3
Today is Monday	Eric Carle	K–2
What a Beautiful Noise	Harry Behb	Pre-K–3
What I Like	Catherine and Laurence Anholt	Pre-K–3
The Wheels on the Bus	Mayann Kovalski	Pre-K–K
Yo, Hungry Wolf! A Nursery Rap	David Vozar	Pre-K–4
Zoo Song	Barbara Bottner	Pre-K–2

LIST 9.30 CHILDREN'S LITERATURE RELATED TO HOLIDAY MUSIC

Away in a Manger	Meryl Doney	1–2
Bring a Torch, Jeanette Isabella	Sandra Boyton	K–3
Children, Go Where I Send Thee	Hyman Chanover	K–3
The Christmas Mouse	Elizabeth Wenning	2–up
The Friendly Beasts	S. Chamberlain	1–2
Good King Wenceslas	J.M. Neale	Pre-K–up
Good King Wenceslas	John Wallner	2–3
The Great Shamrock Disaster	Patricia Giff	1–3
Happy Hanukah, Everybody	Hyman Chanover	K–3
Holiday Singing and Dancing Games	Esther Nelson	Pre-K–up
I Saw Three Ships	Elizabeth Goudge	4–8
Jingle Bells	Maryann Kovalski	Pre-K–3
The Jingle Bells Jam	Patricia Giff	1–3
Little Drummer Boy	Ezra Jack Keats	2–4
My Father	Judy Collins	2–3
The Red White and Blue Valentine	Patricia Giff	1–3
Silent Night	Susan Jeffers	2–5
Sing a Song of Halloween	Strand and Boggs	K–3
Sing Through the Seasons	Biene and Moneli	K–6
A Small Sheep in a Pear Tree	Adrianne Lobel	K–3
The Thirteen Days of Halloween	Carol Greene	Pre-K–2
The Twelve Days of Christmas	Ilse Plume	2–3
A Valentine for You	Wendy Watson	1–2
We Wish You a Merry Christmas	Dan Fox	5–9

LIST 9.31 CHILDREN'S LITERATURE RELATED TO MUSIC HISTORY

African Music: A People's Art	Francis Bebey	10–12
America's Black Musical Heritage	Tilford Brooks	10–12
An Album of Rock and Roll	Trudy Hammer	7–9
The Big Band Years	Crowther and Pinfold	9–12
Black Music in America	James Haskins	7–12
Classical Music	Clive Griffin	9–12
European Classical Music, 1600–1825	Richard Carlin	9–12
Folk Music in Britain, Ireland, and the U.S.	Clive Griffin	4–6
Giants of Jazz	Studs Terkel	Young Adult
History of Western Music	Donald Grout	10–12
I Like Music	Barrie Turner	4–6
It's Rock 'n' Roll	Gene Busnar	9–12
Jazz	Arlo Blocher	6–8
Jazz	Clive Griffin	6–12
Jazz: The Essential Companion	Ian Carr	8–12
The Joy of Music	Leonard Bernstein	10–12
Man's Earliest Music	Richard Carlin	7–12
Menudo	Maria Molina	7–10
Music (Eyewitness Book)	Neil Ardley	4–7
Music of Black Americans: A History	Eileen Southern	10–12
The New Age Music Guide	Patti J. Birosik	10–12
The New Music	Aaron Copland	10–12
Ragtime: Its History, Composers, and Music	John Hasse	10–12
Reggae	Davis and Simon	10–12
The Rhythm and Blues Story	Gene Busnar	6–9
Rock On: The Video Revolution	Nite and Crespo	9–12
Rock Video Superstars	D. and S. Cohen	6–9
Something Queer in Rock 'n' Roll	Elizabeth Levy	K–3
The Story of Folk Music	Melvin Berger	7–9
The Story of Rock 'n' Roll	Pete Fornatale	4–7
Up from the Cradle of Jazz	Jason Berry	10–12
Wham!	Chris Crocker	6–9

LIST 9.32 CHILDREN'S LITERATURE RELATED TO DANCE

Title	Author	Grade
Agnes de Mille	Margaret Speaker-Yuan	7–12
Alice in Danceland	M. Constance Hodges	3–8
All Tutus Should Be Pink	Sheri Brownrigg	1–3
Amy the Dancing Bear	Carly Simon	K–3
Angelina and the Princess	Katherine Holabird	Pre-K–2
Angelina Ballerina	Katherine Holabird	Pre-K–2
Angelina on Stage	Katherine Holabird	Pre-K–2
Ballerina's Holiday	S. Lichtner	5–up
Ballet and Modern Dance: A Concise History	Jack Anderson	10–12
Ballett Dancer	Janet Craig	K–3
Ballet for Boys and Girls	Walker and Butler	7–9
Ballet for Drina	Jean Estoril	3–7
The Ballet Goers' Guide	Clarke and Crisp	10–12
Ballet Kitty	Marcie Anderson	Pre-K–3
Ballet No. 3: Pat's Promise	Sandy Asher	3–5
Ballet Shoes	Noel Streatfeild	4–6
Ballet Steps: Practice to Performance	Anthony Dufort	Young Adult
Barn Dance!	Bill Martin	Pre-K–2
Baseball Ballerina	Kathryn Cristaldi	1–3
Bellyfull of Ballet	Mallett and Bartch	2–8
Bertie and the Bear	Pamela Allen	K–3
The Best-Dressed Bear	Mary Blocksma	Pre-K–2
Black Dance in America	James Haskins	7–12
Blue Tights	Rita Garcia	4–8
Boom-de-Boom	Elaine Edelman	Pre-K–2
Bravo, Tanya	Patricia Gauch	Pre-K–3
Can David Do It?	Sandy Asher	2–4
Cat Dancers	Ron Holiday	9–12
Cinderella	Charles Perrault	Pre-K–3
Cordelia, Dance	Sarah Stepler	1–3
Dance Me a Story	Jane Rosenberg	5–7
Dancer: Men in Dance	Clarke and Crisp	9–12
Dancers (Looking at Paintings)	Peggy Roalf	4–6
Dancershoes	D. and Stephanie Sorine	10–12
The Dancing Class	Helen Oxenbury	Pre-K–1
Dancing Is	George Ancona	K–3
The Dancing Man	Ruth Bornstein	Pre-K–3
Dancing Shoes	Noel Streatfeild	K–6
The Dancing Tigers	Russell Hoban	K–3
Dancing to America	Anne Morris/Paul Kolnik	7–12
Dancing with Indians	Angela Madearis	Pre-K–2
Dumb Old Casey Is a Fat Tree	Barbara Bottner	1–4
Ellen Tibbets	Beverly Cleary	3–5
Emma's Turn	Suzanne Weyn	3–5
Enjoying the Arts: Dance	Nancy Kline	7–9
Frances Dances	Ilene Cooper	3–4
George and Martha Encore	James Marshall	K–3
Going to My Ballet Class	Susan Kuklin	1–3
Harriet's Recital	Nancy Carlson	Pre-K–3
Humphrey, the Dancing Pig	Arthur Getz	Pre-K–3

238

List 9.32 (continued)

The Hurdy-Gurdy Man	Margery Bianco	K-3
I Dance in My Red Pajamas	Edith Hurd	1-3
I Feel Like Dancing	Steven Barboza	Young Adult
I Feel Like Dancing	Steven Barboza	4-6
I Have Another Language: Language of Dance	Eleanor Schick	1-3
In the Spotlight	Karen Backstein	3-5
Isadora Duncan	Ruth Kozodoy	5-9
Just Like Jenny	Sandy Asher	5-9
Life at the Royal Ballet School	Camilla Jessel	7-9
Lion Dancing	Kate Waters	1-5
Listen to the Nightingale	Rumor Godden	5-up
A Little Interlude	Robert R. Maiorano	K-3
Magic Slippers	Gilda Berger	4-8
Max	Rachel Isadora	K-3
Messy Myra	Barbara Bottner	Pre-K-3
Mirandy and Brother Wind	Patricia McKissack	Pre-K-3
Molly's New Washing Machine	Laura Geringer	K-3
Moongame	Frank Asch	K-3
My Ballet Class	Rachel Isadora	Pre-K-3
Nijinsky: Scenes from the Childhood . . .	Catherine Brighton	1-3
The Nutcracker	E.T. Hoffman	1-5
Of Swans, Sugar Plums, and Satin Slippers	Violette Veroy	1-3
The Old Woman and the Willy Nilly Man	Jill Wright	K-3
Oliver Button Is a Sissy	Tomie de Paola	Pre-K-3
101 Stories of the Great Ballets	Balanchine and Mason	7-12
Opening Night	Rachel Isadora	K-3
Our Ballet Class	Stephanie Sorine	K-3
Pepito's Story	Eugene Fern	Pre-K-3
Petrouchka	Vivian Werner	4-7
The Queen Always Wanted to Dance	Mercer Mayer	Pre-K-2
The Red Shoes	Hans Christian Andersen	3-up
Samantha on Stage	R. Sanderson	3-up
Saturday Is Ballet Day	Cathy Beylon	3-5
Shimmy Shake Earthquake	Cynthia Jabar	1-3
Sometimes I Dance Mountains	Byrd Baylor	K-3
Song and Dance Man	Karen Ackerman	Pre-K-2
Sophie and Lou	Petra Mathers	1-3
Stage Fright	Suzanne Weyn	3-5
Star Boy	Paul Goble	K-3
Swan Lake	Anthea Bell	K-3
Swan Lake	Rachel Isadora	1-3
Terpsichore in Sneakers	Sally Banes	10-12
The Skinny Goats	Victor Ambrus	Pre-K-3
Three for the Show	Suzanne Weyn	3-5
Three Sisters	Audrey Wood	Pre-K-3
The Twelve Dancing Princesses	Jacob Grimm	K-4
A Very Young Dancer	Jill Krementz	3-6
What If They Saw Me Now?	Jean Ure	7-up
The World of Dance	Melvin Berger	7-12

LIST 9.33 CHILDREN'S LITERATURE RELATED TO OPERA AND SYMPHONY

Aida	Leontyne Price	4–6
The Alphabet Symphony	Bruce McMillan	K–2
The Barber of Seville	Johanna Jonston	2–5
The Bear Who Loved Puccini	Arnold Sundgaard	Pre-K–3
Beverly Sills	Bridget Paolucci	7–12
A Candle Opera	Richard Sparks	5–10
The Cat's Opera	Ellis Dillon	K–3
The Complete Phantom of the Opera	George Perry	9–12
The Flying Orchestra	Ulf Lofgren	K–3
Grover's Overtures	Machaela Muntean	Pre-K–6
Help, Help, the Globolinks!	Leigh Dean	2–5
Into the Woods	Sondheim and Lapine	9–12
Little Princesses' Symphony Adventures	Vera Sharp	Pre-K–4
Madam Nightingale Will Sing Tonight	James Mayhew	Pre-K–3
The Magic Flute	Margaret Greaves	2–5
Marian Anderson	Anne Tedards	6–10
Metropolitan Opera Stories of Great Operas	John Freeman	9–12
Opera: What's All the Screaming About?	Roger Englander	7–12
Pages of Music	Tony Johnston	K–3
The Performing World of the Musician	Christopher Headington	7–9
Peter and the Wolf	Maria Carlson	Pre-K–3
Pet of the Met	Lydia Freeman	Pre-K–3
The Phantom of the Opera	Kate McMullan	3–7
Rondo in C	Paul Fleischman	K–3
Scheherazade and the Arabian Nights	Constance Allen	1–6
Sing Me a Story	Jane Rosenberg	K–4
The Storybook of Opera	Cyrus Biscardi	7–12
Tales from the Opera	Anthony Rudel	9–12
Winning Scheherazade	Judith Gorog	5–up

LIST 9.34 BOOKS TO INTEGRATE MUSIC WITH SCIENCE AND SOCIAL STUDIES THEMES

All God's Critters Got a Place in the Choir	Bill Staines	1–2
American Indian Music and Musical Instruments	George Fichter	4–8
American Indians Sing	Charles Hofmann	3–6
Baby Beluga	Raffi	K–up
Ben Franklin's Glass Armonica	Byrna Stevens	1–4
Best Loved Songs of the American People	Denes Agay	9–12
Careers in Music	Gene Busnar	7–10
A Computer Went a Courtin'	Carol Greene	K–3
A Cry from the Earth	John Bierhorst	6–8
A Day in the Life of a Rock Musician	David Paige	6–9
Down by the Bay	Raffi	Pre-K–2
The Erie Canal	Peter Spier	K–3
Eskimo Songs and Stories	Edward Field	K–3
"Hot Cross Buns" and Other Old Street Cries	Betty Horvath	K–3
Hurrah, We're Outward Bound	Peter Spier	K–3
The American Songbag	Carl Sandburg	7–12
Music Is Math	Oliver Luck	4–12
Myth, Music and Dance of American Indians	Ruth DeCesare	4–12
National Anthems of the World	Reed and Bristow	9–12
The Pelican Chorus	Edward Lear	K–3
Rise Up Singing	Blood-Patterson	8–12
The Science of Music	Melvin Berger	4–6
Sing a Song of Sound	Vicki Silveres	Pre-K–2
Sing a Whale Song	Chapin and Forster	Young Adult
Songs of the Chippewa	John Bierhorst	4–8
Songs of the Wild West	Dan Fox	7–9
The Star Spangled Banner	Peter Spier	K–6
Stories of Our American Patriotic Songs	John Lyons	4–7
Yankee Doodle: Musical	Aurand Harris	1–7

See Also List 5.14, Operas with Historical Themes

LIST 9.35 CHILDREN'S LITERATURE RELATED TO MUSICAL INSTRUMENTS

Ada Potato	Judith Casely	1–3
Anatole and the Piano	Eve Titus	K–3
André Previn's Guide to the Orchestra	André Previn	7–12
Ben's Trumpet	Rachel Isadora	Pre-K–2
Berlioz the Bear	Jan Brett	K–3
Broadway Banjo Bill	Leah Comaiko	K–3
Brogeen Follows the Magic Flute	Patricia Lynch	1–8
The Buffalo Nickel Blues Band	Judie Angell	3–7
Cooder Cutlas	Elizabeth Frank	7–up
Crash! Bang! Boom!	Peter Spier	Pre-K–1
Crocodile Bear	Gail Jorgensen	K–3
Don't Blame the Music	Caroline Cooney	8–up
Electronic Musical Instruments	Larry Kettelkamp	7–9
Emmet Otter's Jug-Band Christmas	Russel Hoban	Pre-K–3
The Enchanted Flute	James Mayhew	1–3
The Facts and Fiction of Minna Pratt	Patricia MacLachlan	4–6
The Fiddler's Son	Eugene Coco	K–3
The Golden Guitar	Ann Alene	K–3
Here's Hermione	Shiela Greenwald	4–6
Jasper Makes Music	Bety Horvath	K–3
Join the Band	Marjorie Pillar	4–6
Joshua and the Magic Fiddle	Janosch	K–3
The Little Band	James Sage	Pre-K–3
The Little Brass Band	Margaret Wise Brown	K–3
Little Bear and the Oompah-pah	Francesca Crespi	K–3
Loudmouth George and the Cornet	Nancy Carlson	Pre-K–3
The Lute's Tune	Michale French	4–8
The Magic of Music	Lisl Weil	2–3
Meet the Lincoln Lion's Band	Particia Giff	1–3
Music	Neil Ardley	5–9
Musical Max	Robert Kraus	Pre-K
Music in the Wood	Cornelia Cornelissen	K–8
Music Lessons	Harriet Ziefert	Pre-K–3
Music Lessons for Alex	Caroline Arnold	3–5
Nate the Great and the Musical Note	Marjorie Sharmat	2–3
The Old Banjo	Dennis Haseley	1–5
The Old Man and the Fiddle	Macahel McCurdy	Pre-K–3
The Orchestra	Mark Rubin	K–3
Orchestranimals	Vlasda van Kampen	2–3
A Pianist's Debut	Barbara Beirne	3–4
A Piano for Julie	Elanor Schick	K–3
Piano Man	Joyce Sweeney	2–4
Play It Again, Rosie!	Ruth Brook	K–3
Rootin', Tootin', Bugle Boy	Patricia Giff	1–3
Teddy Bear's Bird and Beast Band	Caroline Howe	K–3

List 9.35 (continued)

Title	Author	Grade
The Transformation of Faith Flutterman	Phyllis Shalant	4–6
Trilby's Trumpet	Sarah Stapler	K–6
Trumpets in Grumpetland	Peter Dallas-Smith	K–3
The Truthful Harp	Alexander Lloyd	K–3
Ty's One Man Band	Mildred Pitts Walter	K–3
A Very Young Musician	Jill Krementz	3–4
The Violin Close Up	Peter Schaff	K–3
The Violin-Maker's Gift	Donn Kushner	5–6
The Violin Man	Maureen Hooper	3–7
Viva La Musica	Pete Escovito	4–7
The Voice of the Wood	Claude Clement	K–up
Woodsong	Gary Paulsen	7–up
Yang, the Youngest and His Terrible Ear	Lensey Namioka	3–5
Yankee Doodle Drumsticks	Patricia Giff	1–3
Zin! Zin! Zin: A Violin	Lloyd Moss	K–3

LIST 9.36 CHILDREN'S LITERATURE RELATED TO COMPOSERS AND MUSICIANS

Alex and the Cat	Helen Griffith	1–3
Beethoven's Cat	Elisabet McHugh	4–8
The Bremen Town Musicians	Ruth Gross	Pre-K–2
Brewster's Courage	Deborah Kovacs	2–6
The Buddy Trap	Sheri Sinykin	3–7
Cromwell's Glasses	Holly Keller	K–3
Dear Bruce Springsteen	Kevin Major	K–12
Famous Children (set of 4)	Ann Rachlin	Pre-K–3
Fiddler	Cosgrove	1–3
Great Composers	Piero Ventura	5–9
I Can Be a Musician	Rebecca Hankin	K–3
Journey to Boc Boc	Oscar DeMejo	3–7
Keeping Barney	Jessie Haas	5–9
Kelly 'n' Me	Myron Levoy	7–up
Letters to Horseface	F.N. Monjo	Young Adults
Louis Armstrong: An American Success Story	James Collier	6–10
The Mozart Season	Virginia Wolf	Young Adults
Mozart Tonight	Julie Downing	K–3
Music and Imagination	Aaron Copland	10–12
Music Talks	Helen Epstein	9–12
Nadja: On My Way	Nadja Salerno-Sonnenberg	7–12
Nothing but the Best	Judith Kogan	10–12
Once upon A to Z: An Alphabet Odyssey	Jody Linscott	Pre-K–up
Orphe	Cynthia Boight	9–up
The Philharmonic Gets Dressed	Karla Kuskin	K–3
Play Beethoven	Allison Sage	1–4
Play Mozart	Allison Sage	1–4
Sad Story of Veronica Who Played the Violin	David McKee	K–4
Scott and the Ogre	Marti Plemons	3–6
Skunk Lane	Brom Hoban	2–4
Stephan and Olga	Betsy Day	Pre-K–3
Stolen Moments	Tom Schnabel	9–12
The Super Stars of Rock	Gene Busnar	7–12

LIST 9.37 VIDEOS SUITABLE FOR THE ELEMENTARY MUSIC PROGRAM

All Aboard: A Collection of Music Videos for
   Teaching Socialization Skills
All-Time Favorite Songs
Amazing Grace
American Music Makers
Babes in Toyland
Bangalore and the Stump Drum
Beethoven Lives Upstairs
Beginning Folk Dances
Best Sing-Along Mother Goose Video Ever!
Big Bird Sings
Bremen Town Musicians
Carnival of the Animals (Ogden Nash)
Carnival of the Animals (Saint-Saens)
Children's Classics as Musical Theater:
   Alice in Wonderland
   Puss in Boots
   The Red Shoes
   The Wind in the Willows
Children's Songs Around the World
Clifford's Sing Along Adventure
Cricket in Times Square
The Dancing Princesses
A Day at Old MacDonald's Farm
A Day at the Circus
Diamonds and Dragons Video
Don Cooper's Sing Along Videos:
   Mother Nature's Songs
   Musical Games
   A Pocket Full of Songs
   Songs of the Wild West
   Star Tunes
Ella Jenkins Live at the Smithsonian
Eureeka's Castle: Sing Along with Eureeka
Favorite Music Stories Videos:
   Aida and Barber of Seville
   Hansel and Gretel and The Firebird
   Magic Flute and Scheherazade
   Midsummer Night's Dream and Swan Lake
   Nutcracker and Peer Gynt
   Peter and the Wolf and The Sorcerer's
     Apprentice
   William Tell Overture and Sleeping Beauty
Folkloric Dances of Mexico
Follow the Drinking Gourd
Four-Hour Children: The Concert
Fred Penner Children in Concert Series
   The Cat Came Back
   A Circle of Songs
Grand Canyon Suite
Grandpa
Great Composers and Their Music
Hänsel and Gretel
I Can Dance
I'd Like to Teach the World to Sing

I Like Music
Imagineria
I Want to Be a Ballerina
Joe Scruggs in Concert
Jubal and the Twanging Strings
Kids Make Music
Know the Orchestra
Letter Sound Songs
Let's Be Friends
Let's Make Music: Exploring Rhythm
Lincoln Portrait
Miss Christy's Dance Adventure
Miss Christy's Dancin' Ballet
Miss Christy's Dancin' Jazz
Miss Christy's Dancin' Tap
The Musical Alphabet
Musical Classics for Children
   Adventures of Peer Gynt
   Carnival of the Animals
   The Nutcracker
   Peter and the Wolf
Musical Instruments: A Child's Introduction
Musical Tales Series:
   Coppelia/The Sleeping Beauty
   The Nutcracker/Petrushka
My First Video Series:
   My First Music Video
Nursery Raps with Mama Goose
Nutcracker (Maurice Sendak/Pacific Northwest Ballet)
The Nutcracker (Mikhail Baryshnikov)
The Nutcracker Prince
Old World Lullabies
Once upon a Sound
Peer Gynt
Perfect the Pig/Ty's One-Man Band
Peter and the Wolf
Peter, Paul and Mommy Too!
Pete Seeger's Family Concert
Picture This Sing-A-Long Series
Pictures at an Exhibition
Puss in Boots (National Ballet of Marseilles)
Raffi Concert Series:
   Raffi in Concert with the Rise and Shine Band
   A Young Children's Concert with Raffi
Read and Sing with America
Rhythm People
Richard Scarry's Best Videos Ever:
   Best Learning Songs Video Ever
Ride the Roaring Roller Coaster
Rock-A-Doodle
Rock 'n' Read
Rodeo
School House Rock:
   Grammar Rock
   History Rock

List 9.37 (continued)

Multiplication Rock
Science Rock
Sesame Song Series:
   Monster Hits
   Sing Yourself Silly!
   Rock & Roll!
   Dance Along
   Elmo's Sing-Along Guessing Game
Silent Mouse: The Story of Silent Night
Silly Songs
Sing Around the World
Singing Time!
Song City U.S.A.:
   More Song City U.S.A.
   Song City U.S.A.
Sorcerer's Apprentice
Sparky's Magic Piano
The Sport Animation Series:
   Jaxx Time Tale
   The Story of Dancing Frog
Stars and Stripes and Other American
   Band Favorites
Storytime!
Storytime Musical Treasures:
   The Carnival of the Animals

The Nutcracker
Peter and the Wolf
Symphantasy
Tales & Tunes Series:
   Christmas Tales & Tunes
   Hanukkah Tales & Tunes
   Spooky Tales & Tunes
   Sports Tales & Tunes
There Goes A.....Sing Along Series
   Bulldozer Songs
   Fire Truck Songs
   Santa Claus Songs
   Train Songs
This Pretty Planet
Tubby the Tuba
Wee Sing Series
Wheels on the Bus: Sing Along
Who's Afraid of the Opera:
   The Barber of Seville/Lucia di Lammermoor
   Faust/Rigoletto
   La Traviata/Daughter of the Regiment
   Mignon/La Perichole
Willie, the Operatic Whale
The Wonderful World of Music
Young Person's Guide to the Orchestra

LIST 9.38 VIDEOS SUITABLE FOR THE MIDDLE SCHOOL MUSIC PROGRAM

Africa: A Musical Portrait
Amahl and the Night Visitors
The Art of Listening
Chorus: A Union of Voices
The Civil War
The Cowboys
Dance Theater of Harlem
Famous Composers and Their Music
A Gilbert and Sullivan Sampler:
   The Gondoliers
   Iolanthe
   The Mikado
Grand Canyon
Great Composers:
   Beethoven
   Brahms
   Mozart
   Schubert
History of Jazz
History of Rock and Roll
How Audio Recordings Are Made
I Am a Dancer
The Instruments of the Symphony Orchestra
The Ladies Sing the Blues

Listen! Hear!
Louis Armstrong: The Gentle Giant of Jazz
The Man, the Music, and the Marine: John
   Philip Sousa Marches to Greatness
Making Music: The Symphony Orchestra
   Video
Mexican Dances
Orchestra!:
   Lower Strings, Brass and Percussion
   Piano, the Conductor and Orchestra
   Upper Strings and Woodwinds
The Railroads
Songs of the American Revolution/Songs of
   the South
Songs of the Mississippi Valley/Songs of the
   Old South West
Songs of the Pioneer/Songs of the Western
   Frontier
Steffan, the Violin Maker
Toot, Whistle, Plunk, and Boom (cartoon;
   origin of strings)
Treemonisha
Voice: The Universal Instrument

LIST 9.39   VIDEOS SUITABLE FOR THE HIGH SCHOOL MUSIC PROGRAM

Amadeus
Amazing Grace
American Patchwork Series:
    Cajun Country: Don't Drop the Potato
    The Land Where Blues Began
    Jazz Parades: Feet Don't Fail Me Now
    Appalachian Journey
    Dreams and Songs of the Noble Old
America's Music Series:
    Blues 1
    Blues 2
    Country & Western 1
    Country & Western 2
    Folk 1
    Folk 2
    Gospel 1
    Gospel 2
    Jazz the Dixieland 1
    Jazz then Dixieland 2
    Rock and Roll 1
    Rock and Roll 2
    Soul 1
    Soul 2
America's Music: The Roots of Country Series:
    The Birth of Sound/Singing
        Cowboys and Western Swing
    Honkey Tonk Kings and Queens:
        The Nashville Sound
    Folk Revival:
        Rockabilly to Rockin' the Country
Andrew Lloyd Webber: The Premier
    Collection Encore
Artur Rubinstein
Baryshnikov: The Dancer and the Dance
The Beatles: The First U.S. Visit
Bernstein in Berlin
Blues Masters: The Official History of the Blues
Bubbe Meises: Bubbe Stories
Classical Ballet Series:
    Carmen
    Cinderella
    Don Quixote
    Giselle
    Ivan the Terrible
    La Bayadere
    Macbeth
    The Nutcracker
    Romeo and Juliet
    Sleeping Beauty
    Swan Lake
    The Ultimate Swan Lake
Classic Composers Series:
    Beethoven
    Brahms
    Mozart
    Schubert

Classic Opera Series:
    Aida
    The Barber of Seville
    Don Carlo
    Ernani
    La Boheme
    La Cenerentola
    La Traviata
    Lohengrin
    Madame Butterfly
    Magic Flute
    Tosca
    Un Ballo in Maschere
Dame Kiri Te Kanawa
Essential Opera
Famous Composer Series:
    Haydn
    Mozart
    Schubert
George Gershwin Remembered
Glenn Miller: America's Musical Hero
A Great Day in Harlem
A Hard Day's Night
In the Shadow of the Stars
Jazz at the Smithsonian Series
    Alberta Hunter
    Art Farmer
    Joe Williams
Jazz Masters Vintage Collection
The Music Maestro Series:
    Bach
    Beethoven
    Brahms
    Chopin
    Dvorak
    Grieg
    Haydn
    Mendelssohn
    Mozart
    Schubert
    Tchaikovsky
    Vivaldi
Pavarotti & Friends Together for the Children of Bosnia
Pavarotti & the Italian Tenor
Riverdance: The Show
Rock 'n' Roll: The Greatest Years
The Story of the Symphony:
    Beethoven
    Berlioz
    Brahms
    Haydn and Mozart
    Shostakovich
    Tchaikovsky
Thelonius Monk: Straight No Chaser
Three Tenors: Carreras, Domingo, and Pavarotti
Verdi: Requiem
Yehudi Menuhin

LIST 9.40   CD ROMs RELATED TO MUSIC

Anatomy of Music	5th & up
The Art of Listening	5th & up
Beethoven Lives Upstairs	K & up
Beethoven's 5th	2nd & up
Discovering Music	5th & up
Forrest Gump: Music, Artists and Times	8th & up
Great Composers: Their Lives and Music	3rd - h.s

Volume 1	Bach, Schumann & Rachmaninoff
Volume 2	Handel, Chopin & Debussy
Volume 3	Mozart, Mendelssohn & Dvorak
Volume 4	Beethoven, Grieg & Hanson
Volume 5	Haydn, Tchaikovsky & Ravel
Volume 6	Schubert, Brahms & Strauss

The Guide to Classical Music	5th & up
Introduction to Classical Music	9th & up
Kid Riffs	K & up
Lamb Chop Loves Music	Pre-K to 3rd
Making Music	2nd & up
Mooky-Oke	Pre-K to 2nd
Multimedia Beethoven	7th to adult
Multimedia Mozart	7th to adult
Multimedia Schubert	7th to adult
Musical Instruments	4th & up
Musical World of Professor Piccolo	3rd & up
Music of American History: Apple Pie Music	6th & up
Music Central '96	h.s.
The Music Game	3rd & up
MusicROM Prescriptives: Blues	7th & up
MusicROM Prescriptives: Jazz	7th & up
MusicROM Prescriptives: R & B	7th & up
Robert Winter's Crazy for Ragtime	h.s.
Theatrix-Julliard Music Adventure	K - 4th
Viking Opera Guide	6th & up

LIST 9.41 DISTRIBUTORS OF VIDEOS AND CD ROMs

A few distributors of videos are listed below. There are many distributors. Please see your school librarian for the latest catalogs, or see your public librarian for *The Video Source Book*, National Video Clearinghouse, for a complete listing of distributors for specific videos.

Baker and Taylor
652 East Main St.
PO Box 6920
Bridgewater, NJ 08807-0920
(800) 775-2200

Educational Record Center
3233 Burnt Mill Drive, Suite 100
Wilmington, NC 28403-2655
(919) 251-1235

Library Video Company
Educational Video Buyers' Guide
PO Box 1110/Dept. M-35
Bala Cynwyd, PA 19004
(800) 843-3620

National Geographic Society
Educational Services
Washington, DC 20036
(800) 368-2728

Society for Visual Education, Inc.
Department BV
1345 Diversey Parkway
Chicago, IL 60614-1299
(800) 829-1900

LIST 9.42   PARTS OF THE EAR

The numbered labels on the diagram correspond to the numbered parts of the ear on the list below:

1. anvil (incus)
2. auditory nerve
3. cochlea
4. eardrum (tympanic membrane)
5. Eustachian tube
6. hammer (malleus)

7. inner ear
8. middle ear
9. outer ear
10. round cochlear window
11. stirrup (stapes)
12. semicircular canals

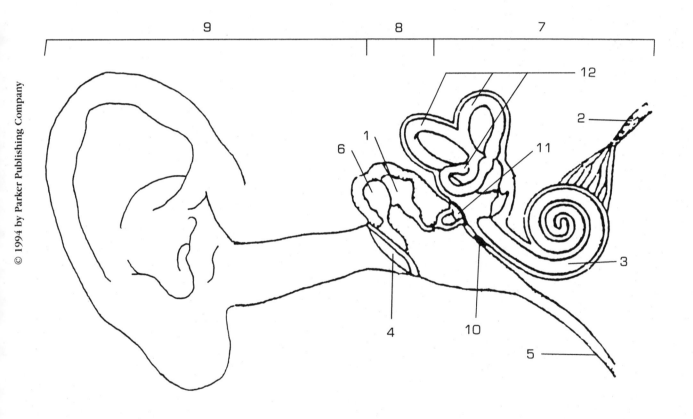

LIST 9.43   ACOUSTICS TERMS

acoustics	the science of sound
ambience	fullness of a sound
amplitude	the loudness of a sound
anechoic chamber	an artificially constructed room which has no reflective sound
attack	the beginning moment of a sound; the first element of the sound envelope
beats	an interference that occurs when two sounds of slightly differing frequencies are sounded simultaneously
Bel	a unit for measuring changes in intensity of sound
cents	1/100 of a tempered semitone
chorus effect	quality produced in a tone by the slight spreading of frequencies
complex tone	mixtures of simple tones (pure tones and partials)
cycle	one complete vibration
decay	the diminishing of the amplitude of a sound to zero; the final element of the sound envelope
decibel	a unit which measures the intensity of sound
difference tone	a subjective tone which is the difference in the frequencies of the two actual tones present
Doppler effect	the apparent shift of frequencies as the sound source moves toward or away from the listener
force	a push or pull which can produce distortion or acceleration
formants	fixed frequency regions which give voices and instruments their individual character
frequency	the number of vibrations per second of any sound
fundamental	the harmonic of the lowest frequency
harmonics	partials of a complex tone
hertz (Hz̄)	cycles per second
infrasound	a sound too low in pitch to be detected by the human ear
intensity	amount of energy in a sound
interference	the result of the superposition of two waves
loudness	how each person senses a sound
masking	when one sound makes another inaudible
medium	substance through which sound travels
monochord	a one-string instrument used to measure string ratios
nodes	in a standing wave, the points along the string that do not move
oscillation	vibration
overtone	partials sounding over the fundamental
partials	simple tones that combine to form a complex tone
period	time required for one cycle
pitch	the highness or lowness of a note, due to its frequency
pure tone	sustained tone of a single frequency; a sinewave
reflected sound	sound waves bouncing off a change of medium

List 9.43 (continued)

resonance	effect which occurs when a number of repeated pulses cause a larger vibration
sawtooth wave	a complex wave made up of harmonics 1, 2, 3, 4, etc. all in the same phase
sinewave	the wave created by a pure tone
sound	small, rapid changes in the ambient air pressure
sound absorption	amount of energy absorbed from sound
sound envelope	attack, sustain, and decay of a sound
sound waves	areas of alternating high and low pressure which move through the air and when collected in the ear are interpreted as sound
square wave	a complex wave made up of harmonics 1, 3, 5, 7, etc. all in the same phase
subjective tones	tones not actually present in the sound, but heard by the human ear
summation tone	a subjective tone which is the sum of the frequencies of the two actual tones present
sustain	the duration of a sound, the second element of the sound envelope
timbre	the quality of vocal or instrumental musical sounds
tone	a musical sound
tone color	see timbre
ultrasound	sounds too high pitched to be heard by human ears
vibration	back and forth motions that are the source of all sounds
watt	a unit of measure for the expenditure of power
wavelength	distance between peaks of successive sound waves
white noise	a mixture of sounds of all frequencies
"wolf" tone	resultant, unpleasant tone emitted when the frequency of a string and the frequency of its resonating body are in close proximity

LIST 9.44   CAREER OPPORTUNITIES IN MUSIC

MUSIC EDUCATION

elementary music specialist
junior high school general music
choral specialist
band director
string specialist
music supervisor of a school system
state supervisor of music
head of music department or music school
college music professor
private studio teaching
conservatory or music school teaching
store studio teaching

CONDUCTING

professional orchestra
civic orchestra
youth symphony
choral
musical director for ballet
staff music director for radio or TV station

COMMERCIAL MUSIC

composer
arranger
performer
music director for film company
music critic
symphony manager
recording industry
instrument repair
piano tuner/technician
music librarian
radio or TV music commentator
music/musical business associations

BUSINESS OPPORTUNITIES

retail music store
music sales
music publishing
instrument manufacturing
music wholesale

RELIGIOUS MUSIC

director of music
church organist

OPERA

singers
orchestra players
general manager
stage director
costume designer
set designer
stage manager
technical staff (electricians, stagehands,
    lighting, etc.)

PERFORMANCE

accompanist
symphony playing
performing popular music
military musician
theater performer
music director for a recreation department

RELATED FIELDS

concert manager

LIST 9.45   MUSIC MAGAZINES

ASCAP in Action
1 Lincoln Plaza c/o ASCAP
New York, NY 10023
(212) 595-3050

AWC (American Women Composers)
News/Forum
1690 36th St. NW, Suite 409
Washington, DC 20007
(202) 342-8179

The Absolute Sound
2 Glen Ave.
Sea Cliff, NY 11579
(516) 676-2830

Acoustic Guitar
PO Box 767
San Anselmo, CA 94979-0767
(415) 485-6946

AGMAzine (American Guild of Musical
Artists)
1727 Broadway c/o AGMA
New York, NY 10019-5248
(212) 265-3687

American Brahms Society Newsletter
Univ. of Washington School of Music DN10
Seattle, WA 98195
(206) 543-0400

American Choral Review
American Choral Foundation, Inc.
c/o Chorus America
2111 Sansom St.
Philadelphia, PA 19103
(215) 563-2430

American Music
Library of Congress Music Div.
Washington, DC 20540
(202) 707-5504

American Music Center Newsletter
30 W. 26th St., Suite 1001
New York, NY 10010-2001
(212) 366-5260

American Music Teacher
617 Vine St., Suite 1432
Cincinnati, OH 45202-2434
(513) 421-1420

The American Organist
475 Riverside Drive, Suite 1260
New York, NY 10115
(212) 870-2310

American Record Guide
4412 Braddock St.
Cincinnati, OH 45204
(513) 941-1116

American Recorder
2586 Cranberry Hwy.
Wareham, MA 02571
(508) 291-0087

American String Teacher
PO Box 170639
Hialeah, FL 33017
(305) 364-0099

Asian Music
Asian Studies Dept.
388 Rockefeller Hall, Cornell University
Ithaca, NY 14853
(607) 255-5049

Audio
Hachette Magazines, 1633 Broadway
New York, NY 10019
(212) 767-6332

Billboard
1515 Broadway
New York, NY 10036
(212) 536-5031

CD Review
Forest Rd.
Hancock, NH 03449
(603) 525-4201

Cadence
Cadence Building
Redwood, NY 13679
(315) 287-2852

Choral Journal
PO Box 6310
Lawton, OK 73506
(405) 355-8161

The Church Musician
127 Ninth Ave. N.
Nashville, TN 37234
(615) 251-2944

List 9.45 (continued)

Clavier
200 Northfield Rd.
Northfield, IL 60093
(708) 446-5000

Conductors Guild Newsletter
5 W. Chestnut Hill Ave.
Philadelphia, PA 19118
(215) 242-8444

Continuo
PO Box 327
Hammondsport, NY 14840
(607) 569-2489

Current Musicology
Columbia University Dept. of Music
New York, NY 10027
(212) 854-3825

Dance Magazine
33 W. 60th St.
New York, NY 10023
(212) 245-9050

Dance Teacher Now
SMW Communications
3020 Beacon Blvd.
West Sacramento, CA 95691-3436
(916) 373-0201

Dialogue in Instrumental Music Education
The Humanities Building
School of Music, University of Wisconsin
Madison, WI 53706-1483
(608) 263-5972

The Diapason
380 East Northwest Hwy.
Des Plaines, IL 60016-2282
(312) 298-6622

Double Reed
University of Idaho School of Music
Moscow, ID 83843
(208) 885-6111

Downbeat
180 West Park Ave.
Elmhurst, IL 60126
(708) 941-2030

Drama-Logue
PO Box 38771
Los Angeles, CA 90038
(213) 464-5079

EAR, Magazine of New Music
131 Barick St., Rm. 905
New York, NY 10013
(212) 807-7944

Eastman Notes
Eastman School of Music
26 Gibbs St.
Rochester, NY 14604
(716) 274-1000

Ethnomusicology
Music Dept. Box 1924
Brown University
Providence, RI 02912
(401) 863-3234

Experimental Musical Instruments
PO Box 784
Nicasio, CA 94946
(415) 662-2182

Fanfare
273 Woodland St.
Tenafly, NJ 07670
(201) 567-3908

Flute Talk
200 Northfield Rd.
Northfield, IL 60093-3390
(708) 446-5000

Guitar Review
Albert Augustine, Ltd.
40 West 25th St.
New York, NY 20010
(212) 924-4651

Historical Performance
Early Music America
30 West 26th St., Suite 1001
New York, NY 10010-2011
(212) 366-5643

The Instrumentalist
200 Northfield Rd.
Northfield, IL 60093
(708) 446-5000

International Musician
1501 Broadway, Suite 600
New York, NY 10036
(212) 869-1330

© 1994 by Parker Publishing Company

List 9.45 (continued)

Jazz Times
7961 Eastern Ave., Suite 303
Silver Spring, MD 20910-4898
(301) 588-4114

Journal of Music Theory
Yale University Music Dept.
PO Box 4030, Yale Station
New Haven, CT 06520-4030
(203) 432-2996

Journal of Musicology
PO Box 4516
Louisville, KY 40204
(502) 459-5222

Journal of Research in Music Education
University of Kansas Dept. of Art and Mus.
    Ed. & Mus. Therapy
311 Bailey Hall
Lawrence, KS 66045-2344
(913) 864-4784

Journal of Research in Singing and Applied
    Vocal Pedagogy
PO Box 32887
Texas Christian University Music Dept.
Fort Worth, TX 76129
(817) 926-4415

Journal of the American Viola Society
Brigham Young University Music Dept.
Provo, UT 84602
(801) 378-3083

Journal of the Arnold Schoenberg Institute
The Arnold Schoenberg Institute
Univ. Park, MC-1101
University of Southern California
Los Angeles, CA 90089-1101
(213) 740-4090

Journal of the Conductors' Guild
PO Box 3361
West Chester, PA 19381
(215) 430-6010

Journal of the Violin Society of America
614 Lerew Rd.
The Chimneys Violin Shop
Boiling Springs, PA 17007
(717) 258-3203

The Juilliard Journal
Juilliard School, Lincoln Center
New York, NY 10023
(212) 799-5000

Keyboard Classics
223 Katonah Ave.
Katonah, NY 10536
(914) 232-8108

Living Blues
University of Mississippi, Sam Hall
University, MS 38677
(601) 232-5574

Music Article Guide
PO Box 27066
Philadelphia, PA 19118
(215) 848-3540

Music Clubs Magazine
444 Seminole Rd.
Babson Park, FL 33827
(813) 638-2629

Music Educators Journal
MENC
1902 Association Drive
Reston, VA 22091
(703) 860-4000

Music Perception
University of California, San Diego
Psychology Dept.
San Diego, C-009
La Jolla, CA 92093
(619) 534-3000

Musical America
825 Seventh Ave.
New York, NY 10019
(212) 887-8383

The Musical Quarterly
200 Madison Ave.
New York, NY 10016
(212) 679-7300

Musician
33 Commercial St.
Gloucester, MA 01930
(508) 281-3110

List 9.45 (continued)

The NATS Journal
SWBTS, PO Box 22507
Forth Worth, TX 76122
(817) 923-1921

*The National School Orchestra Association
 Bulletin*
345 Maxwell Drive
Pittsburgh, PA 15236-2067
(412) 882-6696

The New Republic
745 Argyle Rd.
Brooklyn, NY 11230
(718) 859-4410

New York Magazine
755 Second Ave.
New York, NY 10017
(212) 880-0700

The New York Opera Newsletter
PO Box 278
Maplewood, N.J. 07040
(201) 378-9549

Notes (Music Library Association)
Music Building
Harvard University
Cambridge, MA 02138
(617) 495-2794

Old Time Country
University of Mississippi, Center for the
 Study of Southern Culture
University, MS 38677
(601) 232-5574

Opera Fanatic
c/o Bel Canto Society
11 Riverside Drive
New York, NY 10023
(212) 877-1595

Opera Guide
PO Box 2184
Van Nuys, CA 91404
(818) 786-7372

Opera Journal
WT Box 879
West Texas State University
Canyon, TX 79016-0879
(806) 656-2844

Opera Monthly
PO Box 816
Madison Square Station
New York, NY 10159
(212) 627-2120

Opera News
70 Lincoln Center Plaza
New York, NY 10023-6593
(212) 769-7080

Opera Quarterly
Duke University Press Journals
6697 College Station
Durham, NC 27708
(919) 684-2173

Opus
c/o Schwann
535 Boylston St.
Boston, MA 02116
(617) 437-1350

Pastoral Music
225 Sheridan St.
Washington, DC 20011
(202) 723-5800

Percussive Notes
PO Box 16395, Cameron University
Lawton, OK 73505
(405) 581-2807

Performance Magazine
1203 Lake St., Suite 200
Fort Worth, TX 76102-4504
(817) 338-9444

Performing Arts
3539 Motor Ave.
Los Angeles, CA 90034
(310) 839-8000

Perspectives of New Music
University of Washington School of Music
 DN-10
Seattle, WA 98185
(208) 543-0196

The Philadelphia Musical World and Times
4944 Bingham St.
Philadelphia, PA 19120

List 9.45 (continued)

Piano Quarterly
Rader Rd.
Wilmington, VT 05363
(802) 464-5149

Popular Music in Society
Bowling Green State University
Popular Press Journals
Bowling Green, OH 43403
(419) 372-7865

Prelude
205 17th St.
Pacific Grove, CA 93950
(408) 375-5711

The Quarterly
Frasier Hall 123, Music School
University of Northern Colorado
Greeley, CO 80639
(303) 351-2254

Rolling Stone
1290 Avenue of the Americas
New York, NY 10104
(212) 484-1616

Sacred Music
548 Lafond Ave.
St. Paul, MN 55103
(612) 293-1710

Schwann
535 Boylston St.
Boston, MA 02116
(617) 437-1350

Sing Out! The Folk Song Magazine
PO Box 5253
Bethlehem, PA 18015-0253
(215) 865-5366

Society News Magazine
c/o Contemporary Rec. Soc.
724 Winchester Rd.
Broomall, PA 19008
(215) 544-5920

Strings
PO Box 766
San Anselmo, CA 94979-0767
(415) 485-6946

Symphony
777 14th St. NW, Suite 500
Washington, DC 20005
(202) 628-0099

The Tracker
Organ Historical Society
PO Box 26811
Richmond, VA 23261
(804) 353-9226

Vantage Point
1285 Avenue of the Americas, 3rd Floor
New York, NY 10019
(212) 245-4510

Variety
475 Park Ave. South
New York, NY 10016
(212) 779-1100

Washington International Arts Letter
PO Box 12010
Des Moines, IA 50312
(515) 255-5577

Yellow Springs Review
1645 Art School Rd.
Chester Springs, PA 19425
(215) 827-9111

Zither Newsletter of U.S.A.
6173 North McClellan Ave.
Chicago, IL 60646
(312) 631-2854

All Things Musical
535 Montery Ave.
P.O. Box 3309
Terre Haute, IN 47803
(812) 234-2124

THE PARTS OF THE BOW

1. eye
2. ferrule
3. frog
4. hair
5. ivory
6. screw
7. slide
8. stick
9. tip
10. wrapping

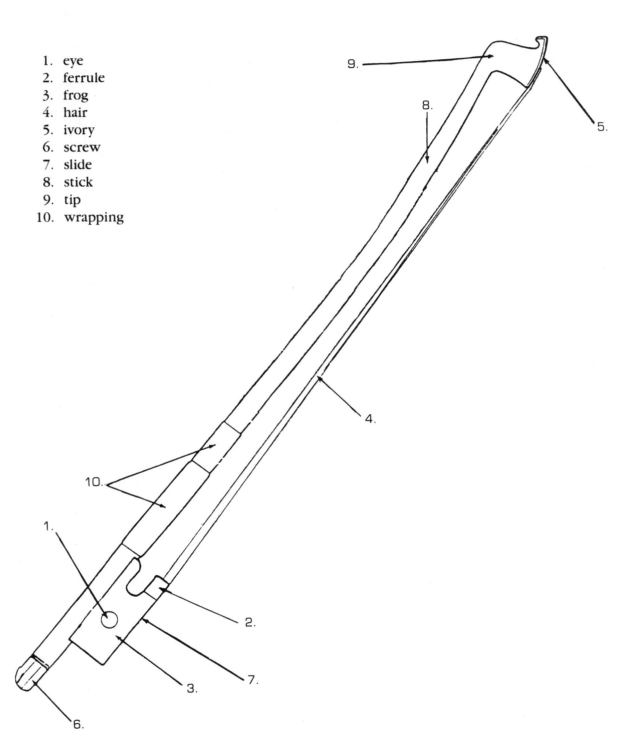

THE PARTS OF THE MODERN VIOLIN

1. bouts
2. bridge
3. chin rest
4. end button
5. f hole
6. fingerboard
7. neck
8. nut
9. pegbox
10. pegs
11. purfling
12. ribs
13. scroll
14. shoulder
15. strings
16. tailpiece
17. top
18. tuners

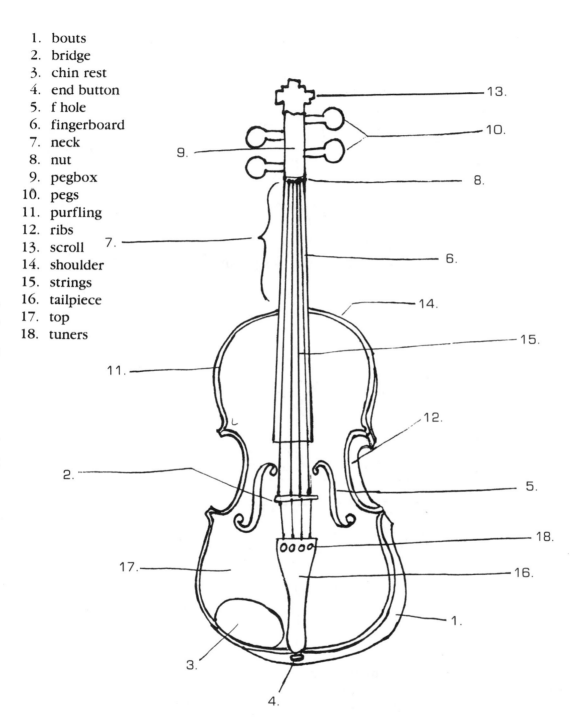

PARTS OF THE MODERN PIANO

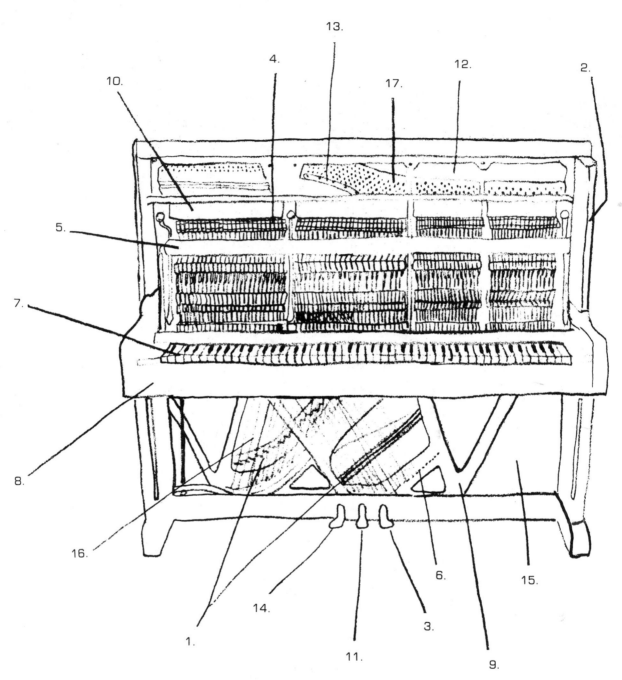

1. bridges
2. case
3. damper pedal
4. hammer
5. hammer rail
6. hitch pin
7. key/keyboard
8. keybed
9. metal frame
10. muffler felt
11. muffler pedal
12. pin block
13. pressure bar
14. soft pedal
15. soundboard
16. strings
17. tuning pin